James Cameron: Interviews

Conversations with Filmmakers Series
Gerald Peary, General Editor

James Cameron
INTERVIEWS

Edited by Brent Dunham

University Press of Mississippi / Jackson

www.upress.state.ms.us

The University Press of Mississippi is a member
of the Association of American University Presses.

Copyright © 2012 by University Press of Mississippi
All rights reserved

First printing 2012

Library of Congress Cataloging-in-Publication Data

Cameron, James.
  James Cameron : interviews / edited by Brent Dunham.
      p. cm. — (Conversations with filmmakers series)
  Includes bibliographical references and index.
  Includes filmography.
  ISBN 978-1-61703-131-1 (cloth : alk. paper) — ISBN 978-1-61703-132-8 (pbk. : alk. paper) —ISBN 978-1-61703-133-5 (ebook) 1. Cameron, James, 1954– Interviews. 2. Motion picture producers and directors—Canada—Interviews. I. Dunham, Brent. II. Title.
  PN1998.3.C352A3 2011
  791.4302'33092—dc23   2011020888

British Library Cataloging-in-Publication Data available

Contents

Introduction ix

Chronology xxi

Filmography xxv

How to Direct a *Terminator* 3
    Thomas McKelvey Cleaver/1984

The 1984 Movie Revue: James Cameron Interviewed by David Chute 8
    David Chute/1985

Writer-Director Shows the Special Effect Energy Can Radiate 15
    JoAnn Rhetts/1986

Aliens: An Out of This World Communication with Director James Cameron 19
    Victor Wells/1986

James Cameron Takes the Plunge 23
    Alan Jones/1989

James Cameron Takes a Second Plunge 29
    Alan Jones/1989

Aliens: James Cameron Interview 35
    Nigel Floyd/1992

The Hero's Journey 41
  Syd Field/1992

Approaching the Sequel 50
  Syd Field/1992

Iron Jim 57
  John H. Richardson/1994

Rich and Strange 71
  Ray Greene/1995

20,000 Leagues Under the Sea: The Movie Director as Captain Nemo 77
  Bill Moseley/1998

A Drive of Titanic Proportions 110
  Academy of Achievement/1999

The Final Frontier 133
  Anne Thompson/2000

James Cameron: The Second Coming 139
  Jenny Cooney Carrillo/2002

Sound of Silence 144
  John Reading/2002

James Cameron 147
  Adrian Wootton/2003

My Titanic Obsession 169
  James Rampton/2005

King of All He Surveys 174
  James Rampton/2006

James Cameron: A Life in Pictures 178
  Francine Stock/2009

James Cameron   189
    Tavis Smiley/2009

James Cameron Interview: *Avatar* Blu-ray; Also Talks *Titanic 3D* and *Avatar 2*   200
    Sara Wyland/2010

James Cameron Interview! Talks *Avatar* Re-release, Sequels, 3D Conversions, and Working with Del Toro   207
    Jim Dorey/2010

Index   215

Introduction

It was one day on the set of *The Abyss* that James Cameron almost died. At the bottom of a gigantic underwater set, Cameron ran out of oxygen. His First AD was supposed to monitor his O_2 levels while he was under but failed to do so on this particular occasion. Cameron knew he couldn't ascend with all his gear on so he stripped most of it off, including his helmet. As he rose, a safety diver saw the situation and tried to assist Cameron by sticking a spare regulator in his mouth. However, the regulator was faulty and Cameron ended up sucking water into his lungs instead of much-needed oxygen. Cameron struggled even more, realizing the safety diver's assumption that the regulator was working just fine. Reading Cameron's resistance as effects of "the bends," the safety diver wouldn't let go of the drowning director. Cameron punched the safety diver, who released him immediately, and swam the rest of the way to the surface. Both the AD and the safety diver were fired. Thus, we are provided in a single anecdote a general overview of James Cameron as one of the most self-reliant, as well as successful and innovative, filmmakers of the past three decades: If it weren't for other people, James Cameron would've been just fine.

As a filmmaker, James Cameron has spent more than thirty years (unintentionally) developing a personal mythology that is just as well known in the industry as his films are to the public. Perhaps this mythology could best be boiled down to "extreme." His lifestyle outside making movies is often described as adrenaline-fueled, whether it's his passion for deep-sea diving, riding motorcycles, or driving out to the desert to play with guns. His films are often record-breaking, both in their massive budgets as well as their eventual box office returns. His work ethic is focused, driven, and uncompromising, very much a "if you can't stand the heat, get out of the kitchen" approach which has polarized his collaborators from day one: they either feed off his energy and the desire to be pushed further, or they take his abuse personally and vow to never work with him again. In addressing the stories of his on-set tyranny, Cameron begins his justification with a slightly snobbish edge but finishes it with a bit of vulnerability: "What people call obsession or passion, for me it's just a work ethic. I think it comes from an insecurity that I'm not good enough."[1] As Hollywood's "king of the world," Cameron now holds the record for the two highest-grossing films of all time (unadjusted for inflation). Perhaps, then, his previous insecurities about inadequacy can finally be put to bed.

There are two distinct and complimentary sides of James Cameron: science and art, inherited from his parents. As biographer Rebecca Keegan posits, "Their wildly different dispositions would combine uniquely in their son, who became equal parts calculating gearhead and romantic artist."[2] Cameron himself agrees with this analysis: "My mother was a housewife but she was also an artist. My father was an electrical engineer. So right there you have a collision of left and right hemisphere thinking and I think I got equal parts of both."[3] Growing up, Cameron couldn't decide which career path to take (science or art); his heart was drawn in both directions equally. It wasn't until his mid-twenties that he decided to combine the two in the ideal medium: cinema. Even a cursory glance at his films provides evidence that his mechanical and his emotional sides have enjoyed their marriage going on thirty years. When his imagination yields a fantastical image that has yet to be materialized on screen (e.g., the liquid metal Terminator in *T2*), his scientific brain rises to the challenge. While most writers and directors are at the mercy of the industry's current state-of-the-art technology, their imaginations inhibited by what is "possible," Cameron might stand alone as the only filmmaker who creates technical innovations to accommodate his ideas. In 1993, following George Lucas's example with ILM, Cameron went so far as to create his own special effects studio, Digital Domain. Furthering this notion of Cameron's approach as equal parts science and emotion, he often attempts to inject his technology-driven films with the heart and soul of multidimensional characters and Academy Award–nominated performances. It's arguable that instead of a generic, "guns and ammo" extermination film, *Aliens* wouldn't have been the success that it was without Cameron's portrayal of Ripley as both female warrior and motherly savior. Likewise, it's doubtful that *Titanic* remained the number one movie in America for four months straight because of the special effects; the likely culprit was the resonant love story.

Cameron's big break came in 1979 when he began working for Roger Corman's New World Pictures as a model maker. Ever the opportunist,

Corman began producing a film that was unabashedly exploiting the success of *Star Wars* called *Battle Beyond the Stars*. As an anonymous presence in the model department, Cameron took a chance in his design for one of the film's spaceships. When Corman was unsatisfied with the ship's current design, he demanded that the model department propose new ideas. Knowing Corman and his cinematic sensibilities, Cameron took a bold step and presented "a spaceship with tits" to match the ship's computer's female personality. It worked and James Cameron soon emerged from the model shop as the Art Director for *Battle Beyond the Stars*. "Then, I clawed my way up from there, as meanly and brutally as I could."[4] It was during work on his second film New World Pictures called *Galaxy of Terror* that Cameron had the idea to be a director. In typical Cameron fashion, his desire to be a director was not a power play, he simply disapproved of the way his sets were being lit and photographed. Ever proud of his work, he felt obligated to make it right and do it himself rather than let someone else ruin it. It's been this perfectionism that's come to define Cameron's career. While working on *Galaxy of Terror*, a chance visit by an Italian producer would earn him his first directing gig. Soon, no one would be ruining Cameron's sets.

After convincing Roger Corman to let him become *Galaxy of Terror*'s Second Unit Director, Cameron was attempting to film an insert shot of a severed arm covered in writhing maggots. They used mealworms instead of maggots and when they called "action!" none of their larvae actors hit their marks. In an attempt to liven things up, Cameron rigged the prop arm for electricity and as soon as it was plugged in, those little mealworms danced like they were supposed to. Italian producer Ovidio Assonitis just happened to be visiting the set when he witnessed James Cameron apparently directing the mealworms with such success. Assonitis was looking for a director for his low-budget production *Piranha II: The Spawning*, a sequel to another New World Pictures B-horror film. And so, James Cameron got his first job as a director—at least for a couple weeks before he was fired. Crestfallen, Cameron took the firing as an indication that his talents were not found in directing after all. A few months later, he flew to Rome to confront Assonitis about his termination and to see the footage he shot (Assonitis had made it a practice to take the dailies off to be developed before Cameron could see them). After finally convincing Assonitis to see the rough cut of the film, Cameron saw that his footage actually worked just fine, which added to his theory that Assonitis had not fired him for incompetence but for a chance to direct the picture himself. Having regained some confidence in his abilities as a director, Cameron still had an itch to scratch. Before he left Rome, he spent his nights sneaking into the editing bay and re-cutting the film; not necessarily because he knew there was a *Citizen Kane* to be found but because he knew his name was going to be on it and he wanted to make it as presentable as possible—getting any future work after this would be difficult if his only credit as a director was trash. The final edit that was released was not Cameron's but his personal validation was already secured. Later, he would jokingly call it "the finest flying-piranha movie ever made."[5]

If the auteur theory is given any credence, certainly James Cameron could be considered an ideal candidate. While the theory aims to identify the true author of a film, cinema is perhaps the most collaborative art form, making this search frustrating if not impossible. From the outset, the auteur theory presents contradictions and incites endless debates, even when the subject being considered simply directs the films. Because he wears so many hats while making his films, Cameron, more than most others, actually might deserve the "A Film By" credit. Cameron is known for doing multiple jobs on a set, again, not because there's no one to do it, but because he'd rather do it right himself than let someone else make a failed attempt. In an interview with the *New Yorker*, Cameron fesses up to his "control freak" reputation: "I always do makeup touch-ups myself, especially for blood, wounds, and dirt. It saves so much time."[6] As an auteur, the consistency to be found within Cameron's work is much more grounded in ideas rather than a particular visual style.

Thematically, Cameron has shown in film after film that certain ideas and possibilities weigh heavily on his mind. Nuclear weapons, for example, play either minor or major parts in almost all of his feature films. We learn from these interviews that growing up during the Cold War, and especially the Cuban Missile Crisis, has had an immense impact on his point of view. In a recent biography, it is revealed that when Cameron was eight years old, he found a pamphlet detailing how to build a civilian fallout shelter. "I realized that the safe and nurturing world I thought I lived in was an illusion, and that the world as we know it could end at any moment."[7] This sense of fatalism pervades Cameron's films; the inevitability of these self-inflicted apocalypses is constantly teased but never without a glimpse at their prevention. If Cameron provides any clemency to his audiences from his dire visions, it is a buffer of time: the apocalypse will come soon but not quite yet. In *The Terminator*, Cameron set the "end times" to begin thirteen years in the future (1997); in his one and only TV series, *Dark Angel*, which first aired in 2000, we are shown the end of civilization takes place in 2009.

This pessimism surrounding "the future" becomes another thread connecting his films. As Cameron states, the function of futuristic or sci-fi films has always been about contemporary self-reflection as opposed to narratives meant to predict the future. Cameron explains this to Ray Greene in their discussion of the social commentary found in *Strange Days*. "Historically, science fiction has always been terrible at actually predicting the future. What it's great at is giving you a different way of looking at your life now."[8] In films such as *The Terminator* and *The Abyss*, we are shown possible outcomes for our haphazard pursuance of bigger and better technologies. In an interesting paradox, however, for all James Cameron's impressive contributions to the advancement of technology (underwater camera systems, computer-generated effects, Mars landing vehicles, etc.), his films often warn humanity of its "not-so-bright" future if technology is pushed too far. "[T]he more we rely on technology, the more we have to rely on each other in our basic capacities as humans to bond together emotionally—in friendship or in love."[9] In further explaining his seemingly contradictory worldview, Cameron defines himself as "optimistically paranoid," a position that is also actively expressed in his films. "I'm very optimistic about the human animal and our potential, and I'm paranoid about some of the darker potential inherent in these technologies."[10]

One might assume that anyone who is paranoid of a nuclear attack would also be concerned about environmental issues, but until *Avatar*, Cameron hadn't shown us his "inner tree hugger." Before an image of a peace-loving, flower-wearing, and pacifist James Cameron enters the mind, take into account the following quote: "I suppose you could say I believe in peace through superior firepower. I don't believe that the human race is going to suddenly evolve to the point that we can all join hands and sing 'Kumbaya.'"[11] This ethos could definitely describe Cameron's oeuvre as a filmmaker but what about *Avatar*? In this case, superior firepower did not prevail and it was atrocities committed by humans against the Na'vi that flipped the typical sci-fi notion that humans are always innocent. In addition to the film's obvious didactics about conservation and a respect for nature, Cameron's post-*Avatar* life has been busy with more political and environmental activities. Cameron began a campaign surrounding *Avatar*'s DVD release with trips to the Xingu River in the Amazon where a "real life" *Avatar* situation is occurring. Beyond that, Cameron also met with senators in Washington, D.C., gave speeches at Earth Day rallies and hit the political talk-show circuit with appearances on shows like *Hardball* with Chris Matthews. Cameron has also recently visited western Canada to bring awareness to the oil mining there, not simply to stop the drilling but to make the process as efficient and safe as possible—lessons learned from the BP disaster in the Gulf of Mexico, a disaster that Cameron also offered to help advise on the clean-up. The *Avatar* DVD was purposely released on Earth Day as a catalyst for dialogue about the environmental issues, Cameron says, the scientific community is trying warn us about. For Cameron, the problem starts with the public actually believing that there is a problem to begin with and blames the right wing for their instigating denial amongst the population. "If we can't even talk about the problem, what are we going to do about it?"[12]

Of course, although his films deal with the end of the world (or the threat thereof), there is always a figure present to save the day. It just so happens that the hero in Cameron's universe doesn't fit the typical mold established by decades of Hollywood mythmaking. This "thinking outside the box" approach to heroism is shown by his employment of strong, capable female protagonists. Sarah Connor (Linda Hamilton) from the *Terminator* series is given the same respect and archetypal narrative arc as so many male heroes that came before (and after) her. Her transformation from diner waitress to combat soldier is often thought to be one of the greatest female characters, especially considering she's ensconced in the testosterone-soaked action genre. Again, in his second film, *Aliens*, Cameron inherits Sigourney Weaver's character, Ellen Ripley, the first film's only survivor, and injects her with a complexity that earned Weaver her first Oscar nomination, a rare occurrence indeed for the sci-fi genre and doubly so for a woman. These two examples of strong female characters would be enough to prove James Cameron's predilection for "girl power" but they're not alone. *The Abyss*'s Lindsey Brigman (Mary Elizabeth Mastrontonio), *True Lies*' Helen Tasker (Jamie Lee Curtis) and *Titanic*'s Rose (Kate Winslet) all follow the same pattern of women characters that emerge as thoughtful and well rounded, as opposed to the traditional "object of desire." Inspiration for these strong female characters is perhaps attributed to Cameron's mother, Shirley, an individual whose own life reminds us of a James Cameron heroine. "While a mother with three kids under age eight, Shirley would join the Canadian Women's Army Corps, happily trooping off on weekends in fatigues and combat boots to assemble a rifle while blindfolded and march through fields in the pouring rain."¹³ Continuing his string of capable heroines is a character named Max (Jessica Alba) from Cameron's first major post-*Titanic* project: a TV series he co-created called *Dark Angel*. Similar to his films before *Dark Angel*, this maiden voyage into television centers on a bleak future, wiped out once again through the employment of destructive technology. Ultimately, despite an avid fan base and critical praise, *Dark Angel* would only last two seasons. Cameron was initially disappointed and frustrated with this ill-fated foray into TV but it was announced in 2010 that a television spin-off of *True Lies* was being developed for the FOX network and with Cameron acting as Executive Producer.

For all the love and attention paid to his filmmaking, Cameron's passions don't simply end there. As a boy, and ardent science fiction reader, Cameron dreamed of going to outer space. Throughout the years, Cameron has sustained this interest in space exploration: he joined NASA's Advisory Council in 2002, developed his own Mars rover vehicle, designed a 3D camera system for upcoming expeditions to Mars and, a few years ago, began developing a 3D IMAX film about life and work aboard the International Space Station. Plans for that film fell through as interest in the red planet waned after a couple unsuccessful Hollywood productions (*Red Planet* and *Mission to Mars*, both 2000), and the final blow to the project came after the *Columbia* spaceship disaster in 2003. Growing up, he realized that while exploring the cosmos might be a bit unrealistic, the oceans provided a more accessible and equally exotic venue for exploration. As a boy in Canada and living nowhere near an ocean, he was forced to begin his underwater life becoming scuba certified in a YMCA pool in Buffalo, New York. These days, Cameron not only gets to dive in a real ocean, he gets to explore the mysteries of the deep with million-dollar submersibles. Cameron has described his never-ending curiosity as the main drive behind all his ventures, and deep-sea diving certainly has provided opportunities for that curiosity to be entertained. In fact, some might be surprised exactly how much diving means to him: between filmmaking and diving "if I had to choose one over the other, I would probably dive."¹⁴ Luckily for his fans, James Cameron doesn't have to give up filmmaking to pursue his aquatic hobbies. Starting with *The Abyss*, and later with his documentaries, Iron Jim got smart and combined his two favorite things: diving and movies. And, as is rumored, the director's next installments of the *Avatar* franchise will take place under Pandora's oceans, thus continuing his aquatic and cinematic obsessions.

Before the release of *Avatar*, James Cameron was basically absent from Hollywood for over a decade. People assumed that Cameron's "exile" after *Titanic* was a product of insecurity and a fear that he would never be able to follow up the biggest movie of all time. The truth is, he simply took advantage of his "king of the world" status to do as he pleased. To Tavis Smiley, Cameron explains that stage fright was the last thing on his mind, "It was more like I had my FU money; I could do whatever I wanted at that point. I didn't think my directing career was going to go away just because I went off to do these other things, and it didn't."[15] "These other things" would become six underwater documentaries, including three more dives to the sunken *Titanic*, an exploration of Hitler's flagship, the *Bismarck*, and a study of deep-sea life forms living in the most hostile environments on Earth. Not only did these films allow Cameron to indulge in his amphibious life, he was also busy continuing his techie life by developing a brand new 3D camera system and the ability for these cameras to dive two and a half miles deep to sites like the *Titanic*. With the help of cameraman Vince Pace and his engineer younger brother, Mike, Cameron's love of filmmaking and diving would again be married, like every one of his other projects, in the most extreme way. It was the development of these new camera systems that led to the production of *Avatar*. Despite taking the time to indulge in his passions outside Hollywood, Cameron was also waiting for this new leap forward in technology before he could tackle the immensity of *Avatar*.

Most of the discussion about Cameron's career is dedicated to the films he writes and directs but his few engagements as a producer merit their own consideration. Cameron has produced most of his own films (exceptions being *The Terminator*, *Aliens*, and *The Abyss*), and, despite his despotic control as a writer/director, he has occasionally produced films for other filmmakers. His first producing gig on someone else's project came with *Point Break* (1991), directed by his then-wife Kathryn Bigelow. Their personal/professional relationship worked well on that film and Cameron would also produce her next film, *Strange Days* (1995), based on his original story. That film also marked the first time a James Cameron script would be directed by someone else since *Rambo: First Blood Part II*. "I actually wrote with her in mind to direct it. It was a well-tailored fit."[16] It would take seven years but Cameron next went on to produce Steven Soderbergh's sci-fi drama, *Solaris*, a remake of Andrei Tarkovsky's 1972 original. Excluding some of his post-*Titanic* documentary work, Cameron wouldn't produce for someone else again for another nine years, that being *Sanctum*, a thriller about a cave dive gone wrong and filmed in 3D with Cameron's Fusion cameras, set to be released in 2011. Also on the horizon, Cameron announced that he will be producing pal Guillermo Del Toro's upcoming adaptation of H. P. Lovecraft's *At the Mountains of Madness*.

In his piece here, writer Bill Moseley offers a succinct definition of Iron Jim: "James Cameron is his own man."[17] Beyond a simple comment on his individuality, this statement reflects a lot more about his successes in life. Despite his long history working with the studios, James Cameron can be considered more of an "independent" filmmaker. Like George Lucas before him, he has created an empire of his own where the Hollywood studios work for him. After *Titanic*, Cameron simply walked away from Hollywood, confident that he could pick up right where he left off, even a decade later. In his interview with the Academy of Achievement, Cameron explains his rise in the industry and ruminates on what success actually means. "There are many talented people who haven't fulfilled their dreams because they over-thought it, or they were too cautious, and were unwilling to make the leap of faith."[18] He goes on to comment on the difficulties that occur after that leap has finally been made: "It's going to be grabbing the tiger by the tail and if you have not prepared yourself mentally for it through study, through knowing and hypothesizing what it will be like when you're in that position, you won't be able to deal with it."[19] Upon consideration of Cameron's career and his ferocious rise to the top, perhaps, following his example, it is better to be the tiger and let others try to hold onto you.

This collection attempts to provide a context with which to examine the career and life of James Cameron. The entirety of his more than thirty-year career is represented in some form, hopefully illuminating the breadth of one of the most notorious and successful histories in Hollywood. The interviews contained herein were selected because they satisfied two simple criteria: the diversity of their sources and their ability to provide a specific insight into Cameron's career. Included in this collection are interviews from newspapers big (the *Guardian*) and small (the *Charlotte Observer*), pop culture magazines like *Premiere*, a post-screening Q&A, sci-fi magazines like *Starburst* and *Dreamwatch*, an interview from Collider.com, and an extended interview from Syd Field's book on screenwriting, *Four Screenplays*. Also included are interviews in print for the very first time, including an interview from *Marketsaw 3D*, a blog dedicated to 3D filmmaking, Cameron's appearance on *Tavis Smiley*, and a transcript of BAFTA's "James Cameron: A Life in Pictures." What these pieces provide is a thorough and complex presentation, the ultimate goal being a collection that approaches James Cameron and his work from as many angles as possible. The interviews are presented chronologically to highlight Cameron's evolution as a filmmaker; no one film is favored and a progressive movement is made through the past thirty years. Consistent with the standards set by the University Press of Mississippi and the "Interviews" series, all interviews within are unabridged and unedited from their original source. For the interviews needing transcription, I have done so to the best of my ability.

I would like to thank Leila Salisbury, Valerie Jones, and everyone at the University Press of Mississippi for their support, patience, and understanding. To the authors who have graciously offered their work to this project, I cannot thank you enough: Jenny Cooney Carrillo, David Chute, Jim Dorey, Syd Field, Nigel Floyd, Alan Jones, Bill Moseley, John H. Richardson, and Anne Thompson. Also, many thanks to the publishers or representatives who made the process so pleasant: Ken Bacon at *Box Office Magazine*, Allan Bryce at *Dark Side Magazine*, Joanna Chaundy at the *Independent*, Maria David at the *Charlotte Observer*, Matt McAllister at Total Sci-Fi Online, Kathleen O'Connell at the Academy of Achievement, Gavin Smith at *Film Comment*, Karena Smith at BAFTA, Jim Steranko at Supergraphics, Tony Timpone at the Brooklyn Group, Steven Weintraub at Collider.com, and Helen Wilson at the *Guardian*. I would also like to thank the authors writing for those publications: Thomas McKelvey Cleaver, Ray Greene, James Rampton, John Reading, JoAnn Rhetts, Francine Stock, Victor Wells, Adrian Wootton, and Sara Wyland. A special thanks goes to Judy Fox at Personal Talent Management for bringing Bill Moseley to the project.

BD

Notes

1. Academy of Achievement interview, posted June 18, 1999. http://www.achievement.org/autodoc/page/camoint-1.

2. Rebecca Keegan, *The Futurist: The Life and Films of James Cameron* (New York: Crown Publishers, 2009), 3.

3. Academy of Achievement.

4. Thomas McKelvey Cleaver, "How to Direct a *Terminator*," *Starlog Magazine*, December 1984, 57.

5. David Chute, "The 1984 Movie Revue: James Cameron Interviewed by David Chute," *Film Comment*, February 1985, 59.

6. Dana Goodyear, "Man of Extremes: The Return of James Cameron," *The New Yorker*, October 26, 2009, http://www.newyorker.com/reporting/2009/10/26/091026fa_fact_goodyear.

7. Keegan, 1–2.

8. Ray Greene, "Rich and Strange," *Box Office Magazine*, October 1995, 12.

9. Alan Jones, "James Cameron Takes the Plunge," *Starburst Magazine*, November 1989, 9.

10. Greene, 12.

11. Goodyear.

12. Ted Johnson, "Cameron Confronts Climate Crisis," *Variety*, April 21, 2010.

13. Keegan, 3.

14. James Rampton, "My Titanic Obsession," *The Independent*, August 9, 2005.

15. Tavis Smiley, "James Cameron," *Tavis Smiley*, PBS, December 17, 2009.

16. Greene, 10.

17. Bill Moseley, "20,000 Leagues Under the Sea: The Movie Director as Captain Nemo," http://www.astralgia.com/webportfolio/omnimoment/titanic/cameron/index.html.

18. Academy of Achievement.

19. Ibid.

Chronology

1954 Born on August 16 in Kapuskasing, Ontario, Canada.
1959 The Cameron family moves to Chippawa, Ontario, near Niagara Falls.
1968 At 14, Cameron watches *2001: A Space Odyssey*. It makes an indelible impression on the teenager. Soon after, he and his friend start making films with a Super 8 camera.
1970 Becomes a certified scuba diver in a YMCA pool in Buffalo, New York.
1971 Moves to Brea, California. Studies Physics and English at Fullerton College and California State University, Fullerton.
1978 With his friends, Cameron makes *Xenogenesis*, a sci-fi short film. Marries Sharon Williams.
1979 Begins working as a model builder for Roger Corman's independent studio, New World Pictures.
1980 Works as a model builder and Art Director on New World Pictures' *Battle Beyond the Stars*.
1981 Works as a visual effects artist on John Carpenter's *Escape From New York*. He also becomes the Production Designer and 2nd Unit Director on New World Pictures' *Galaxy of Terror*. Directs his first picture: *Piranha Part Two: The Spawning* but is fired before its completion—his name remains on the credits.
1983 While waiting to film *The Terminator*, Cameron becomes a writer for hire, completing scripts for two sequels to the Rambo and Alien franchises.
1984 Writes and directs the sci-fi action film starring Arnold Schwarzenegger: *The Terminator*.
1985 His screenplay for *Rambo: First Blood Part II* is rewritten and directed by Sylvester Stallone. Marries Gale Anne Hurd.

1986 Cameron directs his first studio film, *Aliens*. The film is a hit, reviving 20th Century Fox and giving Cameron every director's dream: final cut.

1989 Cameron makes *The Abyss*, a dream project based on a story he wrote in high school. The special effects in the film herald the emergence of CG. Marries Kathryn Bigelow.

1991 Produces *Point Break* for his wife, Kathryn Bigelow, to direct. Writes and directs *Terminator 2: Judgment Day*, the first film to cost more than $100 million to make but returned over $500 million in worldwide box office sales.

1992 The success of *Terminator 2* leads to a $500 million, multipicture domestic distribution deal with 20th Century Fox giving Cameron creative freedom and ownership of the films produced. He also completes scripts for *The Crowded Room*, an intimate drama based on a nonfiction book but was never produced, a Stan Lee-approved Spiderman script that would never be made, and, finally, *Strange Days*.

1993 Creates his own special effects studio, Digital Domain, with effects guru Stan Winston whom he previously worked with on *The Terminator*, *Aliens*, and *Terminator 2*. His first daughter, Josephine, with girlfriend Linda Hamilton, is born.

1994 For his first film under the new deal with Fox, Cameron writes and directs the action-comedy *True Lies*, a loose remake of a French film titled *La Totale!*

1995 Produces *Strange Days* for then ex-wife Bigelow based on his script, co-written by Jay Cocks. Cameron also takes his first of many deep-sea dives to the wreck of the Titanic in preparation to make *Titanic*.

1996 Writes and directs *T2 3D: Battle Across Time*. This short film was made to accompany a theme park ride for the Universal Studios parks in Hollywood and Florida. Construction begins on Fox Studios Baja—an entire production facility to house the production of *Titanic*.

1997 Cameron again produces the most expensive movie in history ($200 million): *Titanic*. Despite negative industry buzz about the bloated budget and delayed production, the film remains the number one film in America for a record 16 weeks and goes on to become the highest grossing film of all time. Marries Linda Hamilton.

1998	Steps down as CEO of his special effects house, Digital Domain.
2000	Cameron ventures into a new medium, TV, by co-creating *Dark Angel*. Despite its popularity, the show would be canceled after only two seasons. Marries Suzy Amis.
2001	Twins, Claire and Quinn, are born.
2002	Directs his first underwater documentary *Expedition: Bismarck*, detailing the last days and sinking of the famous WWII ship. Produces *Solaris*, a sci-fi drama directed by Steven Soderbergh. Cameron becomes a member of the NASA Advisory Council.
2003	Directs *Ghosts of the Abyss*, a 3D documentary short and first of three documentaries to further explore the wreckage of the Titanic. Cameron is also Executive Producer on *Volcanoes of the Deep Sea*, a short documentary about the volcanic activity on the ocean floor and the life surrounding it.
2005	Directs *Aliens of the Deep*, about the alien life forms to be found at the bottom of our oceans, and acts as Producer on two more TV documentaries about the Titanic, *Last Mysteries of the Titanic* and *Titanic Adventure*.
2006	Cameron is executive producer and narrator on *The Exodus Decoded*, a television documentary directed by Simcha Jacobovici. Daughter, Rose, is born.
2007	Cameron is executive producer on Simcha Jacobovici's next film titled *The Lost Tomb of Jesus*. This controversial TV documentary claims to have uncovered Jesus' tomb.
2008	*The Terminator* is selected for preservation by the National Film Registry.
2009	After more than a decade away from feature filmmaking, Cameron returns with *Avatar*. With years of research and development, Cameron and his team create a revolution in CG, jump-starting a new and substantial wave of 3D filmmaking. The film goes on to break *Titanic*'s box office record with $2.8 billion in worldwide box office. Cameron receives a star on the Hollywood Walk of Fame the same day *Avatar* is released.
2010	*Avatar* is nominated for numerous awards including four Golden Globes, eight BAFTAs and nine Academy Awards including Best Picture and Best Director. Announces that his next writing/directing projects will be the second and third installments in the *Avatar* franchise.

Filmography

Short Films

1978
XENOGENESIS
Producer: **James Cameron**, R. L. A. Frakes
Executive Producer: Alvin J. Weinberg
Director: **James Cameron**, R. L. A. Frakes
Screenplay: **James Cameron**, R. L. A. Frakes
Production Design: **James Cameron**
Cast: William Wisher, Jr. (Raj), Margaret Undiel (Laurie)
Color, 12 minutes

1996
T2 3-D: BATTLE ACROSS TIME
Production Company: Landmark Entertainment Group, Lightstorm Entertainment, MCA Planning and Development, Universal Creative, Universal Studios Recreation Group
Producer: Chuck Comisky
Executive Producer: Andrew Millstein, Scott Ross
Associate Producer: Jessica Huebner
Director: John Bruno, **James Cameron**, Stan Winston
Screenplay: Adam J. Bezark, **James Cameron**, Gary Goddard
Cinematography: Peter Anderson (3-D), Russell Carpenter (live action)
Production Design: John Muto
Art Direction: Bela Brozek (uncredited)
Editing: Allen Cappuccilli, David de Vos, Shannon Leigh Olds
Music: Brad Fiedel
Cast: Arnold Schwarzenegger (The Terminator), Linda Hamilton (Sarah Connor), Robert Patrick (T-1000), Edward Furlong (John Connor), Earl Boen (Dr. Peter Silberman)
Color, 12 minutes

Feature Films

1979
ROCK 'N' ROLL HIGH SCHOOL
Production Company: New World Pictures
Producer: Roger Corman, Michael Finnell, Anthony Masi
Director: Allan Arkush, Joe Dante (uncredited), Jerry Zucker (uncredited)
Story: Allan Arkush, Joe Dante
Screenplay: Richard Whitley, Russ Dvonch, Joseph McBride
Cinematography: Dean Cundey
Art Direction: Marie Kordus
Set Decoration: Linda Pearl
Editing: Larry Bock, Anthony Masi (documentary), Gail Werbin
Production Assistant: **James Cameron** (uncredited), et al.
Cast: P. J. Soles (Riff Randell), Vincent Van Patten (Tom Roberts), Clint Howard (Eaglebauer), Dey Young (Kate Rambeau), Mary Woronov (Miss Evelyn Togar)
Color, 93 minutes

1980
BATTLE BEYOND THE STARS
Production Company: New World Pictures
Producer: Ed Carlin
Executive Producer: Roger Corman
Associate Producer: Mary Ann Fisher
Director: Jimmy T. Murakami, Roger Corman (uncredited)
Story: John Sayles, Anne Dyer
Screenplay: John Sayles
Cinematography: Daniel Lacambre
Art Direction: Charles Breen, **James Cameron** (as Jim Cameron)
Set Decoration: John Zabrucky, Forrest Chadwick (uncredited)
Editing: Allan Holzman, R. J. Kizer
Music: James Horner
Cast: Richard Thomas (Shad), Robert Vaughn (Gelt), John Saxon (Sador), George Peppard (Cowboy), Darlanne Fluegel (Nanelia), Sybil Danning (Saint-Exmin), Sam Jaffe (Dr. Hephaestus)
Color, 104 minutes

1981
ESCAPE FROM NEW YORK
Production Company: AVCO Embassy Pictures, International Film Investors, Goldcrest Films International
Producer: Larry Franco, Debra Hill
Associate Producer: Barry Bernardi
Director: John Carpenter
Screenplay: John Carpenter, Nick Castle
Cinematography: Dean Cundey, George D. Dodge
Production Design: Joe Alves
Set Decoration: Cloudia
Costume Design: Steven Loomis
Editing: Todd Ramsay
Music: John Carpenter, Alan Howarth
Director of Photography (Special Effects): **James Cameron**
Matte Artwork: **James Cameron**
Cast: Kurt Russell (Snake Plissken), Lee Van Cleef (Hauk), Ernest Borgnine (Cabbie), Donald Pleasence (President), Isaac Hayes (The Duke), Season Hubley (Girl in Chock Full O'Nuts), Harry Dean Stanton (Brain), Adrienne Barbeau (Maggie), Tom Atkins (Rehme)
Color, 99 minutes

GALAXY OF TERROR
Production Company: New World Pictures
Producer: Roger Corman
Co-Producer: Marc Siegler
Director: B. D. Clark
Screenplay: Marc Siegler, B. D. Clark, William Stout (outline, uncredited)
Cinematography: Jacques Haitkin, Austin McKinney
Production Design: **James Cameron**, Robert Skotak
Art Direction: Steve Graziani, Alex Hajdu
Set Decoration: K. C. Scheibel, Bill Paxton (uncredited)
Editing: Larry Bock, R. J. Kizer, Barry Zetlin
Music: Barry Schrader
Cast: Edward Albert (Cabren), Erin Moran (Alluma), Ray Walston (Kore), Bernard Behrens (Commander Ilvar), Zalman King (Baelon), Robert Englund (Ranger), Taaffe O'Connell (Dameia), Sid Haig (Quuhod), Grace Zabriskie (Captain Trantor)
Color, 81 minutes

PIRAHNA PART TWO: THE SPAWNING
Production Company: Brouwersgracht Investments, Chako Film Company
Producer: Chako van Leuwen, Jeff Schectman
Executive Producer: Ovidio G. Assonitis
Director: **James Cameron**, Ovidio G. Assonitis (uncredited)
Screenplay: H. A. Milton
Cinematography: Roberto D'Ettorre Piazzoli
Art Direction: Vincenzo Medusa, Stefano Paltrinieri
Editing: Robert Silvi
Music: Steve Powder
Cast: Tricia O'Neil (Anne Kimbrough), Steve Marachuk (Tyler Sherman), Lance Henricksen (Police Chief Steve Kimbrough), Ricky G. Paull (Chris Kimbrough), Ted Richert (Raoul, Hotel Manager), Leslie Graves (Allison Dumont), Carole Davis (Jai)
Color, 84 minutes

1984
THE TERMINATOR
Production Company: Hemdale Film, Cinema 84, Euro Film Funding, Pacific Western
Producer: Gale Anne Hurd
Executive Producer: John Daly, Derek Gibson
Director: **James Cameron**
Screenplay: **James Cameron**, Gale Anne Hurd, William Wisher (additional dialogue)
Cinematography: Adam Greenberg
Art Direction: George Costello
Set Decoration: Maria Rebman Caso
Costume Design: Hilary Wright
Editing: Mark Goldblatt
Music: Brad Fiedel
Cast: Arnold Schwarzenegger (The Terminator), Michael Biehn (Kyle Reese), Linda Hamilton (Sarah Connor), Paul Winfield (Lieutenant Ed Traxler), Lance Henricksen (Detective Hal Vukovich), Bessa Motta (Ginger Ventura), Earl Boen (Dr. Peter Silberman)
Color, 108 minutes

1985
RAMBO: FIRST BLOOD PART II
Production Company: Anabasis N.V.
Producer: Buzz Feitshans
Executive Producer: Mario Kassar, Andrew G. Vajna
Associate Producer: Mel Dellar
Director: George P. Cosmatos
Screenplay: Sylvester Stallone, **James Cameron**, Kevin Jarre (story), David Morrell (characters)
Cinematography: Jack Cardiff
Production Design: Bill Kenney
Set Decoration: William Skinner, Sig Tingloff
Costume Design: Tom Bronson
Editing: Larry Bock, Mark Goldblatt, Mark Helfrich, Gib Jaffe, Frank E. Jimenez
Music: Jerry Goldsmith
Cast: Sylvester Stallone (John J. Rambo), Richard Crenna (Col. Samuel Trautman), Charles Napier (Marshall Murdock), Steven Berkoff (Lt. Col. Podovsky), Julia Nickson (Co Bao), Martin Kove (Ericson), George Kee Cheung (Capt. Vinh)
Color, 96 minutes

1986
ALIENS
Production Company: Twentieth Century Fox Film Corporation, Brandywine Productions, SLM Production Group
Producer: Gale Anne Hurd
Executive Producer: Gordon Carroll, David Giler, Walter Hill
Director: **James Cameron**
Screenplay: **James Cameron**
Story: **James Cameron**, David Giler, Walter Hill
Characters: Dan O'Bannon, Ronald Shusett
Cinematography: Adrian Biddle
Production Design: Peter Lamont
Art Direction: Terence Ackland-Snow, Ken Court, Bert Davey, Fred Hole, Michael Lamont
Set Decoration: Crispian Sallis
Costume Design: Emma Porteous
Editing: Ray Lovejoy
Music: James Horner

Cast: Sigourney Weaver (Ellen Ripley), Carrie Henn (Rebecca "Newt" Jorden), Michael Biehn (Cpl. Dwayne Hicks), Lance Henricksen (Bishop), Paul Reiser (Carter Burke), Bill Paxton (Pvt. Hudson), William Hope (Lt. Gorman), Jenette Goldstein (Pvt. Vasquez)
Color, 137 minutes

1989
THE ABYSS
Production Company: Twentieth Century Fox Film Corporation, Pacific Western, Lightstorm Entertainment
Producer: Gale Anne Hurd, Van Ling (special edition)
Director: **James Cameron**
Screenplay: **James Cameron**
Cinematography: Mikael Salomon
Production Design: Leslie Dilley
Art Direction: Peter Childs, Russell Christian, Joseph Nemec III
Set Decoration: Anne Kuljian
Costume Design: Deborah Everton
Editing: Conrad Buff, Joel Goodman, Steven Quale (special edition), Howard Smith
Music: Alan Silvestri
Cast: Ed Harris (Virgil "Bud" Brigman), Mary Elizabeth Mastrantonio (Lindsey Brigman), Michael Biehn (Lt. Hiram Coffey), Leo Burmester (Catfish De Vries), Todd Graff (Alan "Hippy" Carnes), John Bedford Lloyd (Jammer Willis), J. C. Quinn (Arliss "Sonny" Dawson), Kimberly Scott (Lisa "One Night" Standing)
Color, 138 minutes

1991
TERMINATOR 2: JUDGMENT DAY
Production Company: Carolco Pictures, Pacific Western, Lightstorm Entertainment, Canal+, T2 Productions (uncredited)
Producer: **James Cameron**
Executive Producer: Gale Anne Hurd, Mario Kassar
Co-Producer: Stephanie Austin, B. J. Rack
Director: **James Cameron**
Screenplay: **James Cameron**, William Wisher
Cinematography: Adam Greenberg
Production Design: Joseph Nemec III
Art Direction: Joseph P. Lucky

Set Decoration: John M. Dwyer
Costume Design: Marlene Stewart
Editing: Conrad Buff, Mark Goldblatt, Richard A. Harris, Dody Dorn (special edition)
Music: Brad Fiedel
Cast: Arnold Schwarzenegger (The Terminator), Linda Hamilton (Sarah Connor), Edward Furlong (John Connor), Robert Patrick (T-1000), Earl Boen (Dr. Silberman), Joe Morton (Miles Dyson), S. Epatha Merkerson (Tarissa Dyson), Castulo Guerra (Enrique Salceda), Danny Cooksey (Tim), Jenette Goldstein (Janelle Voight), Xander Berkeley (Todd Voight)
Color, 137 minutes

POINT BREAK
Production Company: JVC Entertainment Networks, Largo Entertainment
Producer: Peter Abrams, Robert L. Levy
Executive Producer: **James Cameron**
Co-Producer: Rick King, Michael Rauch
Director: Kathryn Bigelow
Screenplay: W. Peter Iliff
Story: Rick King, W. Peter Iliff
Cinematography: Donald Peterman
Production Design: Peter Jamison
Art Direction: Pamela Marcotte, John Huke (uncredited)
Set Decoration: Linda Spheeris
Editing: Howard Smith
Music: Mark Isham
Cast: Patrick Swayze (Bodhi), Keanu Reeves (Johnny Utah), Gary Busey (Pappas), Lori Petty (Tyler), John McGinley (Ben Harp), James Le Gros (Roach), John Philbin (Nathanial), Bojesse Christopher (Grommet), Julian Reyes (Alvarez)
Color, 120 minutes

1994
TRUE LIES
Production Company: Twentieth Century Fox Film Corporation, Lightstorm Entertainment
Producer: Stephanie Austin, **James Cameron**
Executive Producer: Lawrence Kasanoff, Rae Sanchini, Robert Shriver
Associate Producer: Pamela Easley

Director: **James Cameron**
Screenplay: **James Cameron**
Screenplay (*La Totale!*): Claude Zidi, Simon Michaël, Didier Kaminka
Cinematography: Russell Carpenter
Production Design: Peter Lamont
Art Direction: Robert Laing, Michael Novotny
Set Decoration: Cindy Carr
Costume Design: Marlene Stewart
Editing: Conrad Buff, Mark Goldblatt, Richard A. Harris, **James Cameron** (uncredited)
Music: James Horner
Cast: Arnold Schwarzenegger (Harry Tasker), Jaime Lee Curtis (Helen Tasker), Tom Arnold (Albert Gibson), Bill Paxton (Simon), Tia Carrere (Juno Skinner), Art Malik (Salim Abu Aziz), Eliza Dushku (Dana Tasker), Grant Heslov (Faisil), Charlton Heston (Spencer Trilby)
Color, 141 minutes

1995
STRANGE DAYS
Production Company: Lightstorm Entertainment
Producer: **James Cameron**, Steven-Charles Jaffe
Executive Producer: Lawrence Kasanoff, Rae Sanchini
Co-Producer: Ira Shuman
Director: Kathryn Bigelow
Screenplay: **James Cameron**, Jay Cocks
Story: **James Cameron**
Cinematography: Matthew F. Leonetti
Production Design: Lilly Kilvert
Art Direction: John Wamke
Set Decoration: Kara Lindstrom
Costume Design: Ellen Mirojnick
Editing: Howard Smith, **James Cameron** (uncredited)
Music: Graeme Revell
Cast: Ralph Fiennes (Lenny Nero), Angela Bassett (Lornette "Mace" Mason), Juliette Lewis (Faith Justin), Tom Sizemore (Max Peltier), Michael Wincott (Philo Gant), Vincent D'Onofrio (Burton Steckler), Glenn Plummer (Jeriko One), Brigitte Bako (Iris)
Color, 145 minutes

1997
TITANIC
Production Company: Twentieth Century Fox Film Corporation, Paramount Pictures, Lightstorm Entertainment
Producer: **James Cameron**, Jon Landau
Executive Producer: Rae Sanchini
Co-Producer: Al Giddings, Grant Hill, Sharon Mann
Associate Producer: Pamela Easley Harris
Director: **James Cameron**
Screenplay: **James Cameron**
Cinematography: Russell Carpenter
Production Design: Peter Lamont
Art Direction: Martin Laing, Charles Lee
Set Decoration: Michael Ford
Costume Design: Deborah L. Scott
Editing: Conrad Buff, **James Cameron**, Richard A. Harris
Music: James Horner
Cast: Leonardo DiCaprio (Jack Dawson), Kate Winslet (Rose DeWitt Bukater), Billy Zane (Caledon "Cal" Hockley), Kathy Bates (Molly Brown), Frances Fisher (Ruth DeWitt Bukater), Gloria Stuart (Old Rose), Bill Paxton (Brock Lovett), Bernard Hill (Captain Edward James Smith), David Warner (Spicer Lovejoy), Victor Garber (Thomas Andrews)
Color, 194 minutes

2002
SOLARIS
Production Company: Twentieth Century Fox Film Corporation, Lightstorm Entertainment
Producer: **James Cameron**, Jon Landau, Rae Sanchini
Executive Producer: Gregory Jacobs
Co-Producer: Charles V. Bender, Michael Polaire
Director: Steven Soderbergh
Screenplay: Steven Soderbergh
Novel: Stanislaw Lem
Cinematography: Peter Andrews
Production Design: Philip Messina
Art Direction: Steve Arnold, Keith P. Cunningham
Set Decoration: Mike Malone, Kristen Toscano Messina
Costume Design: Milena Canonero
Editing: Mary Ann Bernard

Music: Cliff Martinez
Cast: George Clooney (Chris Kelvin), Natascha McElhone (Rheya), Viola Davis (Gordon), Jeremy Davies (Snow), Ulrich Tukur (Gibarian), John Cho (DBA Emissary #1), Morgan Rusler (DBA Emissary #2), Shane Skelton (Gibarian's Son)
Color, 99 minutes

2009
AVATAR
Production Company: Twentieth Century Fox Film Corporation, Dune Entertainment, Giant Studios, Ingenious Film Partners, Lightstorm Entertainment
Producer: **James Cameron**, Jon Landau
Executive Producer: Laeta Kalogridis, Colin Wilson
Co-Producer: Brooke Breton, Josh McLaglen
Associate Producer: Janace Tashjian
Line Producer: Peter M. Tobyansen
Director: **James Cameron**
Screenplay: **James Cameron**
Cinematography: Mauro Fiore
Production Design: Rick Carter, Robert Stromberg
Art Direction: Nick Bassett, Robert Bavin, Simon Bright, Todd Cherniawsky, Jill Cormack, Stefan Dechant, Seth Engstrom, Sean Haworth, Kevin Ishioka, Andrew L. Jones, Andy McLaren, Andrew Menzies, Norman Newberry, Ben Procter, Kim Sinclair
Set Decoration: Kim Sinclair
Costume Design: John Harding, Mayes C. Rubeo, Deborah Lynn Scott
Editing: **James Cameron**, John Refoua, Stephen Rivkin
Music: James Horner
Cast: Sam Worthington (Jake Sully), Zoe Saldana (Neytiri), Sigourney Weaver (Dr. Grace Augustine), Stephan Lang (Colonel Miles Quaritch), Joel David Moore (Norm Spellman), Giovanni Ribisi (Parker Selfridge), Michelle Rodriguez (Trudy Chacon)
Color, 162 minutes

Documentaries

2003
GHOSTS OF THE ABYSS
Production Company: Earthship Productions, Walden Media, Walt Disney Pictures

Producer: John Bruno, **James Cameron**, Chuck Comisky, Janace Tashjian, Andrew Wight
Executive Producer: Giedra Rackauskas
Segment Producer: Haley Jackson
Creative Producer: Ed W. Marsh
Consulting Producer: Chris Steenolsen
Line Producer: Andrew Wight
Director: **James Cameron**
Cinematography: Vince Pace, D. J. Roller
Production Design: Martin Laing
Art Direction: Leonard Barrit, Javier Nava
Editing: Ed W. Marsh, Sven Pape, John Refoua, David C. Cook (uncredited)
Music: Joel McNeely, Lisa Torban
Cast: Bill Paxton (himself), Dr. John Broadwater (himself), Dr. Lori Johnston (herself), Don Lynch (himself/Thomas Andrews), Ken Marschall (himself/J. Bruce Ismay), **James Cameron** (himself), Mike Cameron (himself), Jeffrey N. Ledda (himself)
Color, 59 minutes

VOLCANOES OF THE DEEP SEA
Producer: Alex Low, Pietro L. Serapiglia
Executive Producer: **James Cameron**
Line Producer: Lilly Antonecchia, Dougal Caron
Director: Stephen Low
Screenplay: Alex Low, Stephen Low
Cinematography: William Reeve
Editing: James Lahti
Music: Michel Cusson
Cast: Ed Harris (narrator), Dr. Richard Lutz (himself)
Color, 40 minutes

2005
ALIENS OF THE DEEP
Production Company: Buena Vista Pictures, Earthship Productions, Walden Media
Producer: **James Cameron**, Andrew Wight
Associate Producer: Christopher A. Debiec
Creative Producer: Ed W. Marsh
Director: **James Cameron**, Steven Quale
Cinematography: **James Cameron**, Vince Pace

Art Direction: Leonard Barrit
Editing: Matthew Kregor, Ed W. Marsh, Fiona Wight
Music: Jeehun Hwang
Cast: Dr. Anatoly M. Sagalevitch (himself, MIR chief pilot/Keldysh expedition leader), Genya Chernaiev (himself, MIR pilot), Victor Nischeta (himself, MIR pilot), Pamela Conrad (herself, JPL astrobiologist), **James Cameron** (himself)
Color, 47 minutes

Television

1988
MARTINI RANCH: REACH
Production Company: David Naylor & Associates
Producer: Tom Huckabee, Bill Paxton
Line Producer: Howard Woffinden
Director: **James Cameron**
Cinematography: John R. Leonetti
Editing: Howard E. Smith
Cast: Kathryn Bigelow, Bobbie Brat, Bud Cort, Jenette Goldstein, Philip Granger, Lance Henricksen, Charlottle McGinnis, Adrian Pasdar, Bill Paxton, Judge Reinhold, Paul Reiser, Mark Rolston, Scott Thomson
Color, 8 minutes

2000–2002
DARK ANGEL
Production Company: 20th Century Fox Television, Cameron/Eglee Productions
Series Producer: Stephen Sassen, Janace Tashjian, Michael Angeli
Series Executive Producer: **James Cameron**, Charles H. Eglee, René Echevarria
Series Co-Executive Producer: Rae Sanchini, Kenneth Biller, et al.
Series Co-Producer: Gina Lamar, George A. Grieve, Moira Kirland, Doris Egan
Series Consulting Producer: Chip Johannessen, David Simkins, et al.
Series Supervising Producer: Patrick Harbinson, Steve Beers
Series Director: Jeff Woolnough, Thomas J. Wright, **James Cameron** (1 episode), et al.
Series Creator: **James Cameron**, Charles H. Eglee

Series Writer: Jose Molina, Moira Kirland, René Echevarria, **James Cameron** (2 episodes)
Series Cinematography: David Geddes, Brian Pearson
Series Production Design: Jerry Wanek
Series Art Direction: John Marcynuk
Series Set Decoration: Tedd Kuchera, Jonathan Lancaster
Series Costume Design: Jennifer L. Bryan, Susan De Laval, Derek J. Baskerville
Series Editing: John Refoua, Steven Polivka, James Wilcox, Stephen Mark
Series Music: Joel McNeely, Amani K. Smith
Series Cast: Jessica Alba (Max Guevera/X5-452), Michael Weatherly (Logan Cale), Richard Gunn (Calvin "Sketchy" Theodore), J. C. MacKenzie (Reagan "Normal" Ronald), Valarie Rae Miller (Cynthia "Original Cindy" McEachin), John Savage (Donald Lydecker)
Color, 43 minutes per episode

2002
EXPEDITION: BISMARCK
Production Company: Discovery Channel Pictures, Earthship Productions
Producer: **James Cameron**, Andrew Wight
Consulting Producer: Chris Steenolsen (uncredited)
Director: **James Cameron**
Cinematography: Christopher Titus King, Vince Pace, D. J. Roller
Editing: Chris Angel, Calli Cerami, Matt Kregor, Fiona Wight
Music: Jeehun Hwang
Cast: Lance Henricksen (narrator), **James Cameron** (himself), Walter Weintz (himself), Curt Lowens (Walter Weintz), Karl Kuhn (himself), Richard Doyle (Karl Kuhn), Heinz Steeg (himself), Kai Wulff (Heinz Steeg)
Color, 92 minutes

2005–2006
ENTOURAGE
Production Company: Home Box Office (HBO), Leverage Management
Series Executive Producer: Doug Ellin, Stephen Levinson, Mark Wahlberg
Series Director: Julian Farino, Mark Mylod, Ken Whittingham, et al.
Series Writer: Doug Ellin, Rob Weiss, Ally Musika, et al.

Series Cinematography: Rob Sweeney, Steven Fierberg, et al.
Series Editing: Gregg Featherman, Jeff Groth, Jon Corn, et al.
Series Production Designer: Chase Harlan, Stephen McCabe, et al.
Series Art Direction: Elizabeth Thinnes, Chase Harlan, et al.
Series Costume Designer: Amy Westcott, Olivia Miles, et al.
Series Cast: Kevin Connelly (Eric Murphy), Adrian Grenier (Vincent Chase), Kevin Dillon (Johnny "Drama" Chase), Jerry Ferrara (Turtle), Jeremy Piven (Ari Gold), **James Cameron** (himself, 4 episodes)
Color, 30 minutes per episode

2005
LAST MYSTERIES OF THE TITANIC
Production Company: Earthship Productions
Producer: **James Cameron**, Andrew Wight
Associate Producer: Christopher A. Debiec, Haley Jackson
Technical Producer: Bernie Laramie
Director: Neil Flagg
Cinematography: David E. West, Ralph B. White
Editing: David C. Cook, Matthew Kregor, Justin Shaw, Fiona Wight
Music: Geoff Levin, Paul Searles
Cast: Laura Anderson (passenger), Lynn Anderson (passenger), Scott G. Anderson (Lookout Frederick Fleet), Mike Arbuthnot (himself), Paul Brightwell (Quartermaster Robert Hichens), John Burke (Host)
Color

TITANIC ADVENTURE
Production Company: Earthship Productions, Independent Television News, Channel 4 Television Corporation, Discovery Channel UK
Producer: **James Cameron**, Mel Morpeth, Andrew Wight
Executive Producer: Jeremy Cross, Philip Armstrong Dampier
Assistant Producer: Christopher A. Debiec, Kathryn Jennex, Irene McMillan
Director: Mel Morpeth
Editing: Bernard Moss, Tony Quinn
Cast: Tony Robinson (himself, presenter), Mike Arbuthnot (himself, marine archaeologist), **James Cameron** (himself), Emily Jateff (herself, marine archaeologist), Lori Johnston (herself, microbiologist), Don Lynch (himself, *Titanic* historian)
Color, 77 minutes

2006
THE EXODUS DECODED
Production Company: Associated Producers
Producer: Felix Golubev, Simcha Jacobovici
Executive Producer: **James Cameron**, Susan Werbe
Director: Simcha Jacobovici
Cinematography: Damir I. Chytil, Richard Fox
Art Direction: Hili Tsarfati
Editing: Graeme Ball, Ian Morehead (uncredited)
Music: John Welsman
Cast: Uzi Avner (himself), Manfred Bietak (himself), John Bimson (himself), **James Cameron** (himself), Philip Davies (himself), William G. Dever (himself), Prof. Christos Doumas (himself), David Faiman (himself), Catherine Hickson (herself)
Color, 92 minutes

2007
THE LOST TOMB OF JESUS
Producer: Ric Esther Bienstock, Felix Golubev, Simcha Jacobovici
Executive Producer: **James Cameron**
Director: Simcha Jacobovici
Screenplay: Graeme Ball, Simcha Jacobovici
Cinematography: J. P. Locherer, John Petrella
Art Direction: Avishay Avivi
Editing: Graeme Ball
Cast: Mark Caven (narrator, UK), Ouriel Maoz (himself), Rivka Maoz (herself), Dr. Shimon Gibson (himself), Tal Ilan (herself), James Tabor (himself), Simcha Jacobovici (himself), Felix Golubev (himself), Frank Moore Cross (himself)
Color, 102 minutes

James Cameron: Interviews

How To Direct a *Terminator*

Thomas McKelvey Cleaver/1984

Starlog Magazine #89, December 1984, 56–57, 66. Reprinted by permission of the Brooklyn Company.

"I was sick and dead broke in Rome, Italy," director James Cameron reminisces, "with a fever of 102, doing the final cut of *Piranha II*. That's when I thought of *Terminator*. I guess it was a fever dream!"

Terminator, the second movie helmed by the Canadian-born filmmaker, also marks the debut of Arnold Schwarzenegger (*Starlog* #88) in a new screen role—as a villain.

"I would have to say that in my febrile youth, I was an absolutely rabid science-fiction fan," Cameron continues, detailing his background. "I read all the classics, all the old Ace paperback novels. When I went to college, I put the brakes on that reading and got into the 'real world,' which made me realize that many science-fiction writers have a much better perspective on life than those writers who are mired in the specifics of day-to-day life. Now, you might say that I've come full circle and am back to being a big science-fiction fan.

"The thing I most like about science-fiction is that it provides a way of exploring issues without upsetting any one group. You can do a story about an oppressed minority, and your readers could range from people who are members of oppressed minorities themselves to people who profit from that oppression; they can read the story and project their views into it and not get upset, while also reading the other side. If you do a story about a Latino and a landlord today, however, then the readers may get upset and take sides without seeing what the story is really saying."

Using science-fiction as a way to comment on today's realities is another aspect of *Terminator*. "The story is set in a present that *is* affected by the near future," says Cameron. "The catastrophe which creates that future happens right around the corner from us today, and the people of that future—the year 2029—know the people from the present. There is a direct relationship between the present and the future that I don't think has been done before. At the risk of telling the audience what they should think *after* they've seen the movie, *Terminator* speaks to the fact that though none of us may think much about the consequences our actions as individuals might have on the future, those actions do have consequences.

"Basically, I want to give the audience an E-Ticket ride [a la the old Disneyland ticket scheme]. I think they want to think a bit during the film, and talk about it afterwards, but not to have to try and figure out what it is they just saw. My 'film school,' if you will, was hitch-hiking to the nearest town and seeing the features at the two theaters there every Saturday. I was well-grounded in being a member of the audience, and I try to remember that; let's remember that we must be in tune with our audience or the movie won't work.

"The greatest goal of a filmmaker is to entertain. If you have something to say, let it be said in such a way that you're not chasing the audience out of the theater. You have to entertain first, but many filmmakers have forgotten that there must be something *more* than entertainment. If you're just going to entertain, why are you doing it? The audience will walk out. And when they come off the emotional rollercoaster, they have *nothing* left. There's more to filmmaking than just selling popcorn."

Comparing *Terminator* with other genre films, Cameron, observes, "There's a love story at its heart; to put it in a nutshell, I would call it a romantic nightmare. More work was spent—from a writing and acting standpoint—trying to make the people believable in an everyday setting, both in the future and the present. These are people who get up, eat their Wheaties, complain about how much money they're not getting at work, then something incredible happens. The future comes down on them like a bag of bricks! The female lead, Linda Hamilton, goes from being a coffee shop waitress, a student, to where you see that she *does* have the potential to be a world leader, which is what she will become. It's a strong role for a woman, not one of the cliché female characters that have been so much in evidence recently."

FX and Filmmaking

"Science-fiction films were notoriously under-budgeted until George Lucas came along," Cameron notes. "What's happened, though, is that filmmakers have become hardware-happy. The earlier movies told their stories through the characters; I think that earlier approach was better. Today's audience is being taken on a rollercoaster ride, where they sit there, waiting to see the next incredible special effect. They don't care what's going to happen next to the people, because the filmmakers didn't create believable characters for whom an audience can really care. With some of the smaller films coming out now, moviemakers are realizing they must concentrate on the people in the story. An excellent example is *The Dead Zone*."

Cameron's view of the writing process that *Terminator* went through contains some insights for those writing SF screenplays. "I wrote the script with a strategy in mind, knowing the movie would be in competition with the big FX films," he explains. "For X-number of special effects, you must spend X-number of dollars at the threshold. Below that, you'll be showing people things they don't want to see. The audience has become visually educated and sophisticated, and even a bit jaded, by the big guys. My strategy was *not* to do special effects from the beginning to the end; the story is set in Los Angeles, 1984, and the main character is the girl next door. Everything plays out from beginning to end against an everyday backdrop.

"I think when a film is under consideration for production, the first and foremost question is: 'Does it work dramatically?' If it doesn't, it will never get to the point of people worrying about how much it costs. A writer should know enough about special FX to be able to stay away from them. The worst thing to do is overburden a script with effects which will scare people away; on the other hand, you must have something visually interesting.

"The writer must be able to figure out how to limit the effects and still tell the story. Start with one matte shot of the castle, for instance, then go inside and let the rest of the scene play on two sets. When you have it on the page and people read it, it makes sense to them. On the other hand, if you write the same scene to go inside the castle, out on the parapet walls, back inside through fourteen rooms and end out on the roof, you have just made that same scene four times more expensive, probably without adding a thing dramatically."

Nevertheless, this philosophy doesn't signify that *Terminator*, while admittedly done on a "lower" budget of $6 million, is a "cheap" FX flick. "We see the future world, briefly, at the film's beginning and end," Cameron says. "Suddenly, it skyrockets to that level of visual effect. There are quite a few matte shots and many miniatures.

"Our major effect, however, is the Terminator itself, the cyborg. The cyborg is an extrapolation from present-day technology. Without getting too specific, the look of the cyborg comes from current engineering techniques. It's not a suit-of-armor type of robot that can't possibly work, but more like a state-of-the-art robot. When you walk out of the theater, I think you *will* believe you've been watching an honest-to-god operating robot."

Much of the difference in the "look" of *Terminator* derives from Cameron's out-of-the-ordinary route to the director's chair. "I guess the one thing that's common to all independent filmmakers is that they really have *nothing* in common," he laughs. "I went to college and majored in physics for two years, then got married and became a truck driver, and decided I really *did* want to be a filmmaker. I had my own production company and did commercials and industrial films. I raised some money and did a pilot for a feature, then used the pilot to get a job as effects cameraman and art director on Roger Corman's *Battle Beyond the Stars*.

"Then, I clawed my way up from there, as meanly and brutally as I could," he grins. "Working for Roger was good training. He's the guy who says, 'We'll make a $6 million movie for $500,000.' After *Battle Beyond the Stars*, I did *Galaxy of Terror* and had about five technical credits, then worked as co-effects supervisor for the FX done for *Escape from New York*, created at Roger's Venice facility."

Visions and Violence

While working on *Battle Beyond the Stars*, Cameron met his soon-to-be collaborator, Gale Ann Hurd, who shares screenplay credit with him on *Terminator* and also serves as the film's producer. "Gale was the assistant production manager on *Battle*," he explains. "I had written a treatment and most of a first draft of *Terminator*, which she became involved in polishing. The initial idea was mine, and the collaboration was her taking the rough edges off. Our strength in doing the movie was pooling our resources and forming an impenetrable barrier to anyone who wanted to take it away from us or change the concept.

"It's always a fight to preserve your vision against the vision of others. If you have five people working as producers, you'll get five completely different concepts of what the story's really about, and often they're completely irreconcilable. You have to fall back on your own instinct. Sometimes, the toughest thing to do is to trust yourself. You might not find that possible in a collaboration if it wasn't a relationship with someone you had worked with and knew. We've been very fortunate with the support of Hemdale and Orion [which financed and distributed the film], since we didn't have that much of a track record; we had directed and produced before, but not on the scale of *Terminator*. Both companies now have high hopes for the picture, but there *were* some times in the early stages where we did think it was going to be scooped out from beneath us."

Hiring Arnold Schwarzenegger to portray the android assassin was a happy accident. "People at Orion passed the script to Arnold," Cameron relates, "with the suggestion that he play the so-called 'hero,' Reese. He and I met, and neither of us felt very comfortable about him in that part. It had never occurred to anyone that he consider playing the villain, but that was the role he wanted! Now, Arnold is a shaven-headed, eyebrowless half-man/half-machine in a black leather jacket with wraparound sunglasses. It does break the mold of what people think about him. And Arnold has come to the point where he realizes he can do what he wants to do as an actor, and he's willing to take chances."

Critics of film violence may take aim at *Terminator*. But Cameron isn't worried. "It's a gun'n'run, shoot-em-up. Many people get shot and killed. But there isn't much gore; the violence is never rubbed in your face. It's done off-screen and used for dramatic effect. I think the audience will realize that all this violence is directed at an unkillable machine, not a man."

With *Terminator* rampaging through theaters, James Cameron is now relaxing and wondering about the fate of some long-planned sequels. "I *have* written the screenplay for *Alien II*," he reveals. "It *does* exist. What will be done with it, no one really knows. I can't really say anything more about *Alien II* than that it does exist." He has also scripted the sequel to *First Blood*. "I suppose there I'll have to go to the theater with everyone else to see what's been done with it."

The 1984 Movie Revue: James Cameron Interviewed by David Chute

David Chute/1985

From *Film Comment*, February 1985, 54, 55, 57–60. Reprinted by permission of David Chute.

James Cameron, writer-director of *The Terminator*, was one of the last cum-laude graduates of the Roger Corman School of Survival Filmmaking—New World Pictures as it existed before Corman sold the company and moved on.

Cameron's stripped-down box-office winner looks like something a Corman protégé might devise: It's almost nonstop, flamboyant action, kicked off when a killer android from the future (Arnold Schwarzenegger) pops up stark naked in contemporary downtown L.A. and begins implacably stalking his assigned victim, Sarah Connor (Linda Hamilton). Her unborn child will lead a revolution against the coming dictatorship of intelligent machines. Michael Beihn plays Reese, the future revolutionary sent back to prevent the killing.

The picture may look New Worldish, but Cameron doesn't. With his neat coiffure, distressed-leather bomber jacket, and pastel-striped shirt, he's more visibly Hollywoody than the Joe Dantes and Jonathan Kaplans and Paul Bartels of legend. But his aesthetic credentials can't be faulted.

DC: I remember reading that your first goal in life was to be a comic book artist—that you grew up wanting to draw Iron Man.
JC: I always wanted to be a raconteur, a storyteller, and I also wanted to create visually and produce images. I was always doing both: I'd be writing stories and also painting, looking for a way to mesh them. Well, comics are a fusion of those two things, so it seemed like a natural. But I'd

been going to movies like a rabid maniac, and at a certain point, I said, "That's what a movie is. It's a visual medium with a narrative intent."

For a long time I was working as a truck driver to support myself while I wrote scripts. Then I quit to make a pilot for a feature film. I raised some money from a consortium of dentists in Orange County. It was an attempt to do a little piece of a big-budget science-fiction film: $20,000 for a ten-minute segment of a movie that was just like something you might see in a theater. It was crudely edited, but there's a visual narrative there and the special effects are pretty good. It showed certain basic skills. On the strength of that I got a job at New World—the old New World, with Roger Corman.

DC: New World has been the classic entry point for new talent in recent years, maybe the only entry point where a passion for movies still meant something.

JC: I was lucky in that the last wave had just left—the Dante–Mike Finnell–Jon Davison wave—and there was a bit of a vacuum. It was around 1979. Roger was doing pictures which for him were rather ambitious, science-fiction films in the $2 million range. They were projects I could excel in, because I had been an illustrator and I had a strong sense of design for fantasy and science fiction.

So things happened very quickly. I worked on *Battle Beyond the Stars*, on everything from special effects to production design to a little bit of second unit to post-production work as a matte artist; I had five credits on that movie. I was co-supervisor of effects on *Escape from New York*, which were done by Roger's effects company as a subcontract deal. Then on *Galaxy of Terror* I did some illustrations as an effects person, and the executives on the picture saw that I had an affinity for that particular project visually. When the art director began to malfunction and had to be disassembled and repaired elsewhere, I was asked to be the suicide-mission volunteer who would take over that function two days into shooting. There were thirty-five sets required; two had been constructed. The set that was due the next day had not been started yet.

They talked in *The Right Stuff* about pushing the outside of the envelope. Well, you do that in a low-budget environment. Some hysteria catches you, and you either wash out and say, "I don't need this," or the challenge gets to you—the challenge of doing it for less and making it great, or great relative to the string and baling wire you had to work with and the ten seconds you had to do it. The advantage of working at this level in film is that you're not risking a career. You can roll the dice. You can put the pedal to the floor. You develop a sort of gonzo mentality. Once you're within a more formal structure, you have to back off from that and learn to delegate responsibility.

DC: Does that habit of a hands-on approach linger, though? Does it pay off later on?
JC: For me it lingers, and I think it absolutely pays off. You see with some filmmakers where they begin to delegate too much authority. They're not in control of the nuances that give texture to a film like *Das Boot*, let's say, where every scene and every shot has some thought behind it. People get the smell of a movie that is too glossy or too packaged. They tend to like underdog movies.

I think *Terminator* has an aspect of that. It was an underdog movie from a production standpoint, and also from a marketing standpoint. People come out of the theater feeling that they got more than they expected from the marketing. That's positive word-of-mouth.

DC: You seem to be fairly pleased with the picture.
JC: *Terminator* was in some ways an ultimate experience for me. I got to conceive the idea, write the script, have a deal made, storyboard the major scenes, go about creating those images in casting and sets and locations, then film it and compare the finished shots to the storyboards and see a satisfyingly similar type of image. For me it was a clean sweep. I got to do everything I wanted to do.

And even beyond that, there was really almost no harmful interference from executives. Our production deal with Hemdale and Orion was structured in such a way that they gave us room to make the picture, and for that we are thankful.

DC: You've said that your initial impetus for the picture was the image of the skeletal metal robot emerging from a fire.
JC: The producer, Gale Hurd, and I set out to make a movie that would function on a couple of levels: as a linear action piece that a twelve-year-old would think was the most *rad* picture he'd ever seen, and as science fiction that a forty-five-year-old Stanford English prof would think had some sort of socio-political significance between the lines—although obviously it doesn't attempt to be that primarily. It coalesced around the image of the robot.

I was thinking of an indestructible machine, an endo-skeleton design, which had never been filmed as such. We'd had things like *Westworld*, where Yul Brynner's face falls off and there's a transistor radio underneath—which is not visually satisfying, because you don't feel that this mechanism could have been inside moving those facial features. So it started from the idea of doing this sort of definitive movie robot, what I've always wanted to see. I had this image of him being covered in flesh and having it burn off, and coming phoenix-like out of the fire.

DC: One of the things that makes the picture rad is that the robot keeps on going so much longer than you expect that it gets to be a great joke. I found myself laughing a lot at *The Terminator*.
JC: It plays completely against your expectation of the moment—and of course I can't enjoy that because I always knew what was going to happen next.

DC: But you've watched audiences react.
JC: Especially really early. Because Orion compressed all their ad money into the week before release, and only did one preview, people went in thinking, "This is going to be Arnold Schwarzenegger as Dirty Harry, maybe with a science-fiction edge to it." But they had no concept of where the road was actually going to take them—and that's great, because to me that's what a movie is. You sit down and it takes you someplace. The best is, if it can take you beyond where you thought you were going to go, and in a way that is not *so* surprising that you don't buy it. If you go back and look, the final version of the robot in *Terminator* is totally prepared for. There's the scene where the Terminator repairs his eye, and you see the mechanisms in his arm. You've known it was there the whole time. But people have just been conditioned to *not* getting what they want at the movies, to always thinking that the filmmaker is going to cheat them—and that if he describes this fantastic machine you're not going to really see it.

At our one—count 'em, one—preview, the audience was very young, twelve to eighteen. And they were hyper, they were screaming, they were ripping the wallpaper off the walls. And I thought, "There is no way they are going to sit quietly through a long character scene like the one in the culvert." But they sat through, in rapt attention. My interpretation is that the overall sense of dread of this character constantly coming back is so well established, they might have been thinking the Terminator was going to walk in while Sarah and Kyle are talking. At least they knew, it had been established that what was said would have some bearing on the action.

DC: Part of the fun of the movie is that it does go further than other movies of this type, but in a playful spirit. It's mean and amoral, but it's also mock-mean; you can get exhilarated rather than knotted up. I think Arnold helps it a lot. He brings an edge of irony to it. He seems to be having fun.

JC: It's a sense of larger-than-life meanness, almost like Darth Vader. It's not like some guy running up and shooting you in the stomach to get twenty-five bucks out of your wallet. Some people have said they found it silly, but I hope it's silly in the good sense of not taking itself too seriously.

DC: It's more like a mood that's being shared between the film and the audience: "Let's have fun."

JC: Exactly. The initial impulse was to make a gritty, street-level science-fiction movie that you would buy as if it was really happening. But Arnold was rather different from what I had envisioned. I'd thought of the Terminator as a more anonymous, saturnine figure—Jürgen Prochnow was one actor I had in mind. With Arnold, the film took on a larger-than-life sheen. I just found myself on the set doing things I didn't think I would do—scenes that were supposed to be purely horrific that just couldn't be, because they were now too flamboyant.

DC: You turn a human being who already seems almost superhuman into a machine, and then you humanize the machine and make people identify with him.

JC: Orion's initial thought was that the poster of Arnold with his chest bared would make women want to come and see the movie. But I don't think anybody sees him in a sexual way in the film. They see him almost from the beginning as this implacable, sexless, emotionless machine—in the form of a man, which is scary, because he's a perfect male figure.

DC: Kids I've seen at screenings of, say, *Dawn of the Dead*, really seem to be rooting for the zombies.

JC: In this film, you have it both ways. You root for Reese and Sarah, you want them to live, you feel the emotions. At the same time, you love to root for the bad guy; you want to see *him* get up again, you want to see him dumbfound the poor cops.

There a little bit of the Terminator in everybody. In our private fantasy world we'd all like to be able to walk in and shoot somebody we don't like, or to kick a door in instead of unlocking it; to be immune, and just to have our own way every minute. The Terminator is the ultimate rude person. He operates completely outside all the built-in social constraints. It's a dark, cathartic fantasy. That's why people don't cringe in terror from the Terminator but go with him. They want to be him for that one moment. But then when we go back to Reese and Sarah, you get the other side of it, what it would feel like to be on the receiving end.

DC: In an article discussing his pseudonym, Richard Stark, the thriller novelist Donald Westlake says, "Stark is a professional writer writing about a professional thief. That's the link between us, the idea of taking a task seriously and doing it the best you can." In other words, these are books about competence. The lead character, Parker, is amoral and brutal, but he never makes a wrong move, he's never distracted, he's never neurotic. That's the vicarious pleasure of the Parker books.
JC: And that's exactly the pleasure of *Terminator*. Because he's computerized he takes the path of least resistance, he's highly efficient, he's unwavering in his purpose, and he always lands on his feet. He may be on fire and rolling off the hood of a car, but he's thinking about his next move.

DC: He goes beyond even what Clint Eastwood represents as Dirty Harry.
JC: With Dirty Harry it's a different thing; it's a fantasy of perfect, real-time justice.
   In the terms of those movies Dirty Harry is always right and only shoots people who deserve it. You can't say that about the Terminator. When I'm asked the question about the violence in *The Terminator*, one of the things I point out is that it doesn't have the implication of going out and making the world better with a .44 Magnum.

DC: The tone of the movie seems enough of a safeguard against anyone taking it literally and imitating it.
JC: There had to be a joking edge to it. I don't think I go as far as someone like Joe Dante or John Landis, though. They're always oscillating between extremes of horror and extremes of humor.

DC: You actually followed in Dante's footsteps by directing *Piranha II: The Spawning*.
JC: Do we have to talk about that? It's the finest flying-piranha movie ever made, but it was a troubled picture. I replaced another director, the effects people did not speak English—it was an Italian production with

an American cast shot in the Caribbean. Plus, it was done by a producer who desperately wanted to be a director.

DC: I gather it was screenwriting that got your career going.

JC: Well, there was a hiatus in the production of *Terminator* where I had the opportunity to write two other scripts, basically on the strength of that one. The first one was *The Mission* a.k.a. *Rambo*, the sequel to *First Blood*. They switched the name after the fact, and Sylvester Stallone changed a few other things after the fact—although that was a given. I was a hired gun and took it for that reason, to see what it felt like to write without hoping you might direct. Then I got involved with Walter Hill and David Giler, who are producing *Alien II*.

DC: It must be a validation for someone who works in action pictures to get hired by Walter Hill.

JC: It's an absolute validation, because I had *The Driver* in mind when I was writing certain scenes *in The Terminator*. Not that I was cribbing; I had only seen the picture once and just had a dim memory of the kinetic forward energy he had in it. And then while I was writing *Terminator*, *The Road Warrior* came out and I said, "This is the next step." Nobody in between had come close. My interpretation of Walter's supporting me is that he wants to see me succeed—so that it can go on to the next stage.

DC: People said of *Alien* when it first came out—and it's also true of *Outland* and *Blade Runner* and *Terminator*—that it presented the future in a very grim light because that's what people find plausible now. The future won't be better than the present, it's going to be all the worst aspects of the present intensified. The current audience seems to take that notion for granted.

JC: It's depressing when you watch the interviews with high school kids the day after *The Day After* and see that they've come to accept the inevitability of nuclear war. In *The Terminator* the fact of nuclear war is thrown away, with the complete understanding that people will buy it. It's just part of the fabric of the story. On the other hand, it tried to say that you take responsibility for your own life, and for the life of society. The Terminator looks like death, and if you want to read into it, it's a death image. Linda Hamilton's character faces that image of death or fate, and survives.

All that has resonance, I hope, with the dark, premonitory character of Reese's future-flashbacks, as I call them, and with the final image of driving off into a storm. It's fate vs. will.

Writer-Director Shows the Special Effect Energy Can Radiate

JoAnn Rhetts/1986

From the *Charlotte Observer*, July 13, 1986. Reprinted by permission of the *Charlotte Observer*.

Once upon a time in America—in late October 1984 to be precise—Orion Pictures dumped onto the market a little science-fiction thriller. Two weeks, the marketing whizzes obviously figured, then *Dune, 2010,* and all the other big-deal Christmas movies would stomp Arnold Schwarzenegger and his nobody costars to steel splinters. No big deal.

The Terminator, however, proved to be a very large deal. A $6.5 million picture about a killer cyborg (Schwarzenegger in the role of his career) sent back from the future to contemporary Los Angeles to assassinate the woman who would someday bear the savior of her race. It grossed more than $25 million in its first four weeks of release. On the road to being named one of *Time* magazine's ten best movies of 1984, it quickly flattened those would-be Christmas blockbusters and eventually finished second only to *The Karate Kid* in 1985 videocassette rentals.

The reason was a man unheard of except by those few who might have seen the surprisingly agile *Piranha II.* James Cameron, the turbo-charged writer-director whose second and third films—*The Terminator* and *Rambo: First Blood Part II*—would eventually haul in more than $350 million at the nation's box offices.

Friday's release of *Aliens,* his speed-of-light, $17 million sequel to Ridley Scott's 1979 science-fiction classic, should push that ante sky-high and make Cameron a household word. In any households, that is, with a love of high-octane action, strong characters (strong women, especially), tonsil-knotting suspense, and wry jokes like the supermarket product identification codes translated into *The Terminator*'s futuristic prison tattoos.

"*Aliens*," says Cameron resplendent on a recent June afternoon in a black open-neck shirt crawling with virulently purple orchids, "is the movie I would have died to see when I was fourteen." The strawberry blond, six-foot-two thirty-one year old director speaks so softly a listener could easily miss his gleeful observations about previous night's terrified preview audience lumping together like fans doing the wave in a football stadium. You wonder how he made himself heard on the set over the screaming marines and blasting machine guns.

How he makes himself heard—according to Michael Biehn, who played the rough-tough love interests of Linda Hamilton in *The Terminator* and Sigourney Weaver in *Aliens*—is by knowing everything there is to know about making movies and by having the unstoppable momentum of ten killer cyborgs.

"He got a lot of his film education from (low-budget filmmaker) Roger Corman," says Biehn. "He seems to know everybody's job on the set better than they do."

The very morning after they'd wrapped *The Terminator*, Biehn walked into Cameron's office and found him gobbling cheese crackers and "furiously scribbling. 'I got a treatment for *Aliens* I gotta get out by 12:30,'" Biehn recalls him saying. "That shows you the energy he has."

Cameron, who was "a major peacenik in the sixties" and who was booed last year by a screenwriting class at a Los Angeles Christian college for making "a little disparaging remark in the best possible taste" about Ronald Reagan, is infinitely more comfortable with the morality of a *Terminator* or an *Aliens* than that of *Rambo*.

Dealing with cyborgs or huge hungry praying mantises, you don't, in Cameron's words, "flounder in morality. You're not killing human beings. You don't have to ask yourself, 'Do they have a family? Did they get drafted?'"

You do have to ask yourself why any director in his right mind—especially a young one who's trying to leave his stamp on the Hollywood hills—would tackle a sequel to a movie as popular and innovative as the original *Alien*.

"Insanity," Cameron says, laughing. "What we did was we tried to deflect any possible criticism by making the film in our style, making it more thematically consistent with *Terminator* than with *Alien*." (He's not using the royal "we"—since last April he's been married to *Terminator* producer Gale Anne Hurd, whom he met after the 1977 Phi Beta

Kappa Stanford graduate joined Corman's New World Pictures as executive assistant to the president.)

And that style? "I think there's an emphasis on action and character. Fast cutting. Good storytelling. Hopefully, trying to stay away from visual pretension as much as possible. Just go for fun and exhilaration and people that you can relate to as human beings, which I think is very important . . . because science fiction has a tendency to be interested in visual things and special- effects and be noninvolving, be sort of a passive entertainment. Whereas what Gale and I like to do is make a film that sort of pulls you in."

"Jim said to me," remembers Sigourney Weaver, who plays beleaguered Officer Ripley in both *Alien* films, "'If you think of the first one as a fun house, this one's the roller coaster.'"

A roller coaster, maybe, at a very weird amusement park, where the skies are all cloudy and gray, you can stroll through the bowels of a mean mommy monster, and everything—but everything—leaks a gloomy moisture,. That constant and annoying drip-drip-drip, though, is emblematic of Cameron's approach to his craft.

"Obviously, a film has no touch-feel; it's all just sound and vision," he says. "But everybody knows what it feels like to have water dripping on you. So if you can create a scene that's so quiet, and you can project yourself into it and know what it would feel like to be standing where the actor is standing, then anything that happens to that character is in a way happening to you.

"Any way in which you can make a film more of a subjective experience for the audience member, the more impact it's going to have. And I think that's what people pay hard-earned dollars for when they go to see a film like this—to participate in it, to have their senses affected, to feel emotions."

As a teenager in Niagara Falls, Ontario—actually, "a little town outside Niagara Falls with forty miles of woods behind our house"—he never missed a Saturday matinee at the two local theaters. Stanley Kubrick's landmark *2001: A Space Odyssey* made him sick. "It had such an effect on me that I was physically ill from the vertigo sequence," he remembers. "I also wanted to find out how it was done, so I started studying photography and special effects."

The oldest of five children of an electrical engineer and a homemaker ("there's always been a sense of her trying to do more and being frustrated, trapped by the family"—which probably explains his movie superwomen), Cameron was a straight-A high school student.

"Then I kind of dropped out and became a biker for a while, worked in a machine shop, drove a truck. Then I went to college (California State University at Fullerton) for a couple of years and majored in physics."

He joined Corman's manic movie factory as a miniature builder on *Battle Beyond the Stars* (1980). Initially, Hurd, now thirty, was less than bowled over. "I thought he was very aggressive for a model-builder," she remembers. "Here's this guy who was ordering everyone around, and he wasn't even in charge."

"Trust Gale to notice that," says Cameron. "She's definitely the one for seeing the psychodynamics of leadership.

"But let's face it, at New World (other veterans of Corman wars include Jack Nicholson, Martin Scorsese, Francis Ford Coppola, Peter Bogdanovich, and John Sayles), it was put up or shut up, sink or swim *the first day*. The other thing was there were no rigid preconceptions about what you should be doing (like making spaceship walls from fast-food Styrofoam trays—one of Cameron's innovations). You could do pretty much whatever you could convince other people you could do.

"It was a matter of wearing a lot of different hats and getting a lot of experience very quickly. I made more enemies there in two weeks—it took me years to get it straightened out."

Although, says Cameron, "It's very unhip from a Hollywood standpoint not to have your next four pictures mapped out," he has no plans beyond an immediate Hawaiian vacation with his wife. Hurd's production companies will produce all Cameron's projects, but she'll work on other pictures as well. In development is *The Silent Man*, her drama about a boy caught in the turmoil of South Africa's troubled Soweto.

And there's always the possibility of a tiny terminator. A baby, says Cameron in tongue-in-cheek Hollywood-ese, "is another thing we're . . . negotiating. My people are talking to her people."

Aliens: An Out of This World Communication with Director James Cameron

Victor Wells/1986

From *Prevue Magazine*, August 1986, 42–46. Reprinted by permission of J. Steranko, editor-publisher of *Prevue Magazine*.

"There are three kinds of pictures: high-budget movies, low-budget flicks, and no-waste films. I'm a no-waste filmmaker," says James Cameron, underscoring the fact that, in a business where the average product costs more than $10 million, a careful, imaginative artist can generate maximum box office with minimal expenditure.

The triple-threat entrepreneur began his career with Roger Corman, working in various capacities, art directed *Battle Beyond the Stars*, co-supervised special fx for John Carpenter's *Escape from New York*, acted as production designer and second unit director for *Planet of Horrors*, and directed *Pirahna II*.

Additionally, Cameron is an accomplished illustrator whose efforts have ranged from creating movie ad campaigns to storyboarding the films he directs. In 1984, besides co-scripting *Rambo: First Blood II*, he wrote and directed *The Terminator*, a breathtaking SF thriller that scored internationally with critics and audiences, catapulting the thirty-three-year-old powerhouse into the forefront of contemporary filmmaking.

His latest project, *Aliens*, is the much-awaited follow-up to the 1979 smash hit, *Alien*. Sigourney Weaver reprises her role as Warrant Officer Ripley, the sole survivor of the spaceship *Nostromo*'s encounter with a deadly extraterrestrial. After more than a half-century in suspended animation, she returns to Earth where her story of the ordeal is not believed. The alien planet has since been colonized, and, with contact mysteriously lost, she undertakes a mission back, accompanied by a team of super-Marines armed with high-tech weapons. Realizing her greatest nightmare, she discovers the hostile world overrun with the terrifying creatures—including variations of the Face-hugger, Chest-burster, and a giant Queen alien, thirteen feet high and twenty feet long.

Cameron discussed the genesis of the new film, his approach to creating a sequel to one of the cinema's biggest blockbusters, and Ripley's chances of surviving a second clash with science fiction's most fearsome juggernauts.

Prevue: Sequel-making is a dangerous undertaking, especially when the original is as effective as *Alien*. Obviously, you found a direction that will break new ground.
Cameron: That was the idea; *Aliens* had to be completely different, while still being an extension of the first film—or the *prequel*, as I call it. The writer, Dan O'Bannon, and the director, Ridley Scott, established a set of elements which can't be violated. But, they only created *part* of a universe, which primarily dealt with life and death within the confines of a spaceship.

Prevue: What was your focus in opening up the concept?
Cameron: To begin with, *Alien* happened in space. The characters literally existed in a vacuum—they had no past or life *beyond* that film. Ripley, of course, was the only survivor because she was a very strong female, and that impressed me very much. I wanted to take the character further, to know Ripley as a person, to see some depth and emotion. The movie is about her, *every scene*. It gets inside her mind, takes her back to face her own worst nightmare—and conquer it, so to speak. In a way, *Aliens* is about her revenge.

Prevue: You were asked to make the film in October 1983, before preproduction had even started on *The Terminator*. A year later, you wrote a treatment, then submitted a finished script in February 1985. But, Sigourney Weaver didn't get involved until a few months before filming began. Didn't she modify some of the graphic violence you planned?
Cameron: Let's say she was helpful in recreating Ripley by advising me about what the character would or wouldn't do. By the time she came to it, the screenplay was a *fait accompli*, but she didn't rampage through it, saying this or that *won't* work. She thought it was consistent with the character she had created.

Prevue: You have Ripley lead a combat team against the aliens on their planet.
Cameron: Yes, it was very physically demanding for Sigourney. At first, her character knows nothing about weaponry or fighting, but learns from the soldiers, ultimately becoming the center of the battle to survive. Now she's faced with not only saving her own life, but others' lives, too; people she cares about very much. At the end, she's completely on her own, and must use what she's been taught to stay alive.

Prevue: Your fascination with weaponry really shows through in *Aliens*. They have a familiar look about them, but are modified with futuristic touches. The "Pulse" gun, for example, is a combination Thompson submachine gun and Franchi SPAS 12-pump action shotgun mechanism that can shoot *both* kinds of ammunition. The "Smart" guns, with the helmet-mounted sights like those designed for helicopter pilots, look like MG-42 Spandau-type machine guns. Could *Aliens* qualify as a science fiction combat film?
Cameron: Among other things! I see it as a dark, action piece with a very human center. I like the idea of a futuristic military movie, but not with *Star Wars*' Imperial Storm Troopers running around in fantastic costumes, just "ground pounders," dog soldiers who've been around from the time of the Roman legions to Vietnam.

Prevue: You've also managed to extract some humor from your warriors.
Cameron: Actually, I had a hard time making it *less funny*, so it *didn't* play like a comedy. There's the constant wisecracking, defying authority, complaining about the job with military characters. But, hopefully, audiences will respond, because if they're not sympathetic with the characters, they can't be scared. And the quickest way to make them sympathetic is by being funny. Then, there's the camaraderie between the people who put their lives on the line every day, which also interests me. Couple that with near-super weaponry, and you've got science fiction in the grand tradition—future war.

Prevue: The conflict takes place on Acheron, a name Dante used in his description of the Ninth Circle of Hell. What's your vision of the alien planet?
Cameron: A raw, primal world, constantly windswept with freezing rain—unlike anything on Earth, except for certain familiarities, like

clouds and mountains. The colors, the light, the contours, everything so harsh and hostile that even the rock formations have been eroded into tortured shapes, all dark and shadowy so that things sometimes *appear* to be there—even when they're not.

Ron Cobb, who worked on *Alien* and Syd Mead of *Blade Runner* both contributed conceptual designs, along with production designer Peter Lamont of *Octopussy*. All of us looked for logical reasons why things should be like they are, and the more real they are, the more the audiences will be involved.

Prevue: And frightened, too.
Cameron: Yes. Real fear has to touch a primal spot deep in the brain. Several scenes play on the fear of being trapped in a very tight space with a lethal presence nearby, but unseen—the intense, claustrophobic environment where characters build tension between themselves.

Prevue: But enhanced by the same kind of cinematic velocity that made *Terminator* so explosive.
Cameron: Well, there's nothing quite as exciting as trip-hammer editing and the incredible forward momentum from an action sequence that's really well-orchestrated—A follows B in a kind of domino principle where, once something starts, *nothing* can stop it.

Of course, I underline the action aspect of the story, and the film's last half is a real pressure cooker: the planet, the characters, the bio-mechanoid visuals, the new creatures plus the textural reality of the first film. It's a two-hour roller coaster ride that begins with an electric shock—and never lets up!

James Cameron Takes the Plunge

Alan Jones/1989

Starburst Magazine #135, November 1989 (vol. 12, no. 3). Reprinted by permission of Alan Jones, horror critic, author, and broadcaster.

The Abyss has predictably polarized critical opinion. *Rolling Stone* said, "It out *ET*'s *ET*," while *Film '89* commented on how bad the script was. The dispassionate view probably lies somewhere in the middle ground between the two. What no one can dispute, though, is how director James Cameron has once more pushed the movie making state-of-the-art to new limits. No one else comes even close to Cameron's hardware sensibility or his clearly defined understanding of what plot motors heighten suspense and emotional responsiveness.

In *The Terminator* and *Aliens*, thrills, excitement, and shock were Cameron's driving forces. But in *The Abyss*, while those calling cards are still in evidence, Cameron's slant is more on our human depths than any horrors lurking beneath the ocean.

Cameron remarked, "I wanted to make *The Abyss* because I was interested in a cold, dark, threatening, and very sterile environment. How, as human beings, we are pushing our mental and physical limitations to adapt to that environment. We are using technology to push ourselves further into ever more hostile environments including outer space. But the more we rely on technology, the more we have to rely on each other in our basic capacities as humans to bond together emotionally—in friendship or in love. These factors keep us from destroying each other and allow us to survive in situations we wouldn't have a hope in otherwise."

A lot has happened to James Cameron since we last spoke on *Aliens*. He divorced his producer wife Gale Anne Hurd with whom he formed GJP (Gale Jim Productions), the company behind *The Abyss*, and he married Kathryn Bigelow, director of *Near Dark* and *Blue Steel*.

He has just emerged from the most grueling assignment any director has ever undertaken where the word "Action" was replaced with the command "Right gentlemen, let's get wet!" And he has suffered very badly at the hands of a misinformed American press who reported he was about to be lynched by his stars at any given moment during the six months it took to get *The Abyss* on screen.

Hard to Please Everyone

Now in a relaxed and contemplative mood in his hotel suite at the Savoy in London, I asked Cameron to set the record straight and put all these events in perspective, especially with regard to the controversial ending of *The Abyss*.

He shrugged, "What I've found after making four movies is how hard it is to please everyone. And one shouldn't even aspire to that. If you make a movie along given guidelines, you're condemned for not being original. But when you attempt to throw off conventions and formulas, the same people say it doesn't fit the accepted party line. Reviews for *The Abyss* were pretty evenly divided between the positive and negative. I preferred that to them all being mediocre. But there were enough people who got the gag, which I found very satisfying."

He added, "Working in such a high-budget range I do have a certain responsibility to the financiers. But my responsibility is to adhere to the script they deemed commercial enough to back in the first place. Once the decision is made, and they give me the resources, I don't second guess if the scene I'm shooting will impede or advance the cause of future commerciality. I can't do that even if other directors can. The technical and emotional problems on the set are bad enough without the additional worry whether the market place will be ready for your movie in a year's time."

The original concept for *The Abyss* came from a short story Cameron wrote in high school. He continued, "It was even titled *The Abyss* at that early stage and it was based on the idea of fluid breathing which I had just found out about at a science seminar."

Underwater Rat!

"Years later, when I wrote the script for the movie, I contacted the scientist responsible for the research in this area. He demonstrated his theories with rats swimming around in an oxygenated fluid. I did a tremendous amount of reading up on him, and the subject, and I asked him how he did it. Well, he showed me, and we copied it on film."

The rat sequence may be real, but the same idea is simulated later by actor Ed Harris who held his breath in a similar colored liquid. Cameron added, "Human research is restricted by the Food and Drug Administration in America because the substance is a fluorocarbon emulsion and it isn't approved for use on people. Basically what that means is you can't drink it. The FDA hasn't allowed for the fact you can inhale it safely which apparently causes no side effects because it's biologically inert and nontoxic.

"The substance absorbs oxygen twenty times more than water does and carbon dioxide more readily as well. So it acts as a transfer medium for gases. You aren't the first person to ask me about it because the rat scene does seem to transfix the audience. People assume it's faked because they can't work out exactly how it's done—therefore it has to be a special effects trick." Cameron admitted to being worried about all the other "Dive-In" movies being made while he plunged into *The Abyss*. But he said, "My cause for concern vanished when I found out what they were about. I had to give the audience enough credit to be able to distinguish between my film and the other relatively straightforward horror shockers. My concern was whether it was being sold ambiguously as containing horror elements. I'm still worried about these wrong impressions—hence this publicity tour where I can redress and emphasize the differences."

The bearded director had these fears compounded the moment he arrived in Britain. He continued, "When asked by the girl at passport control why I was here, I said to promote my movie. She asked me what it was and when I told her she replied, 'Oh! It looks absolutely horrifying.' She was responding to the studio-approved trailers and television presentation. What *The Abyss* is really about is a message that isn't coming through loud and clear for a reason I don't understand. I suppose everyone naturally assumes it's in the same mode as my last two movies."

The Abyss's Theme

It was never Cameron's intention to make *The Abyss* a horror film. He made it solely to explore the benign alien avenue as he stated, "My idea for NTI—Non Terrestrial Intelligence—contact was conceived right after *Aliens*. Why should I want to make *Aliens* again underwater? I'd done it once, I was very happy with it, so why repeat it? I wanted to make the definitive monster movie with *Aliens* and I think I succeeded. I certainly didn't want to challenge my own area. *The Abyss* was always conceived as being exactly what it is."

But, he added, "In a way, what's bothersome, and I guess it's my own limitations as a film-maker, it's structurally inherent the creatures have to be benevolent. They have to be an idealization of a peaceful society or else the story makes no sense.

"Is it my fault audiences don't grasp the fact that these creatures have to be protected from our violently human negative influences? Coffey, Michael Biehn, is the monster of the piece—but people still manage to get to the last fifteen minutes and be amazed it has an uplifting ending. I find this truly incredible because all the manifestations of the aliens are benign.

"When the mothership comes up from behind the cliff and Mary Elizabeth Mastrantonio touches it, the music, her expression, and the production design are saying something quite clear. When the NTIs send the pseudopod water tentacle as a probe into the rig, it communicates with the crew. It's quite equivocal it's meant to be wondrous, because the crew's reaction is to laugh and smile. The thing is attempting a positive communication. How can audiences propel themselves beyond that to a point where they think the creatures are threatening?! The movie defines itself well before this.

"The sense of disappointment some people have when the aliens turn out to be nice says a lot about the audience for movies now. The signals sent out from the beginning are ones of benevolence. I can understand the misinterpretation of the initial contact with the USS *Montana* submarine, as it isn't clear it hits the turbulent wake of the mothership. But I'm at a loss understanding why others don't understand!"

The End and Tsunamis

The one universal criticism of *The Abyss* is the dissatisfaction with the end special effect and the loss of a major sequence showing the aliens flooding cities who pose a nuclear threat to life on Earth. This is what Cameron had to say on the subject.

He commented, "It's the nature of the beast to keep pruning and improving. I was never quite satisfied with the visual reality of the tidal wave. My primary concern was not breaking the microcosm of the immediacy of the characters. Going to a third party vantage point wasn't dramatically consistent with the rest of the movie and I liked the idea of saving the sunlight and the bright airy surface world for the finale. I was ambivalent when I wrote the ending, as your mind can downplay the negative aspects of a scene in the writing. But when I saw it in dailies, I axed it, despite the effects people working on it for some time."

He continued, "It's standard filmmaking procedure to attempt more things than you ultimately use. I don't know why people are making such a big deal about it, really. Perhaps the three-dimensional realization of the alien city takes away the fantasy feel, as it looks more ethereal underwater. But that's like the beautiful undersea creatures whose luminescence fades in the open air. It's consistent with reality and thematically it ties in with the ending. The creatures elect to surface and meet us on our terms after witnessing a spectacular human sacrifice. It's terrifying for them to do so after they've been threatened by us, but they see the incredible polar opposite of Michael Biehn in Ed Harris, and they acknowledge the love between him and his estranged wife. From that one guy, with their limited experience, they judge us in a good light as a result. That's what the ending means to me, not how plastic it looks.

Secrecy and Its Publicity

"A curious thing happened while making *The Abyss*," revealed Cameron. He expanded, "The more we emphasized the secrecy of the film, the more people tended to look for negative information. The first news from the front was *Premiere* magazine's article which set the tone for all future journalism for quite some time. It was a wildly inaccurate piece to the point of being total fabrication in certain specific instances. Yet I would get the article quoted back to me as if it were gospel. I was amazed and now I'll never believe anything else I read about a film in production unless I know a good source. It reached a point where the actors were interviewed, but their quotes were ignored and the journalists wrote what they felt like. Very bizarre.

"None of the actors hated me at all. They were eager to promote the movie and they'll work with me again if I ask. They enjoyed the experience at the time—it's only this revisionist mentality that's been imposed from the outside. What exacerbated the problem, and it took me a while to understand why it was occurring, was the actors always wanted to talk about the most dangerous aspects of the shooting as those were the areas where they were challenged the most. They wanted credit for going through this great learning adventure. The press always gave it a negative interpretation as if the actors were complaining. I use this metaphor: if you went on a trip up the Amazon and saw a poisonous snake, by the time you got back to tell everyone, it's bound to have been changed into 'I almost got bitten by a snake and I nearly died!' Who wants to hear you were perfectly safe when the entertainment factor can be increased by a little embellishment?"

Cameron said the shooting of *The Abyss* was hard work underwater but never boring. He added, "It was different for the actors. For them it was like being in World War I. They were in the trenches for three weeks, so to speak, and then they had about two hours of dangerous excitement after we had got the lighting right. I'd get to the set in the morning—actually the evening because we were forced to shoot nights for the last half of the entire underwater schedule as our tarp ripped open and let sunlight in—and try to figure out what we could shoot as there was always a problem with what was scheduled. If we needed to shoot a wide master of the set, there was bound to be a failure in the pumping system, and the tank would be clouded to the point we only had ten feet of visibility.

"So we'd sit and huddle and work out what actors weren't in New York and what we could do instead . . . Every single day there was a glitch usually due to the tank system. We planned the shot, readied the equipment, then worked solidly underwater for ten hours. The actors were never submerged for longer than two hours per day. The crew put in all the hours instead and we had to decompress at the end of each day. My version of the daily grind was always being busy and driving ourselves beyond fatigue. The actors' version of that reality would be they sat around with nothing to do for days on end."

James Cameron Takes a Second Plunge

Alan Jones/1989

Starburst Magazine #136, December 1989 (vol. 12, no. 4). This is the conclusion of the interview in the November 1989 issue. Reprinted by permission of Alan Jones, horror critic, author, and broadcaster.

The Abyss was filmed at the never-completed Cherokee Nuclear Power Station outside Gaffney, South Carolina. Said Cameron, "The reactor was never installed in what became our tank, so there was no danger of lurking radioactivity. The project ran out of funds while 50 percent complete and their white elephant loss was our opportunity gain. The station core was flooded with seven million gallons of water and it gave us the control to build an elaborate set that in the ocean would have been much cruder by necessity.

"At sea we would have had to literally build Deepcore, the oil drilling facility, and it would have to have been much smaller to allow for enough structural integrity for it to be plopped on the bottom of the ocean. This recourse would have limited us to half the size of the set we wound up with. In Gaffney we could build the set first and then flood it.

"We could never have found the right arrangement of cliff and wall either. Most of the exterior action takes place outside Deepcore and that was our major set. For Ed Harris's descent to the bottom of the abyss, the cliff wall adjacent to Deepcore was extended up to the tank surface to create a single long fall of fifty feet. This was the only time we doubled Ed—he did everything else. It wasn't dangerous, it just required a specific skill on behalf of the diver, an ability to equalize one's inner ear space very rapidly during the descent."

Underwater Training

"All the actors went through a rigorous training period," explained Cameron. "It started as a vacation and then we shipped them off to Grand Cayman in the Caribbean. I enrolled them all in a training program and put them on a very sophisticated dive charter boat. I knew all the instructors personally and they had the right qualifications to teach the actors the basics. There's an art to teaching someone to dive. It's 30 percent instruction and 70 percent psychology as you have to get people relaxed and enthusiastic about the environment and downplay the fear factor. What I've found pretty consistently with everyone I've enticed to learn is you go through a threshold of panic and claustrophobia into quite the reverse—a feeling of euphoria and the ability to fly almost. The second part of the program is the instructors holding people back so they don't do anything dangerous with their new-found discovery of underwater freedom."

After a week in the Caymans, where the actors became certified open-water scuba divers, it was back to the South Carolina studio. Cameron continued, "The last two weeks of training were carried out in the number of tanks there. There was the big one, a smaller one two hundred feet long and twenty-two feet deep holding two million gallons which we used for interiors and miniature shots, and adjacent to that there was a baby one about the size of a small swimming pool. This was connected by a long canal four feet wide to the main tank, and I often used the analogy of baby salmon spawned in the baby pool swimming out to the big ocean. Here the actors learned helmet diving and were taught by professionals how to use them properly. I had to go through that too as I had no idea how to adapt either. We picked it up quite quickly as the basic skills of scuba stand you in good stead with helmet diving. You just have to learn about buoyancy control and the gas laws."

He added, "Ed Harris got the short end of the stick because he was cast after the Cayman trip. He didn't want to leave his wife, Amy Madigan, who was filming in Chicago. So he was certified after learning the skills in a mid-western lake."

Facing the Abyss

At various points in Cameron's hi-tech cross between *Close Encounters of the Third Kind* and *Voyage to the Bottom of the Sea* each character must face their own personal abyss. But as German philosopher Friedrich Nietzsche said, "When you look long into an abyss, the abyss also looks into you."

These emotional factors are dealt with by Ed Harris and Mary Elizabeth Mastrantonio, who rise to the occasion of being Cameron's story backbone with heartbreaking power. Cameron is pleased at how well this subtext emerged. He said, "The consensus seems to be it worked very well. It possibly worked too well, actually, as the goals of the Sci-Fi aspect aren't as interesting as a result.

"The most emotional scene in the movie is when Lindsey elects to drown and it doesn't rely on any special effects. From an evolutionary standpoint as a film-maker I feel it's my cue to get away from effects-based movies. *The Abyss* is a relationship story, a survival adventure and a Sci-Fi hybrid. It's an uneasy concept for many to handle and all critical complaints seem to stem from the fact it can't be classified because it doesn't fall into a definable mould. I find it very curious."

No Fish!

What about the fact that there's no fish in *The Abyss*? Cameron smiled, "That's accurate you know. Les Dilley, the production designer, and I researched depths of four hundred meters in the Caymans. We took photos and videos and what you see in the film is exactly what we saw. Okay, the film is supposed to take place at two thousand feet but we assumed it would be the same. Sea life sharply thins out the lower you go. Oceans are like engines motored by sunlight. Plankton grows near the surface, small fish feed on it and larger fish feed on the smaller ones etc. Anyway I didn't want to make a film about the wonders of sea life. That's been done."

He added, "*The Abyss* is a more personal film than *The Terminator* or *Aliens*. The latter was always tainted as a creative entity on my part anyway by being a sequel. But although I had the desire to make a film about the ocean, it's not as personal as some have tried to suggest, with respect to the two leads mirroring my situation with producer Gale Anne Hurd."

"Our divorce was coincidental and our separation postdated the script writing. Life imitated art—but it didn't affect our working relationship. We started on *The Terminator* as two professionals. During *Aliens* we went through a period of being more than that. And now we've reverted back to how we started when we first met. The situation has never been difficult for us, but it seemed to get people wondering if it would affect the movie."

Once again Michael Biehn stars in a James Cameron movie. How does he feel being Biehn's personal employer? He said, "Is it that unusual? I like working with key actors. If Martin Scorsese always uses Robert De Niro, why can't I use Michael—especially as we work so well together? I have equal relationships with other actors, too, from *Aliens*—but I didn't use them in *The Abyss* because I didn't want it perceived as a retread.

"I worked with Michael again because I was able to give him a part totally opposite to anything he'd done for me before. He did feature in a few extra scenes I cut—setting up the oil rig crew, searching through the sunken *Montana*, and where he went crazy in a confrontation with Ed Harris who diffuses the situation. But none were a great sacrifice. From the moment Coffey's hand starts shaking, the audience is immediately set up for what's coming. It's just a question of when. I could have made a film just about him and one man's disintegration under claustrophobic pressure. There were a lot more miles I could have gone storywise. But I don't deal with it cursorily—more like a rock skimming over a water surface. The audience sees key instances of his psychosis and they fill in the rest in their minds. I didn't want everything boringly spelt out."

Wolfgang Petersen's *The Boat* would be the nearest the cinema has got to the claustrophobia expertly conjured up by Cameron in *The Abyss*. Was he influenced by it at all? He said, "Only to the extent that I admired the film and its ability to create a sense of confinement. I saw it after completing *The Terminator* and what I responded to were things I already liked—the idea of wide lens photography putting you subjectively into an environment. I saw how effectively it could be applied and I used the approach in *Aliens* after dabbling with it in *The Terminator*. Water slushing around a set always gives a heightened sense of realism and that was the lesson to be learned from *The Boat*. I created the same gritty reality with *The Abyss*. Everything was covered in grease, the metal was cold and water constantly dripped out of necessity to make the fantasy more believable."

Computer Graphics

"The computer graphics turned out very well and that was the film's potential Achilles' Heel," admitted Cameron with regard to the pseudopod animation. He continued, "I even debated cutting the scenes before we began, but early test footage from ILM looked so promising we plunged straight in.

"What ILM did now defines the state-of-the-art for the future of computer graphics. The integration between the live action and the animation was so seamless and realistic. The stained glass knight in *Young Sherlock Holmes* was the best previous application and ILM have obviously learned a lot since."

As for the hot pink neon color scheme for the aliens, Cameron said this: "I wanted colors which didn't occur naturally underwater. Anything red, yellow, or magenta was banned because, although they occur in coral reef fish, these wavelengths don't propagate well through water. The neon gave the ships a more unearthly feel."

Cameron says he hasn't got the whole *Abyss* experience in perspective yet. And ask him what the hardest part of the £45 million plus epic was and he'll say all of it. He continued, "In *The Right Stuff* it was called maintaining an even strain. Well we were under an even strain for months on end. The underwater shooting pushed us to limits even I couldn't endure. I'm not an athlete and here I was trying to direct after an hour decompressing on pure oxygen. At the end of the day I had to go home and take aspirin to breathe yet more pure oxygen in my bedroom at night, so the nitrogen would be cleansed out of my system before diving another ten hours the next day. I spent 550 hours in a diving helmet to make *The Abyss*—way beyond all limits of what one associates with the job. I'll never do it again. Are you listening? Never!"

But that's one of Cameron's greatest strengths. He always pushes everything to the outside of the envelope. But he lamented, "That may be true but I don't always get the equivalent value on screen for going the extra miles. Here's an example. We did something never done before in motion picture history. We had actors in diving suits speaking dialogue being recorded live underwater. The audience doesn't perceive that as outstanding because we've seen twenty years of helmet movies and it has always been faked. It doesn't even occur to people it was done differently with fabulous equipment. And it may not seem all that remarkable to you. But it was. Look for the bubbles in the water when the actors speak and you can tell. We just didn't get the spectacular showmanship value out of it versus the difficulty level. But when we adopted the motif to do everything as realistically as possible, that was the logical end result."

Genuine Sound

He added, "We spent a lot of time on the sound. It's the one area of filmmaking where things are only getting better. The depressing aspect of visual filmmaking is you have a pristine idea, then you write it as a script and it starts to get compromised a little. Then you do the production design which, for expense reasons, isn't quite what you had in mind. It all slides on a downward curve while the sound side just keeps getting better, as it's less subject to entropy."

But as far as James Cameron is concerned, *The Abyss* is a dramatic and artistic success. He said, "It's what I set out to do. It's a financial success in America although not on the same scale as *Batman*."

As for his future plans, he won't make any comments—but he does lay to rest one persistent rumor . . .

"I have nothing to do with *Bladerunner II*. I wouldn't be interested and I don't want to go around cleaning up after Ridley Scott for the rest of my life! Nor will I sequelize my own films. My only plan for the future is not to have too many technical considerations next time. I don't want hardware to break my focus on the actors which was the great danger on *The Abyss*.

"The only concrete plan I have is to executive produce my wife's new film, *Johnny Utah*, for Columbia. And I'm only doing that so I can watch her do all the work and just lie back body checking anyone who dares to interfere!"

Aliens: James Cameron Interview

Nigel Floyd/1992

From *Dark Side Magazine*, February 1992, 14–18. Reprinted by permission of Nigel Floyd.

With the release of the *Aliens: Special Edition* video, curiosity has been aroused about alternative versions of other James Cameron films, including the rumored "extended play, dance mix" of *The Abyss*. Nigel Floyd dips into his Cameron interview files to give you the official version, straight from the director's mouth, on those re-cut, extended, and alternative versions.

Piranha II: Flying Killers (1981)

Nigel Floyd: Did you get a directing credit on *Piranha II: Flying Killers*, sometimes known as *Piranha II: The Spawning?*
James Cameron: Yeah, I did, kind of against my will. I wanted them to take it off, but they wouldn't do it. The release prints were made in Italy, at Technicolor in Rome, and I was in L.A., so there was nothing I could do.

NF: Was it re-cut?
JC: I only shot half the picture. I got fired after a few weeks. The producer took over the picture, and he shot all these scenes of naked women that had nothing to do with the script. And I didn't even write the script. So the position I have to take is, it wasn't my script and I didn't really direct it, so I have limited responsibility for whatever is wrong with it, which is a lot.

You see, the thing is I thought it was actually going to be kind of a comedy. When somebody first told me the idea, and I had already seen the first film, which was a little bit tongue-in-cheek, I thought this could actually be interesting. You know: somebody is walking down the sidewalk, they get hit by a cloud of flying piranha, and three seconds later a steaming skeleton hits the ground. It could be kind of funny, in a real macabre, George Romero kind of way.

But also it was really a lot more pragmatic than that. Somebody asked me to direct a movie, you know, and I wouldn't have cared if it was Gonzo's revenge, which it wasn't certainly much above, if it was at all.

The Terminator (1984)

NF: Were there any scenes you didn't use in *The Terminator*?

JC: There was a sequence at the end, which I shot but wouldn't use, because the technical quality wasn't good enough. There was actually a double narrative ellipse. As Sarah Connor (Linda Hamilton) is being wheeled out of the factory on the stretcher at the end, you found out that the place where the final showdown took place was a computer factory. There was also a shot of a computer chip, and a guy picking it up. And then, as Sarah is leaving in the ambulance, the camera boomed up and you see that the name of the factory, Cyberdine Systems, is the same as the company that built the killer cyborgs in the future.

The Abyss (1989)

NF: Did you actually shoot the "tidal wave" ending, which is in the novelization?

JC: Yes, that was a shot. It was never completed, because at a certain point we realized, once again, that we were somewhere in the neighborhood of twenty minutes too long, for what the market would bear. Given the fact that I would still have to fight and dance and pretend to hold my breath until I died, you know, the market still isn't going to bear anything more than about two hours fifteen or two hours twenty.

So we knew we had a similar problem, and again it was a question of which scenes broke focus. It was a very similar solution to *Aliens* in a sense; the tidal wave scene, although it was positioned differently in the film, near the end as opposed to near the beginning in *Aliens*, still had the same problem of moving away from the central characters and breaking the immediate emotional, subjective focus of the film.

And in screening the film, even though we liked the scenes and they were quite impressive visually, the film came to a kind of level of intensity that was at an intellectual level rather than an emotional level. At its best, the film had a slightly kind of transcendent quality in those scenes; at its worst, it took us away from the emotional core of the film.

On the one hand, it had things to recommend it, and on the other hand, it had negatives, and my feeling was we shouldn't have anything that has negatives. So that was the kind of the logical process that was used to winnow the picture down.

NF: If you were to do a Special Edition of *The Abyss*, are there other scenes that you would reinstate?
JC: Oh yeah, there are scenes throughout the body of the picture—that whole tidal wave sequence was only three minutes long. We've done a rough cut of the proposed extended play, dance mix—we call it the dance mix. Well, let's face it, the music industry really pioneered the concept of different versions for different formats and for different end users. And that's the kind of world we're moving into in a more general sense, giving people more choices and letting them be more selective.

Anyway the extended version is twenty minutes longer and there are extra scenes throughout the body of the film: for example, there's more character set-up at the beginning, there's a little more action in the middle, and there's the laying of the groundwork for the tidal wave, because it only works in a certain context, of an intensifying nuclear conflict at a world-wide level.

NF: The British censors made you remove one short scene from *The Abyss*, the one of the rat being immersed in the oxygenated fluoro-carbonated emulsion. Even if you were to produce an extended version, this would still, for legal reasons [The Cinematograph Films (Animals) Act 193], be missing from the British version.
JC: That was removed because an old veterinarian passed an edict saying—with absolutely no experience in the matter whatsoever—that a rat breathing an oxygenated fluoro-carbon emulsion was experiencing pain, for which there was no experimental evidence whatsoever. It had to do with an act passed in the 1930s having to do with animals and filmmaking. Now because that's a 1930s act, it applies only to theatrical pictures, it has no weight with respect to video, so our position at the studio is that we can release the video uncut.

They thought they were being very finessefully surgical by removing only shots where you actually saw the rat submerged in the liquid, not the whole scene. Which did preserve some of the narrative, but still it was horrible because the whole point was to see that it was possible to do this, in no uncertain terms.

NF: And did the rat survive?
JC: Oh, the rat was my pet for a year and a half afterwards. It died at the equivalent rat age of, like, ninety-five, about a week ago, actually. So the experience didn't shorten its life any.

The Cutting Room Floor

NF: Who actually owns the material on the cutting room floor?
JC: The studio owns all the elements of the picture, the work print, all the sound elements, whatever it might be.

NF: So in theory, if you approached them and said "I'd like to release the extended dance mix of the film," and they said, "NO chance," there would be no way you could do it.
JC: Exactly, there would be no way that I could circumvent their desires. On the other hand, there's no way they could do it without me. My contract on *The Abyss* was a final cut contract, and under the definition of final cut, anything that they change for any market, at any time, in perpetuity, would be a violation of that final cut, without my permission. So I can't do it without them, but they can't do it without me, so we have to be nice to each other. It's like a marriage where you're trying to protect the children.

Future Tense—Cameron on *Terminator 2*

"The thing that has really amazed me," says an obviously pleased Cameron, "is that people are paying money, and queuing round the block to see a movie about *Judgment Day*, which is the end of the world."

In fact Cameron's $88 million blockbuster is billed as *Schwarzenegger/Terminator 2: Judgment Day*, but the director's point is still a valid one. "It's kind of a wolf in sheep's clothing," he explains. "I knew going in that I had Arnold, and the vast publicity machine that supports him, behind me. So it didn't matter what kind of *T2* I did. It could have been the worst sort of mayhem you can imagine, and people would still have queued to see it. It was a question of what to do with that nuclear bomb..."

Of course we all now know that what Cameron has done is to transform Schwarzenegger's remorseless killer cyborg into user-friendly technology, the kind even a child could control. So while *T2* delivers all the expected hardware, explosions, and mass destruction, its heavy metal body contains a beating human heart.

This is what we have come to expect from Cameron: *Aliens* centered on Sigourney Weaver's efforts to save her surrogate daughter, Newt, from the mean mother alien; and in *The Abyss* Cameron created a benign, super-intelligent underwater alien, the beauty and "humanity" of which contrasted starkly with the paranoid human aggression of Michael Biehn's military madman.

Even the original *Terminator* focused primarily on the relationship between time-travelling freedom fighter Michael Biehn and threatened waitress Linda Hamilton. Cameron's science-fiction films have never been just about hardware; his human stories are the velvet fist within the steel glove.

In *T2*, twelve years have passed since the action of the original. Haunted by nightmares of a nuclear apocalypse, Hamilton has spent the intervening years training her son John (played by newcomer Edward Furlong) to become the rebel leader of the future. But the Skynet computers which failed to prevent John's conception have now sent an advanced, liquid-metal T-1000 cyborg back from the machine-ruled future to finish the job. Hamilton and Furlong must now rely on the help of a reprogrammed T-800 model (played by Arnie) to protect them . . .

Even if it had been possible simply to stage a bigger and better re-run of what Cameron calls *Arnold the Annihilator*, the director thinks it would have been pointless: "The idea of a relentless cyborg killer is pretty boring when you get down to it. How many permutations of The Terminator kicking down doors and shooting everybody can you explore? So the gamble was to see if people would accept the idea of a 'good' Terminator, which to me is such a delicious contradiction in terms. To take the most single-mindedly destructive, dispassionate, and conscienceless killing machine and turn that around was a great dramatic challenge—and a lot of fun."

Paradoxically, while Schwarzenegger's once-lethal cyborg has become an ex-Terminator, the human beings cannot be reprogrammed. Images abound of children playing destructive video games or brandishing toy guns, suggesting a destructiveness that is innate in the human psyche. For Cameron, this is the core of the movie.

"Every single boy on the planet plays with toy weapons. There are no exceptions, it's universal. My interpretation of that is in the line, where the Terminator stales flatly, 'It's in your nature to destroy yourselves.' It's very simplistic, but it's really damning, because it basically says that, in taking that impulse to its extreme, the nuclear war comes from the same aggressive drive that's built in genetically."

"That's the fundamental problem, and to address it in any other way is to miss the point. The first step to any solution is to acknowledge the beast within, because only then can we see that everything else is a manifestation of that basic destructive urge. The irony is that The Terminator has no beast within. His fundamental nature is not destructive—he's very pure. He could be the saint of destruction or the perfect pacifist."

Unlike The Terminator, however, the human beings in the story are able to exercise free will, and in doing so can change the course of history. As when Sarah Connor—having fled with her son to the comparative safety of the desert—chooses to go back into the eye of the storm. Fired by her recurring nightmare of a nuclear holocaust, Sarah decides to kill the inventor of the computer chip which, in the future, will set in motion the chain of events leading to global nuclear war.

"The thing that fascinates me about history," says Cameron, 'is that no matter how grand the landscape it is always made up of human moments. All of history can turn on a moment, an impulse. And that's one of the things that the movie is about. The one person, Sarah Connor, who used to be a waitress, who was basically pretty insignificant, not born to royalty, not a president, not someone with power, someone with no portfolio whatsoever, can change history because of her actions."

Terminator 2 confirms Cameron's place at the cutting edge of science-fiction filmmaking, both in terms of state-of-the-art technology and effects, and in terms of new and challenging ideas. Is this subversion (or rewriting) of a popular genre a conscious thing?

"I don't think of it as subverting the genre," concludes Cameron, "as much as elevating it. I think that all I'm doing cinematically is what the best literary science fiction has always done, which is to make some quite cogent comment on society, human nature, and our possibilities for the future."

The Hero's Journey

Syd Field/1992

From *Four Screenplays* (New York: Dell Publishing, 1994), 79–89. Reprinted by permission of Syd Field, author of *Screenplay*, *The Screenwriter's Workbook*, and *The Screenwriter's Problem Solver*.

Terminator 2: Judgment Day

The eighteenth-century English poet Samuel Taylor Coleridge declared that when you approach a work of art, you must leave your perception of reality behind and approach the work on its own merits, its own level. He described it as "the willing suspension of disbelief." We must willingly suspend our disbelief no matter how far the subject matter strays from what we know to be true, or not true. No matter how outrageous the premise, no matter how unpredictable the characters, situations, reactions, or plot developments are, all have to be left behind when we approach "the work."

I thought about this when I was considering the films for this book. In 1991 there were 424 movies released in Hollywood; 150 were made and distributed by the major studios, and the other 274 were made and released by the independents. Of all those films, roughly a third were action/adventure.

Action is big business in Hollywood, and creates a very large market internationally. Not to include an action film in this book would be like trying to ignore an elephant in a closet.

The only trouble is that I find most of the action films produced and released in Hollywood totally unbelievable. The situations are absurd, and most of the characters are one-dimensional and predictable. Of course, you don't go to an action film to see a good character study. If you look at the "good" action films released in the past few years, *Lethal Weapon 1*, *2*, or *3*, or *Die Hard*, or *The Last Boy Scout*, all are exciting with big and spectacular action sequences, but the characters are usually flat and one-dimensional. In short, it's very difficult for me to "suspend my disbelief" willingly.

Then I went to see *Terminator 2*. I wasn't expecting very much. I had seen *The Terminator*, and while the premise was different and original, I didn't think too much of the film. But *Terminator 2* was a different story. I was totally engrossed, literally glued to the edge of my seat, and in those two plus hours in that darkened theater I willingly suspended my disbelief. I mean, how could I not accept the premise that the world had self-destructed in August 4, 1997, and the ruling machines of an epoch beyond the apocalypse had sent back a "terminator" to destroy the one person who could possibly change that particular future?

I sat watching these spectacular action sequences unfold, utterly absorbed in the most amazing special effects I had ever seen, and I *knew* this was a film of the "future." The story concept was unique and original (which you usually don't find, especially in a sequel), and I found that I liked the characters: they were engaging and sympathetic, even though they were becoming "machines" dedicated to altering the future. But what I found the most interesting was the Terminator, the Arnold Schwarzenegger "character," a machine, a cyborg.

When I started thinking about this I found myself confronting a real dichotomy: Number one, how could I willingly suspend my disbelief and accept this robot as a real, living character? And two, how could I be so emotionally moved by his sacrifice, by his very commitment to life? For this is no ordinary man-in-a-suit robot; this is a robot who acquires the highest human values, who willingly gives up his life to save his comrades and humanity from the devastation of the future. His action transforms the future. Action is character; what a person does, not what he says, is what he is. Joseph Campbell declares, "A hero is someone who has given his or her life to something bigger than oneself," like Oedipus and Hamlet. And "if a machine can learn the value of a human life," Sarah Connor states in the last line of the movie, "maybe we can, too." That line reverberated in my mind for days after I heard it.

It's a thoughtful, provocative way to end the film. If you think about it, it is the Terminator "character" who embodies the classic values of Aristotelian tragedy and undertakes the hero's journey. Was this intentional? I asked myself. Can this robot, this cyborg, played by an Austrian actor, be the prototype of the new American hero?

The more I thought about it, the more intrigued I became. I didn't know too much about James Cameron except that I was impressed with his innovative skill as a filmmaker. It seemed he always had an interesting premise, whether it was *Aliens*, *The Terminator*, or *The Abyss*. *Aliens* was a masterpiece of shock and suspense. I had heard so much about it that I found myself deliberately holding back my emotions, constantly reminding myself that this was only a movie so I wouldn't get too freaked out. Of course, it didn't help too much. I jumped as high as everybody else. Yes, I was very impressed with the way he created suspense, the way he crafted his films.

Creating suspense on film is a special art. Very few filmmakers have the talent really to pull it off. Hitchcock, of course, was the master, and it was the hub of almost all his films. Val Lewton was another who could pull it off. *Cat Woman of Paris* is a classic exercise in film terror: The suspense comes when you least expect it. Jim Cameron is one of those natural filmmakers—like Hitchcock, Welles, Lewton, or Stanley Kubrick, to name a few—who are masters at generating terror and suspense in their movies.

In addition to being an artistic success, *Terminator 2* was also a financial success. It was the highest-grossing film in the world when it was released. It grossed more than $497 million worldwide, of which $205 million was the domestic return; the rest came from the foreign market. It's easy to see that, in the near future, the foreign marketplace will be a key factor in determining which films will be selected for production in Hollywood. *Terminator 2* was definitely a film I wanted to analyze for this book.

I wanted to find out more about Jim Cameron, so I called his office, spoke to his very capable assistant, and we set up an interview. But it was not going to be that easy. After a series of broken and rescheduled appointments—because of "Jim's new deal," it was explained—we finally agreed on a day and time.

It was a long ride to the far end of the San Fernando Valley, where Jim Cameron's company, Lightstorm Entertainment, was located at the time. I pulled up to the nondescript building that looked like any other office warehouse, parked in the visitors' parking lot, and walked inside. It was cool and efficient. "Jim hasn't arrived yet," I was told (I arrived some ten minutes early), so I sat down to wait. The phones were ringing off the hook, and there was a sense of energy and excitement in the air that I couldn't quite identify.

When I opened *Daily Variety* and the *Hollywood Reporter*, the industry's trade papers, and read the headlines, I suddenly understood all the previously canceled appointments. Spread across the top of the page, in big, bold headlines, I read: "CAMERON TAKES FOX BY STORM," and underneath, "Director Signs for $500 Million!"

The article explained that James Cameron had signed a deal with 20th Century Fox to produce some twelve movies over the next five years. It's an extraordinary deal—$500 million for twelve movies! Even the most jaded Hollywood executives have to think about that one. For the people at Fox, however, it made a lot of sense. Cameron is one of the "most talented and commercial directors working in the marketplace," says Joe Roth, the former studio chairman. Together, *Aliens*, *The Terminator*, *The Abyss*, and most recently *Terminator 2: Judgment Day* have grossed more than $652 million worldwide.

The deal gives Cameron creative control over his pictures. He has earned it. *Terminator 2* reflects Cameron's uncanny ability to combine creative thinking with scientific technology.

I had just finished reading about "the deal" when Jim Cameron drove up in a black, late-model Corvette. Tall, lean, and friendly, Cameron briefly introduced himself, asked for five minutes to check things out, and disappeared. He had just shaved his beard, and he looked much younger than he did in the pictures I had seen of him.

I was ushered upstairs into the large conference room, very plush and very high-tech, dominated by a beautiful conference table. On the walls were posters of Jim Cameron's films, and along one wall was a long oak table displaying five small silver alloy models of the Terminator 1000. Right next to these models, and totally contrary to the "look" of the room, was a beat-up and obviously well-used diving helmet: "I spent some 560 hours in that forty-pound diving helmet," Cameron later explained, talking about *The Abyss*. Along the far wall were two pinball machines, both based on the *Terminator* movies, and a beautiful, polished oak bar surrounded by plush and comfortable chairs. The entire room was magnificently decorated, and everything was expertly arranged under a sloping wood beam ceiling. It was beautiful.

We sat at one end of the large conference table, had coffee and coffee cakes, and began talking about *Terminator 2*. The more Cameron talked, the more impressed I became. Immediately, through our conversation, I saw that this man is a natural filmmaker, a man of science and art, with a passion for research and detail.

Jim Cameron grew up in Kapuskasing, a little town just outside Niagara Falls in Ontario, Canada. When he was fifteen, he saw Kubrick's *2001: A Space Odyssey*. "As soon as I saw that," he recalls, "I knew I wanted to be a filmmaker. It hit me on a lot of different levels. I just couldn't figure out how he did all that stuff, and I just had to learn."

"So I borrowed my dad's Super-8 camera and would try to shoot things with different frame rates just to see how it looked." This, of course, is much different from picking up a Super-8 in a high school in a large city like L.A. or New York. "If you pick up a Super-8 camera there, it's because you're going to film school," he said. "For me, it was completely innocent. I had a fascination with it, but I couldn't see myself as a future film director. In fact, there was a definite feeling on my part that those people were somehow born into it, almost like a caste system. Little kids from a small town in Canada didn't get to direct movies."

When he was in his teens his family moved to Orange County in Southern California, and "from a pragmatic standpoint, I could have been in Montana. There is no film industry in Orange County, and since I didn't have a driver's license, it made Hollywood as far away as another state.

"I liked science," he continued, "and thought I might want to be a marine biologist, or physicist. But I also liked to write, so I was pulled in a lot of different directions. I liked the idea of an ocean even though I'd never seen or been in one. But I had been certified as a scuba diver when I was sixteen in a swimming pool in Buffalo, and I dived in the local rivers and lakes.

"I loved the idea of being in another world, and anything that could transport me to another world is what I was interested in. To me, scuba diving was a quick ticket to another land."

He continued talking about his fascination with other worlds, and as he was speaking I could see the evolution of his films: The two *Terminators*, *Aliens*, *The Abyss*, all deal with other worlds.

"I enrolled in junior college and studied physics," he continued, "along with all the math, calculus, chemistry, physics, astronomy, which I loved. And while I made good grades, I knew that's not what I wanted to do with my life, so I switched to being an English major and studied literature for a while. Even so, I couldn't make up my mind what I wanted to do, so I simply dropped out. I worked in a machine shop for a while, then as a truck driver, a school bus driver, and painted pictures and wrote stories at night."

Gradually he began to see that the medium of film could accommodate his interests in both science and art, and with the help of a little book called *Screenplay* he "figured out how to write a screenplay, just like all the big guys, so a friend and I sat down and wrote a little ten-minute script. We raised the money to make it and shot it in 35mm; it was all effects and models and matte shots, all this wild kind of stuff."

"It was a bit like a doctor doing his first appendectomy after having only read about it. We spent the first half day of the shoot just trying to figure out how to get the camera running. We rented all this equipment—the lenses, the camera, the film stocks, everything—then took all the gear back to this little studio we had rented in Orange County.

"Now, I knew in theory how the threading path worked, but we couldn't get the camera to run to save our lives. There were three of us, and one of the guys was an engineer, so we simply took the camera apart, figured out how it worked, traced the circuitry, and then realized there was something in the camera that shut the camera off in case the film buckled. Later, when we returned the equipment, we were talking to the rental guys and they said something about 'a buckle trip,' and I said, yeah, yeah, I know about that, not telling them that we had disassembled their camera and spread it out on the table and figured it all out. It was like the Japanese doing reverse engineering."

I asked him about his background in special effects and he told me he "was completely self-taught in special effects. I'd go down to the USC library and pull any theses that graduate students had written about optical printing, or front screen projection, or dye transfers, anything that related to film technology. That way I could sit down and read it, and if they'd let me photocopy it, I would. If not, I'd make notes. I literally put myself into a graduate course on film technology—for free. I didn't have to enroll in school, it was all there in the library. I'd set it up to go in like I was on a tactical mission, find out what I needed to know, take it all back. I just had files and files stacked on my desk of how all this stuff was done."

It is this kind of analytical approach to film projects that separates Jim Cameron from other filmmakers. "I've always felt that people seek out the information and knowledge they need," he said. "They seek it out and find it. It's like a divining rod to water; nobody will give you the pathway. It's something you have to find yourself."

It's so true. In seminar after seminar, workshop after workshop, people all over the world tell me that success in Hollywood is based on "who you know," not what you do. I tell them that's not true at all.

"People ask me how do you get to be a film director," Cameron continued, "and I tell them that no two people will ever do it the same way, and there is nothing I can say that will help you. Whatever your talents are, whatever your strengths and weaknesses, you have to find the path that's going to work for you. The film industry is about saying 'no' to people, and inherently you cannot take 'no' for an answer.

"If you have to ask somebody how to be a film director, you'll probably never do it. I say, probably. If that pisses you off, and then you go out and say, 'I'm going to show that Jim Cameron; I am going to be a director,' that gives you the kind of true grit you need to have in order to go through with it. And if you do become a film director, then you should send me a bottle of champagne and thank me."

There is no "one" way to find your true path in Hollywood. Whether you're a screenwriter, director, actor, producer, whatever, each person has to find his or her way. Success in Hollywood is not measured on talent alone. Persistence and determination are the keys to success; then comes talent.

Cameron got a job working for Roger Corman's New World Pictures, building miniatures. He was the art director and special effects cameraman on *Battle Beyond the Stars*, and was production designer and second-unit director on *Galaxy of Terror* (1981).

Corman's "frantic, frenzied," high-energy school of filmmaking was "like being air-dropped into a battle zone," Cameron recalls. "It was the best, fastest, strongest injection into filmmaking I could have gotten."

He became special effects supervisor on John Carpenter's *Escape from New York* (1981), then directed *Piranha II: The Spawning*, filmed in 1981, though not released until 1983.

After that he wrote and directed *The Terminator*. When I asked how it came into being, Cameron paused for a moment, looked at the pinball machine against the far wall, and smiled slightly. "If you want to know the truth, the evolution of *The Terminator* is somewhat dishonest. I had just directed my first movie, *Piranha II*, but the truth is that I'd actually gotten fired from the shoot after a couple of weeks. Officially my friends knew I was a film director, but that really wasn't true within the industry because I couldn't get my phone calls returned, even from the people at Warner Bros., and they were the ones who put up the negative costs of *Piranha II*. I couldn't get a call back from anybody. I was absolutely dead in the water. I knew that if I was ever going to direct a movie again, I was going to have to create something for myself. So writing a screenplay became a means to an end, a way of visualizing what the movie would be.

"I had to contour whatever I wanted to do into how I could sell myself," he continued. "I have a strong background in special effects. So my natural inclination would be to go toward science fiction. But realistically, I knew the most money I could probably raise to make a picture would be $3 million or $4 million. So I knew it would have to be contemporary, had to have a contemporary location, and I would have to shoot it nonunion. So I started putting things together. I've got effects, I want it to be science fiction, but I want it to be a contemporary story. So how do I inject the fantastic element into a contemporary story? I didn't want to "make a fantasy, like a magic mirror communicating with another dimension. I wanted it to be gritty realistic, kind of hardware-based, true science fiction, as opposed to fantasy science fiction.

"I'd always liked robots, so essentially I came up with the idea of time travel and catching glimpses of the future. From a budget standpoint that would be controllable. But if I thrust myself entirely into that world, then I was suddenly talking about a $15 million, $20 million, or $30 million picture. If I kept it limited in terms of what I saw through flashbacks or dream sequences or whatever, and I injected one element from that world into our own, I felt it was controllable.

"Then I hit on the idea of the future being determined by something that's happening now, someone who's unaware of the results of their actions finds out they have to answer for those actions—in the future. So what's the most extreme example of that I can think of? If the world has been devastated by nuclear war, if global events are predicated on one person, who is the least likely person you can imagine? A nineteen-year-old waitress who works at Bob's Big Boy (a fast-food restaurant in Southern California).

"That was the premise, and it started to unfold from that. The easiest way to undo what she had done would just be to kill her, just erase her existence, which is not the most subtle approach to the story. It's true that the future could come back and tell her what was going to happen, but being they were machines, they were thinking in a very binary mode.

"So I started creating some juxtapositions that seemed interesting to me. This incredible nightmare would be glimpsed through little windows of contemporary reality.

"The story evolved from that."

What about The Terminator? I asked.

He paused a moment, reflecting. "I first started thinking about the film in two stages," he continued. "In the first stage the future sends back a mechanical guy, essentially what The Terminator became, and the good guys send back their warrior. In the end, the mechanical guy is destroyed; but up in the future, they say, well; wait a minute, that didn't work, what do we have left? And the answer is something terrible, something even they're afraid of. Something they've created that they keep locked up, hidden away in a box, something they're terrified to unleash because even they don't know what the consequences will be—they being the machines, or computers, whoever's in charge.

"And that thing in the box becomes a total wild card; it could go anywhere, do anything, a polymorphic metal robot that is nothing more than a kind of blob. I saw it as this mercury blob that could form into anything. Its powers were almost unlimited, and they couldn't control it.

"That scared me. Just sitting there writing the story scared me.

"That's what *The Terminator* was going to be about. But already I could see that it was starting to slop over the boundaries I had set for myself. And I thought, no, I'll get killed. If I try this now it'll be too ambitious; I'll get creamed. I've got to scale back, got to go for something tighter, simpler. So I took out the liquid metal robot.

"Besides, there was no way I could accomplish something like that. In all my effects experience, nobody had really come up with a way of doing it. Maybe in a future film context you could advance that technology and get it looking better, but at that time, in 1983, the answer was a definite no. So I decided against it."

That was the first major creative choice Cameron had to make before he could move forward with his idea. The next key decision he had to confront was that "I didn't want the robot to look like a man in a suit. If this robot was something that was supposed to fit inside a human form, we could not accomplish that visual by putting it outside a human form, then trying to imagine that it was also inside. It just wouldn't work. Nobody had ever created a robot that wasn't a suit. *Star Wars* [George Lucas] had been done a few years earlier, and since then there had been a whole history of film robots that were basically guy-in-suit robots. So for me, the special effects challenge was getting something believable that could have existed inside a human form. That was the real challenge."

The Terminator was filmed and released and became "a sleeper hit." It literally made Arnold Schwarzenegger a superstar and paved the way for the sequel, which took seven years to come to the screen.

It was a hero's journey.

Approaching the Sequel

Syd Field/1992

From *Four Screenplays* (New York: Dell Publishing, 1994), 90–97. Reprinted by permission of Syd Field, author of *Screenplay*, *The Screenwriter's Workbook*, and *The Screenwriter's Problem Solver*.

Where the Writer Begins

Writing a film sequel is always difficult. If you think about the sequels that are successful—the *Rocky* series, *Lethal Weapon*, or *Aliens*, to name just a few recent examples—they always start with the same characters and generate a new story line. They break new ground.

Most film sequels are not successful because they try to put the characters into the same, or similar situations. Look at *Die Hard 2*. Basically it was the same type of story, but instead of setting it in a building like *Die Hard*, they set it in an airport. The action, with only a few modifications, was exactly the same. I'm sure the template of structure was identical. "If it works well," the old Hollywood saying goes, "do it again."

How did Cameron approach the sequel to *Terminator 2*? After all, there were seven years of intense legal battles between *The Terminator* in 1984 and *Terminator 2*. Carolco, the producing company, and Orion, the distributing company, both claimed they owned the sequel rights, and fought for years until they reached an agreement. How did you bridge that kind of gap? I asked him.

He paused for a moment, took a sip of coffee, and said that "from a writing standpoint, the things that interested me the most were the characters. When I was writing Ripley for *Aliens* there were certain things known about her and her experience, but then we lost track of her. In the sequel I was picking her up at a later point and seeing what the effects of those earlier traumas were. With Ripley there was a discontinuity of time, but experientially it was continuous for her because she just went to sleep, and when she woke up, time had gone by.

"It was much different, much more interesting with Sarah. I had to backfill those intervening nine years, so I had to find efficient ways of dramatically evoking what had happened to her. The tricky part was having it all make sense to a member of the audience who didn't remember or hadn't seen the first film. Basically, I had a character popping onto the screen in a certain way, and therefore had to create a back story for that character. I told myself I had to write the script just like there had never been a first film. The sequel had to be a story about someone who encountered something nobody else believes, like the opening scene of *Invasion of the Body Snatchers*, where Kevin McCarthy swears he's seen something shocking, and nobody believes him; then he starts telling the story.

"In *Terminator 2*, the first time we meet Sarah, she's locked up in a mental institution, but the real question is, is she crazy? The advantage of a sequel is that you can play games you can't play in the original. For example, I know the audience knows the Terminator is real. So they're not going to think she's crazy. But the question still remains: Is she crazy? Has the past ordeal made her nuts? I wanted to push her character very far.

"The strange thing that happened in the wake of the film is that a lot of people made the mistake of thinking I was presenting Sarah Connor as a role model for women. Nothing could be farther from the truth. I wanted people to invest in her emotionally, to feel sorry for her, because she had been through such hell. And people made a straight-line extrapolation from Ripley to Sarah.

"They're very different characters. Ripley's been through a trauma, but she has certain innate characteristics of leadership and wisdom under fire; she's a true hero. Sarah's not really a hero. She's an ordinary person who's been put under extreme pressure, and that makes her warped and twisted, yet strengthened, in a sad way. It's like you don't want this to happen to her. The initial image of her had a big scar running down the side of her face, and we actually did makeup tests with scars, but it would have been a real nightmare to deal with a scar like that in production on a day-to-day basis. I really wanted her to look like Tom Beringer in *Platoon* (Oliver Stone). And Linda was up for it, because the last thing she had done was play Beauty in *Beauty and the Beast* for three years. It's a tribute to her as an actor that she was able to pull off that severity without the help of any makeup whatsoever."

In theater the main ingredient of modern tragedy is an ordinary person who is in an extraordinary circumstance; the situation creates the potential for tragedy. Sarah Connor is no hero; she's an ordinary person who just happens to be placed in extraordinary circumstances. The situation has the potential for tragedy, but in this case, the Terminator, the Schwarzenegger "character," becomes the hero.

That was another major problem Cameron had to confront in the sequel. "There's a strange history that happened with the first film," he explains. "A year or two after *The Terminator* came out, people remembered the film fondly. They remembered Schwarzenegger from the other roles he had played, like *Commando* or *Predator* (Jim Thomas, John Thomas), where he was running around with a machine gun in his hand, spraying bullets everywhere, like he had in *The Terminator*. But there was this curious blurring of distinction that he was the bad guy in *The Terminator*.

"That made me very nervous," he says. "I knew the 'bad guy being the hero' could get me into some pretty dangerous territory, morally and ethically. I absolutely refused to do another film where Arnold Schwarzenegger kicks in the door and shoots everybody in sight and then walks away," he said, choosing his words carefully. "I thought there must be a way to deflect this image of bad guy as hero, and use what's great about the character. I didn't know exactly what to do, but I thought the only way to deal with it would be to address the moral issues head-on."

For the screenwriter, the challenge is to find a way to deal with this situation so it springs out of the story context and is based on the reaction of character. The dramatic need, the dramatic function of the Terminator is to terminate, to kill anybody or anything that gets in its way. Because he is a cyborg, a computer, he cannot change his nature; only a human or another robot can change the program. So to change the bad guy into a good guy requires changing the dramatic situation, the circumstances surrounding the action. Cameron had to find a way to change the context yet keep Terminator's dramatic need intact.

"The key was the kid," Cameron explains. "Because it's never really explained why John Connor has such a strong moral template.

"For me, John was pushed by the situation where he sees the Terminator almost shoot the guy in the parking lot. I think everybody invents their own moral code for themselves, and it usually happens in your teens based on what you've been taught, what you've seen in the world, what you've read, and your own inherent makeup."

John Connor intuitively knows what's right "but can't articulate it," Cameron continued. "John says, 'You can't go around killing people,' and the Terminator says, 'Why not?' And the kid can't answer the question. He gets into a kind of ethical, philosophical question that could go on and on. But all he says is, 'You just can't.'

"I thought the best way to deal with this was not be coy about it and hope it slides by, but to tackle it head-on, make this a story about why you can't kill people," continued Cameron.

He paused a moment, stared at the blinking light on the telephone. "What is it that makes us human?" he asked. "Part of what makes us human is our moral code. But what is it that distinguishes us from a hypothetical machine that looks and acts like a human being but is not?

"Essentially you've got a character associated with being the quintessential killing machine; that is his purpose in life. Devoid of any emotion, remorse, or any kind of human social code, he suddenly finds himself in the strangest dilemma of his career. He can't kill anybody, and he doesn't even know why. He's got to figure it out. He's got to, because he's half human. And he figures it out at the end. The Tin Man gets his heart.

"Once I clicked into that, I saw what the whole movie was going to be about."

Every screenwriter knows that there are four major elements that make up the visual dynamics of screen character. One, the main character or characters must embody a strong *dramatic need*. Dramatic need is what your main character wants to win, gain, get, or achieve during the screenplay. What drives your character through the obstacles of the story line, through the conflicts of plot? In the case of Sarah Connor, John Connor, and the Terminator, the dramatic need is to destroy the future by destroying the one vital computer chip that will determine that future. To destroy that computer chip they will have to destroy the creator of that chip, Miles Dyson, along with the manufacturing entity, Cyberdyne. They will also have to destroy the Terminator 1000, sent back from the past to protect the future. It is this dramatic need that pushes the entire story line through to its completion.

In some screenplays a character's dramatic need will remain constant throughout the entire story, as it does in *Terminator 2*. In other screenplays, the dramatic need will change based on the function of the story. In *Witness*, for example, the dramatic need of John Book changes after Plot Point I. The same thing happens in *Thelma and Louise*, as mentioned in Chapter Four. If the dramatic need of the character changes, it usually will occur after the Plot Point at the end of Act I.

The second element that makes good character is a strong *point of view*, the way your character views the world. Point of view is really a belief system. "I believe in God," for example, is a point of view. So is "I don't believe in God." So is "I don't know whether there is a God." All these are belief systems.

What we believe to be true is true. For Sarah, nothing can alter her belief that the future is already here. On August 29, 1997, the nuclear holocaust will be unleashed and sweep across the planet like some wild wind destroying everything in its path. That we know from *The Terminator*. This inevitability defines Sarah's point of view and motivates everything she does.

The third thing that makes good character is *attitude*—a manner, or an opinion. People express their attitudes, or their opinions, and then act on them: Dr. Silberman has the opinion that Sarah Connor is loony and acts on that. And he's not ready to change that opinion, no matter what she says or does, at least not for another six months of her incarceration.

The fourth component that makes good character is *change:* Does the character change during the course of the screenplay? If so, how does he or she change, and what is the change? Can you trace this character arc from beginning to end?

In discussing *Terminator 2*, Sarah "does not change that much," Cameron said, "although she goes through a kind of epiphany after she experiences her character crisis [the moment when she cannot kill Miles Dyson]. But her crisis happens relatively early in the story."

But what if your character is a robot? If you consider the prospect of an emotional change occurring within a robot, you find there's an immediate contradiction. A robot cannot change unless it has been reprogrammed by someone or something outside itself. (As we shall see, a scene had been written where the Terminator is reprogrammed, but it was omitted from the final cut.) In this case, as Cameron has mentioned, there will be a major change within the Terminator. At the beginning of the screenplay, Schwarzenegger's dramatic need is simple: to protect and save John Connor. That is the first directive of the warrior machine, to preserve itself so it can function.

During the story there is a change in the Terminator's "character," and his dramatic need changes to fit the moral beliefs of John Connor. And we know the Terminator cannot change his need, he "cannot self-terminate"; he needs John Connor to do that for him. This means that the Terminator has to disobey his own built-in program.

To do that, Cameron said, "he must make a command decision, and it is the only true act of free will that he has in the entire film."

Wait a minute. A robot with free will? Even though that's a contradiction, it's the basic issue that concerned Cameron in approaching the sequel. If you look at the two films you'll see there's a thematic continuity that runs between them, because both deal with the conflict between destiny versus free will.

If these films are about anything, Cameron maintained, it's an exploration of the eternal conflict between destiny and free will. How do you get that to work? I asked him.

Cameron took another sip of coffee, put down the cup, and asked, "At what point is everything we do in life preordained in some way?" In other words, if we can go forward in time and look back on it, if we can jump around in time, then isn't everything we do in our life already part of a movie that's already been shot? Or is there a way you can change it? Can you get it to a certain point on the decision tree and then go the other way?

He paused for a moment, thinking. "Basically, what I did in *Terminator 2* is say that everything is meant to be a certain way. At least to that point in time where they're sending somebody back from that future. But can you grab that line of history like it's a rope stretched between two points, and pull it out of the way? If you can pull it just a little bit before it rebounds, and cut it exactly at that moment, then you can change it and go in a different direction. Like catastrophe theory. If you do that you get a future that no longer exists at all, except in the memories of the people that are here now. They have a memory of a future that will never happen, which is curious, because it defies our Newtonian view of the world. But it is possible.

"That became my point of departure," he said, smiling slightly. "It's like the Terminator's been born from the forehead of Zeus but he's an anomaly in our time because he's the only one who has memories of a time that will never exist. He becomes an integral part of the ongoing fabric of the world, and it's his existence here that prevents that particular future from ever popping into existence. In a spiritual sense, it would be like a manifestation of God changing the path."

I took a sip of coffee, and as I put down the cup I casually mentioned that there seemed to be a spiritual awareness creeping into the American screenplay. As we study the forces of destruction to our environment; sense the wanton violence raging throughout the land; experience the decay of the cities, the dissatisfaction with politics and politicians, the failure of the American Dream, the helplessness of the homeless, it seems we're becoming more and more aware that a spiritual aspect is missing from our lives. There's a longing to incorporate into our lives some kind of spiritual perspective about the moral order of the universe.

Cameron agreed, then continued, "There's a million ways to look at all these different paradoxes and ellipses. As a matter of fact, in the first script I wrote a scene where Sarah is driving along, talking to herself on the tape machine, and she says, 'But if you had done this then this would have happened, and if you did that then that would have happened and then you wouldn't have even existed, and I could go crazy thinking about it. I just have to deal with what's in front of me.'

"Ultimately, it gets back to morality," Cameron concluded. "Because if the universe can't be explained, if everything can't be known, then we'll never know what's right or what's wrong. We can only know what we feel is right and wrong, which is why I like the idea of the kid spontaneously creating a sense of what's right and what's wrong. It's the same way in *River's Edge* (Neal Jimenez) when the little kid is about to shoot his brother, and he suddenly realizes he can't, you don't do something like that. Even if nobody's ever told him, he knows it.

"As I got ready to write the screenplay," Cameron said, "I kept asking myself, What's the real goal of this movie? Are we going to blow people away and get them all excited? Is that it? Or is there a way we can get them to really feel something? I thought it would be a real coup if we could get people to cry for a machine. If we could get people to cry for Arnold Schwarzenegger playing a robot, that would be terrific.

"That was the fun of the whole thing. It wasn't all the chases and special effects and all that stuff, though I get off on that on a day-to-day basis. I love sitting at the KEM [the editing machine] and making cuts and getting the action working, but when I look back I feel the real thrill was being able to contour a response that was totally opposite from what we got the first time. And to just have fun with that. To play against the expectations. You've got to do that in a sequel."

And that's where we begin.

Iron Jim

John H. Richardson/1994

From *Premiere Magazine*, August 1994, 44-49, 52, 54-55, 97. Reprinted by permission of John H. Richardson.

By February the town was starting to talk—James Cameron was at it again. When he made *The Abyss* he went over budget and over schedule, missing his release date by four weeks. When he made *Terminator 2: Judgment Day* he broke budget records and kept three editors working frantically to make a July 1 release. This time he wasn't just pushing the envelope—he was ripping it to shreds, he was *vaporizing* it. He'd been shooting *True Lies* for five months and counting. Word around town put the budget at $120 million. "They say he's totally out of his mind," said one rival filmmaker, "spending more money than anybody ever spent in the history of man."

With Cameron anything is possible. Fired from his first film, he broke into the editing room and cut the film back to his original vision. That was before the runaway success of the two *Terminators* and *Aliens* gave him imperial power. Nowadays he directs his crew through a bank of speakers pitched to concert volume: "That's exactly what I don't want," he booms. If they mess up, he says, "That's okay, I've worked with children before." The crews respond by printing up T-shirts with semi-jokey slogans: "You can't scare me—I work for Jim Cameron." And when it comes to showdowns with movie studios, Cameron is a master. *T2* co-producer B. J. Rack recalls the first screening they held for executives of Carolco Pictures: "Jim was mixing the soundtrack, and I had a bad feeling—I said, Are you going to be ready?' He said, 'Yeah, yeah'—and he made them wait. Until 4 A.M. The audacity! And they waited—they were *sleeping on the floor.*"

But reports from the *True Lies* set were full of superlatives. Cameron had reinvented special effects on *The Abyss* and *T2*. Now, armed with his own personal computer-effects studio, Digital Domain, he was once again creating—in the words of editor Mark Goldblatt—"eyepopping, mind-blowing visuals." He was shooting a Harrier jet attack on a Miami high-rise that looked so real even Marine pilots wouldn't be able to tell the hardware from the software. And there was a chase scene on Florida's Seven-Mile Bridge that made the stuff in *The French Connection* look like bumper cars. "It's a huge movie," says Arnold Schwarzenegger, once again Cameron's star. "It's *T2*-type of action, but even more creative—things you've never seen before."

The production was immense—the head of the studios in Santa Clarita where *True Lies* was partly shot said Cameron probably picked a facility thirty miles outside of L.A. because no studio in the city had enough *parking*. Cameron's traveling circus was dogged by protests from Florida to Rhode Island. In Newport the city council had to call a special vote to grant *True Lies* an exemption from the city's noise code. Local activist Maureen O'Neil complained to the press, "I don't particularly want my neighborhood simulating Sarajevo."

But all of the whispers, even the nastiest, were tinged with awe. The studio behind *Wyatt Earp* was intimidated enough to change its release date and leave a little space between the western and *True Lies*, even with Kevin Costner playing Earp. As one envious young producer put it: "They say it's going to be the Holy Grail of action pictures."

James Cameron was born in Kapuskasing, Canada, a town just north of Niagara Falls. His father was an electrical engineer who worked for a paper mill. He was a strict disciplinarian and Cameron grew up hating to be told what to do, so he became a master builder and told *other* kids what to do. They constructed rafts, slot cars, go-carts, rockets, forts, boats, a catapult that hurled boulders so large they made craters when they landed. On one occasion they built a submersible "sea lab" and sent mice deep under the Niagara River. When a neighbor stole some of Jim's toys, Jim and his brother, Mike, sawed through the branches that held up his tree house. Hospitalization was required.

Cameron's mother was an artist and encouraged him to paint; she helped get his work shown in a local gallery when he was a teenager. His mother inspired the sympathy for independent women that marks all of Cameron's work. "I always felt this frustration that she was chained to the house by the kids," he says.

When he was around fifteen, Cameron saw *2001: A Space Odyssey*. "I saw it ten times because I couldn't comprehend how they did that stuff," he says. He started building models and experimenting with 16mm film. At night he would lie in bed, listen to "really bad music," and visualize space battles. After a stint at Fullerton College ("I didn't know if I wanted to be a scientist or an artist"), in California, he dropped out and married a waitress. He drove a truck for the local school district and lived in a little house with a yappy little dog.

Then he saw *Star Wars*. "I was pissed off," he recalls. "I wanted to *make* that movie. That's when I got busy."

Really busy. He haunted the USC library, reading doctoral dissertations on optical printing, front projection, and rear projection. "All I was interested in was visual effects," he says. "I didn't know who Humphrey Bogart *was*." He started buying lenses and taking them apart to find out how they worked. He built his own dolly track, fooled around with beam splitters—all in the living room of his little suburban house. "My wife thought I was crazy," he says. "The guy who used to like to smoke dope and go to the river and drink beer and drive fast cars, all of a sudden had gone psychotic on her. She was *afraid* of me."

Armed with some models he had made with the help of two friends, Cameron obtained an interview at Roger Corman's New World Films: "I figured I'd get in there and then I'd spread like a virus." Which is exactly what happened. "Three weeks after I started I had my own department, I was hiring people," Cameron recalls. "And everybody else that worked there just *hated* me."

After about two years with Corman, Cameron got his first shot at directing. The movie was *Piranha II: The Spawning*. He arrived on the set in Jamaica to find a crew that only spoke Italian and a production so poorly prepared and underfinanced that there wasn't even a costume for one of the stars, Lance Henriksen. At dinner one night, he and Henriksen bought the uniform right off their waiter. To make sure there were enough rubber piranhas, Cameron stayed up late every night making them himself. "I remember thinking, Who is this guy?" Henriksen recalls.

Cameron found himself under constant attack by the film's principal producer, an Italian named Ovidio G. Assonitis. He refused to show the director dailies but told him, "'It's shit, nothing cuts,'" Cameron says.

Cameron kept brooding about the film. Was it true the footage didn't cut? Finally he flew to Rome and confronted Assonitis in his office. According to Cameron, "He sat behind the desk with a letter opener in his hand, like he was afraid I was going to jump over the desk." (Assonitis could not be reached for comment.)

That night, Cameron went back and used a credit card to break into the editing room. "So here I am," he recalls. "I'm looking at all these boxes and I see the word *fine*, which is Italian for 'end,' so I figure these must be the trims. I teach myself how to run the Cinemonta, which is their version of KEM, and I just start recutting the picture." He went back night after night, until the film was the way he wanted it. Ultimately, Cameron took away a lesson he would never forget: "It made me mistrustful of other people who have creative power on a film," he says. "*Very* mistrustful."

And that's when Jim Cameron started to become Jim Cameron. Alone in Rome, feeling "pissed off and alienated" and so broke he survived by stealing complimentary breakfast rolls left on trays in the hallways of his hotel, he got sick with the flu. He had been playing with an idea about a robot hit man from the future. Now, waking one night from a fever dream, he *saw* him, like a snapshot. Later he "drew a sketch of half a Terminator, which looked very much like the final one, crawling after a girl who was injured and couldn't get up and run," Cameron says. "He had a kitchen knife and he pulled himself over the floor with it, dragging his broken arm. I thought that was a really horrific image."

When he got back to L.A., Cameron told his agent his idea about a robot hit man. The agent said, "Bad idea, bad idea. Do something else." Instead he fired the agent. He began writing. Wisely, he anchored the sci-fi with human details taken from his own life. He gave his heroine, eventually played by Linda Hamilton, his first wife's job, turning the Bob's Big Boy where she had worked into Bob's Big Buns, and later even cast her yappy little dog. When the script was finished he sold Gale Anne Hurd the rights for one dollar—and the promise that she would never let anyone else direct it.

The Terminator—with Cameron attached to direct—was turned down by all the major studios. Finally, when John Daly's Hemdale got interested, Cameron talked Henriksen into pitching the project in costume. "I went to Hemdale with gold foil from a Vantage pack over my teeth and a cut on my head, and kicked the door open," Henriksen says. Daly bit, captured by "the script, the drawings, and by Jim's complete passion for the project," he says. Orion Pictures bought the distribution rights.

At first, Cameron focused on finding someone to play Kyle Reese, the good guy who crosses time to save the world. "The Terminator was not given much attention," says Daly. "He was just a robot." Then Orion executive Mike Medavoy ran into Arnold Schwarzenegger at a party. "He told me about *The Terminator* and said it didn't have a leading man, so I read the script with that in mind," Schwarzenegger remembers. Cameron was skeptical. "He was like, 'Yeah, I'll meet him,'" says actor Michael Biehn, who was eventually cast as Reese, "but if you have Arnold play Reese you're going to need King Kong for the Terminator."

When they met, Schwarzenegger and Cameron hit it off. Schwarzenegger kept drifting back to the Terminator. "I kept saying he had to be able to change the weapons blindfolded, and shoot without blinking his eyes, and how he should walk and look with his head tilted forward," says Schwarzenegger. "Then Jim said, '*You* should play the Terminator.' I was, 'Oh, I came for the other thing.'" Cameron whipped out a pencil and started drawing. Schwarzenegger was impressed: "You could almost act off the drawing—the coldness of the character."

All of his friends and advisers told Schwarzenegger not to do it, the conventional wisdom being that it was career suicide to play a villain. Finally, Schwarzenegger decided to ignore his advisers. "I ended up thinking, I'll give it a shot, because this is so well written and the guy is so determined."

But Schwarzenegger had a commitment to do *Conan the Destroyer* and wouldn't be free for four months. So Cameron signed on to write *Rambo: First Blood Part II* and *Aliens* simultaneously—while also doing rewrites of *The Terminator*. With a calculator, he divided the amount of time he had by the number of pages he had to write and spent the next four months jumping between three different desks, putting on different music for each script. When he wasn't writing, he was prepping *The Terminator*, happily showing off his plans to everyone involved. "He was almost childlike," Biehn says, "like a kid in a candy store."

The Terminator began shooting in February 1984. Cameron arrived on the set with the confidence of a seasoned pro. "He was like an encyclopedia of technology, and if a shot was a half inch off the way he visualized it, he would go crazy," Schwarzenegger recalls. But he wasn't just a gearhead; he won over the actors by giving them room to work. And he surprised everyone by demonstrating the stunts himself: "He would show it to you without any padding," Schwarzenegger says. "He was totally mad."

One thing about Cameron was . . . different: He could be unusually blunt, especially about the kiss-ass culture of Hollywood. Mess with him and he'd saw off the branches under your tree house. "He's not the kind of guy who will try to say things in a diplomatic way," Schwarzenegger says. "If you do something right, he'll say it was disastrous but probably a human being could do no better. If he was dealing with machines, they could do better. So you walk away going, 'I guess he likes it.'"

Shortly before the movie was to be released, Cameron became disheartened by Orion's attitude; in fact, he says the studio was outright dismissive. "The guy from Orion says, 'When you have a down-and-dirty action thriller like this, it usually plays for two weeks—it usually drops by 50 percent the second weekend, and is gone by the third week,'" he recalls. Even after the picture opened at number one and got surprisingly good reviews, Cameron asserts, Orion refused to support it with a beefed-up ad campaign. "They treated me like a piece of dogshit," Cameron says.

When *The Terminator* was in the theaters, another blow came from an unexpected quarter: Science fiction writer Harlan Ellison threatened to sue, claiming *The Terminator* had ripped off two episodes of *The Outer Limits* that he'd written, "Soldier" and "Demon With a Glass Hand," as well as "I Have No Mouth, and I Must Scream," an award-winning short story. Their plots concerned robots, time travel, altering the past to save humanity from a holocaust, and a future world where "machines are born to kill." Gagged for many years by a secrecy clause, Ellison is now speaking about it for the first rime: "He got all my best stuff, but the wonderful thing is, he combined it in a new, fresh, and interesting way. I would have been very flattered—all he had to do was get on the phone." Over Cameron's objections—time travel and robots are common sci-fi themes, he says—Hemdale and Orion gave Ellison an "acknowledgment to the works of" credit and a cash settlement, telling Cameron that if he wanted to fight they'd back him. But if Ellison won, they'd sue *Cameron*. The director is still bitter: "I could've risked getting wiped out or I could let the guy have his fucking credit."

But Cameron had made a classic. Schwarzenegger's "steel reaper" is as compelling as a nightmare, and the love story between Biehn and Hamilton made it surprisingly popular with women. The film also displays a devilish wit unusual for an action film. Consider the scene, for example, in which the Terminator goes *Un Chien Andalou* one better by carving out part of his damaged eye—and then reaches up to fluff his hair. The result: *The Terminator* never stopped, gaining cult status on video and TV. "No matter what picture I did after that," Schwarzenegger says, "people would say, 'When are you going to do another *Terminator*?'"

Between pictures, Cameron played—and played *hard*. He went diving, flying, ballooning, anything that put a little space or speed between him and the ground. Everyone who knows Cameron has a story about him and fast cars. "I go to Jim's party in my brand-new Acura NSX, and Jim looks at me and says, Nice car,'" says Henriksen. "When Jim says, 'Nice car,' that's a challenge. So I said, 'Jim, why don't you take it for a spin?' Jim takes it out for ten minutes, and when he comes back all the rubber on my back tires is gone."

Fast planes are good too. Actor Bill Paxton tells of a time Cameron, shooting a video, lashed a camera to the wings of an ultralight plane, undid his seat belt to get a better grip, and pointed the plane straight down. "He goes into a three-thousand-foot dive and drops to three feet off the deck," recalls Paxton. "I go, 'My God, another couple of feet . . .'

"If you're going to hang out with Jim," he adds, "you better have your life insurance."

And then, of course, there are the women. After working with her on a professional basis for four years, Cameron took Hurd for an evening at the Charthouse, in Malibu. Add beach and moonlight, and the working relationship became a romance—with a Cameronian twist, iron-man dates: "We went off-road on a four-wheel drive," says Hurd, "took the hot-air balloon out, and a huge wind came up, and we ended up crash-landing. We went horseback riding, ice skating, we shot AK-47s out in the desert." And that was all in *one weekend*. As the romance ripened, Cameron and Hurd would race each other to meetings, Hurd in her Porsche and Cameron in his new Corvette (purchased with his *Terminator* fee), talking on cellular phones and playing one of Cameron's favorite games, ditch-'em. One day she'd try to shake him, the next he'd fly to shake her. "We'd be smoking down the freeway at 120 miles an hour," Cameron says, "talking the whole time like nothing was happening."

Later, Cameron would divorce Hurd and marry Kathryn Bigelow, director of *Near Dark* and *Point Break* and then divorce her and move in with Linda Hamilton—all formidable women much like the *macha* heroines of his movies. The director explains his string of wives by saying he picks women who don't need him, so naturally one day they realize they don't need him. Hurd says that when she was going through troubles, Cameron just gave her too much damn space. "He's tough," explains Mike Cameron, "and toughest on the people he cares about the most."

Cameron's next two movies, *Aliens* and *The Abyss*, established his reputation as both a brilliant world-class director and a potentially out-of-control visionary-crackpot. With *Aliens* he started thinking really big. "I had been on *Close Encounters of the Third Kind*, so I thought I'd seen the biggest set ever built," says Henriksen. "Then I got to *Aliens*."

The film provided Cameron with plenty of opportunities to hone his fighting skills. To begin with, Twentieth Century Fox didn't want Hurd to produce *Aliens*. In one meeting, she recalls, "they basically said, 'How can a little girl like you do a big movie like this?'" They won that battle and set off for England, where they had to contend with a scornful British crew that was convinced it was working on a crappy sequel to a great (British-directed) thriller. Cameron fired his cinematographer early on and Hurd threatened to fire others when a mutiny surfaced. The crew took to calling Cameron Grizzly Adams, and tea breaks were taken with metronomic regularity.

Fox wasn't exactly overwhelmed by the project—the studio thought its summer hit was going to be *SpaceCamp*. Instead, *Aliens* made $83 million and established Cameron as a hot director. It also showed a mind at work, with thematic passion and a mordant sense of humor (listen closely at the end of the credit roll for the slurp of that baby facehugger). Clearly, Cameron wasn't just doing time on Planet Action—he wanted it all, and art too.

But it was *The Abyss*—which Cameroids call, probably accurately, the toughest shoot in film history—that showed just how obsessed Cameron really is. Inspired by a recurring nightmare of a vast wave rolling unstoppably toward shore, it is a wildly ambitious story that ranges from the troubled love of a man and woman to the nature of humanity and war, expressed through some of the most pregnant nautical metaphors since Herman Melville.

But the genius of *The Abyss* isn't so much what's onscreen (which is, alas, flawed) but what it took to get it there. With just four months of preproduction, Cameron and Hurd faced the task of building the largest underwater set ever constructed, a set so huge each section of it weighed forty tons. They found an abandoned nuclear plant and filled its two containment units with a total of 10 million gallons of water, designed a filtration system to keep the water clear, craned in a tarpaulin big enough to keep the water dark, and then began *inventing* underwater filming equipment. With Mike, who had spent the past fourteen years as an aeronautical engineer, Cameron worked on deciding what they needed for the "talking helmets," farmed the assignment out, and turned to developing a "diver propulsion vehicle" for the cameras that eliminated the need for underwater cranes and dolly tracks. The Sea Wasp DPV earned the brothers the first of five patents they have been awarded so far on technical film equipment. They come up with ideas in the following way, Mike says: Jim dreams up his shot, figures out what he needs to execute it, then finds out if the thing exists. If it doesn't, he tells Mike to make it. And when his brother says that from an engineering standpoint it can't be done, "Jim says, 'Don't use the word *engineer* around me ever again.'"

The DPV done, Cameron decided to reinvent special effects, turning to Industrial Light & Magic to help create the "pseudopod" water creature; the effect took eight months to produce, but the process gave ILM a huge jump on the use of computer graphics for film, making movies like *Jurassic Park* and *Terminator 2: Judgment Day* possible. Cameron wrote the script so that if the effect didn't work, he could cut the movie without it.

Filming underwater proved to be incredibly arduous. The water was so highly chlorinated that it burned skin and turned hair white. Even the mundane details were complicated—how does a script supervisor work underwater? (By covering each page in plastic.) How do you take a bathroom break underwater? (By peeing right in your wet suit.) The actors were stretched to the breaking point. When the camera ran out of film in the middle of her death scene, Mary Elizabeth Mastrantonio stormed off the set, screaming, "We are not animals!" Ed Harris tells (in *The Abyss's* fascinating laserdisc special edition) of a day so hard, he burst into tears on the drive home. Neither actor would return calls for this story.

It was on *The Abyss* that Cameron began to get a reputation for abusing his crews. One crew member, who asked to remain anonymous, says: "He just has this tunnel vision to get what he wants done. His crew gets battered and he doesn't care." Cameron loyalists—and there are many—cope through black humor. "One of the Jim jokes on *The Abyss*," says crew member Ed Marsh, "was, 'I'm letting you breathe, what more do you want?'"

Cameron admits that he's "very, very hard" on his crews—and he doesn't apologize a bit. "If an NFL coach didn't browbeat the guys and say, 'You fucked up and you didn't do this' . . . I mean, it's perfectly acceptable in sports that mistakes and laziness should not be tolerated. If you're working on a big movie, it must imply that you're the best—you presented yourself as a varsity athlete. So fucking be one. That's my philosophy." Asked if he fires many people, Cameron gives a dry laugh. "I would never do anything as merciful as firing someone. For fucking up, you have to stay till the end."

Cameron's friends all talk about this side of him, alternately worrying over it and excusing it. They say that Cameron gets frustrated because he can do every job on a movie set better than anyone working for him. They say that he's so passionate about his films that sometimes, when the budget simply can't accept a shot he wants, he *pays for it out of his own pocket*. And they all say that no one works harder than Cameron himself—at least three people have described how, after a long day underwater, Cameron was required to spend an hour decompressing, and he would hang upside down to relieve the strain of the helmet and watch dailies underwater on a video monitor. (Paxton says that by the time the actor visited the *Abyss* set, Cameron had figured out how he could push the limits of the Navy dive tables and spend less time decompressing.)

What's striking, ultimately, is how tender and defensive people are about him. Mike Cameron probably puts it best: "I've been the recipient of a lot of his derogatory remarks, and it does hurt your feelings. But he really is a bighearted guy. The people who are close to him know that, and they just kind of tolerate the viciousness." Maybe the reason they are so willing to forgive is that, as everyone says, Cameron's furies are never personal. "His movies have an ego, and you don't fuck with his movies," says Biehn, "but *he* doesn't have an ego. When he throws a tantrum, it's almost like the movie is throwing a tantrum."

Despite all the tension, Cameron still took time for his brand of fun. One person said he raced his Corvette around the underwater tank, though Cameron's response to this anecdote was, "Not true, but a good idea." However, there's no doubt he continued his lifelong avocation of torturing his little brother—in this case, casting him as a drowned corpse. According to Mike, "He said, 'You're going to go down twenty-five feet, you're going to open your eyes because dead men don't close their eyes, we're going to put a live crab in your mouth, and when it's time to shoot we'll tell you "Action" and you let the crab out of your mouth.'" They did five takes. "Two times, I had to crush the crab because Jim was taking too long setting the lights. I'm sure it was a sheer delight for him."

After a frantic postproduction and many fights with the studio, *The Abyss* ended up a case of too much too late. Its biggest problem was the ending—or, rather, the endings. There were at least three, each more extreme than the previous one, until it practically exploded with its own ambition, and all the really great stuff—the magical pseudopod, the unbelievably intense love-death sequence, Ed Harris's powerful final descent—was snuffed out by a burst of Message. In the end, *The Abyss* made only $54 million and got mixed to negative reviews. Hollywood snickered.

Seven years after the release of *The Terminator*, it was finally time to make *T2*. Cameron had been toying with the idea almost since the first movie wrapped. "Arnold and I were talking about making another picture," says Cameron. "I said, Well, I'm not going to make the same film. You're going to be a good guy.' He thought it was kind of a wacky idea, but he liked it." Cameron had also dreamed up the shape-shifter idea for the T-1000, but it hadn't been technically possible until *The Abyss*. The real problem was making the deal—there was bad blood between Schwarzenegger and Hemdale's John Daly. Ultimately, Hemdale got into financial trouble at the same time that Carolco's high-rolling Mario Kassar was pursuing Schwarzenegger. "I said [to Kassar], Hemdale has no money,'" Schwarzenegger recalls. "'Go for it right now, and we'll do it [for Carolco].'" Once the deal was in place, Cameron sat down and started writing.

Again the scope of the film was vast—for the night-freeway chase scene, the production was caught short when its cabling was stolen and had to rent every electrical cable it could get its hands on to light four miles of freeway. The T-1000 effect cost $5.5 million and took eight months of work for three and a half minutes of screen time.

Despite the tech-heavy nature of the movie, Cameron hit the set determined to get the acting just right. Schwarzenegger says, "He worked harder on the different emotions, talked us through it more, insisted on rehearsing." But he was still doing whatever it took to get the shot he wanted. For the scene in which a helicopter flies below an underpass, Cameron felt that the shot had to be done twice to get both forward and rear angles.

But the budget—which reportedly started in the $70 million range—was soaring. Carolco executives called Schwarzenegger for help. "They said, 'We hope we have your support.' I would say, 'There's no way.'" One of the sequences Carolco wanted cut, Schwarzenegger says, was the roadhouse scene, in which his character gets introduced. "Only a studio guy would cut a scene like that out."

Meanwhile, Cameron and Carolco fought over the ending. Cameron's ending (which can be seen on one version of the laserdisc) puts Hamilton in age makeup many years in the future. Carolco demanded a screening, and, as Kassar flew to George Lucas's Skywalker Ranch in a helicopter through a storm, Cameron started the screening without him. Afterward he snatched up the preview cards and refused to show them to Kassar. But the viewers all said the same thing: Lose the ending. Finally, Cameron relented, and the existing ending was added. The result, of course, was one of the biggest hits of all time, a commercial and artistic success.

Like the others, *T2* spawned its own crew T-shirt: TERMINATOR 3–NOT WITH ME.

After *T2*, Cameron put together a $500 million deal that would give him total power over his films, even ownership of the negative. He also started a company called Digital Domain, based on an idea he got driving in his car—it would "domesticate the highfalutin digital effect," so that even realism-oriented filmmakers could use it. If you wanted a house in the middle of a cornfield, you could grow the corn right in the computer. Cameron called up ILM whiz Scott Ross, who said computers couldn't do that yet. Cameron replied: "I know. We'll make it happen." IBM pitched in the money, and now Digital Domain is working on *Interview with the Vampire*, providing miniatures, mattes, composites, morphing, and even digital enhancement of special effects makeup. Cameron was also having a baby with Linda Hamilton *and* working on a script for his ex-wife Kathryn Bigelow. Then Schwarzenegger called him up and said, "I have the picture you have to do next."

The film Schwarzenegger had in mind was a French film called *La Totale!*, a comedy about a man who pretends to be a boring joe when really he's a secret agent. The problem is, he's done such a good job of pretending that his wife is nearly ready to leave him. Cameron liked it and wrote a script, only to find his shiny new self-financing deal freezing up when he couldn't get any completion-bond company to insure him. After some wrangling, Fox and Cameron agreed to an acceptable budget and Fox put up more cash.

Then the *studio* threw out the numbers. "Once we got into the logistical problems, we knew we weren't going to make that schedule," says Jon Landau, Fox's senior vice-president of feature production. The actors were prepared. "When you make a deal with Jim's company, they don't hire you with an out date," says Jamie Lee Curtis, who signed on as Schwarzenegger's wife. It was made very clear to me in an unspoken way that I shouldn't be making plans for the last day of the movie."

Filming began during a heat wave last year. Working at the Santa Clarita studios, the crew started with interior scenes between Curtis and Schwarzenegger.

"[The first scene] was just two people getting ready for work, that wonderful dance that married people do, where they're oblivious to each other," says Curtis. For three weeks they established the relationship, shooting in a simple and linear way. Then the action started.

"It's not the ordinary scenes you see with car crashes," says Schwarzenegger. "Imagine riding a horse through a hotel lobby and into an elevator, going up the elevator with the horse and people in tuxedos and dresses, then going on to the roof."

And that was the easy stuff—in Miami, Cameron shot the Harrier jet. "The first time I saw that, my jaw dropped," says Curtis. "They took a real Harrier jet and mounted it on top of a hydraulic—it looked like an upside-down spider, with all these legs moving up and down. They were up there for three weeks, with every piece of equipment—a Technocrane, a Lenny arm, a Powerpad. It's outrageous what he did. And it went flawlessly."

Then on to the massive limo-and-helicopter chase on Florida's Seven-Mile Bridge, which took weeks to film. Cameron asked Curtis to perform the final stunt herself. It involved hanging from a wire under a moving helicopter a hundred feet off the water. "Will you be there?" she asked. "I'll be shooting you," he said. So up they went, the director acting as his own cameraman, "hanging out of the helicopter door with nothing but the Seven-Mile Bridge and lots of water and manta rays underneath him."

As the scope of the film expanded, so did the stress. To keep things moving, Cameron ordered the troops around like Patton—via those speakers. The crew dubbed him Mr. Microphone. "People who would screw up constantly would hear about it in a very direct manner," says Tom Arnold, who plays Schwarzenegger's sidekick.

Occasionally, Cameron went too far even for Schwarzenegger. One day, he said that anyone who went to the bathroom could just keep walking—and he wasn't kidding. "That's over the top," Schwarzenegger admits. "*He* would rather pee in his pants than leave the scene when things are clicking. But an electrician doesn't feel as dedicated as he does."

But again, Cameron's fanaticism inspired his troops. Says Schwarzenegger: "There was one thing that blew me away about the guy—there was a particular action scene that required a weapon to be fired in a very tight area. I asked Jim about it, and he said, 'Well, we'll find out if it's safe.' And he gets in this area and has the weapons guy fire it past *his* face a couple of times—the fact is, he has *balls*, man. He'll do anything."

Filming was endless—*True Lies* shot so long that Paxton worked on it for a while, went off and played the lead in another movie, and came back to shoot some more. Tia Carrere, who plays an art dealer, signed on for seven or eight weeks' work and ended up cashing checks for seven months. "It kept going and going, like the Energizer bunny," she says. Cameron admits to 130 shooting days, give or take a few, but add second unit and the occasional unofficial first unit and it's anyone's guess; the rumor is 180 days. (Cameron insists that *True Lies* isn't the most expensive picture in history—*Spartacus* was, he says, "adjusted for today's dollars.") "Fox was sweating bullets, just like Mario did," says one insider. "But what could they do? They want more pictures from him, plus the dailies were great."

Finally, in March, Fox announces that principal photography is finished. A week later, in a small editing room in Santa Monica, Cameron watches a shot of fingers fumbling for an electronic bug. He turns to his editor. "Cut to it with the fingers already on the bug, so she's not fumbling. If it doesn't cut smoothly, then play with it some more."

Cameron jumps to another editing room, then another. Despite a deadline so tight that within a few days he'll end up pushing his release date two weeks, Cameron seems relaxed, even happy. He jokes that "all my available RAM is taken up by *True Lies* dailies," but he seems confident about the movie, and he has even managed to keep things going with Linda Hamilton since she moved out with their baby daughter during preproduction. "Maybe that's what it takes," he says. "We're both pretty happy with the arrangement for right now. And the baby is outstanding, beautiful—total engineer." He shows a one-sheet he came up with for *True Lies*—a hand grenade with a wedding ring for a firing pin. The tag line reads, "Even perfect marriages have their blow-ups." Suddenly it all comes clear: Cameron is probably the only person in the world who can make gearhead action-romances that aren't just sincere, they're autobiographical.

Cameron and his editor watch Schwarzenegger in a tender moment, trying to break through his teenage daughter's shell. "She's very subtle," Cameron says. "She's listening to what he's saying, but she's not going to blurt out, 'Oh, Daddy.' That's excellent, let's go to Six. I like her in Four too."

Then it's off to dailies—yes, despite the wrap announcement, Cameron is *still* shooting. In a few days Schwarzenegger—already at work full-time on another movie—will quietly slip out to shoot one last scene.

Maybe the last. "I called [Cameron] a perfectionist once," says Tom Arnold. "And he said, 'No, I'm a greatist. I only want to do it until it's great.'"

Rich and Strange

Ray Greene/1995

From BOXOFFICE *Magazine*, October 1995, 10–12. © BOXOFFICE Media, LLC. Reprinted with permission.

In actual fact, the following interview with James Cameron was solicited by BOXOFFICE based on false assumptions. We were present at NATO/ShoWEST last March when the writer/director/producer received NATO's "Producer of the Year" award and gave a stirring address about the role of exhibition in the face of new technological developments. We were also aware of *Strange Days*, Cameron's latest producing venture (directed by Kathryn Bigelow), which, in capsule form, seemed to fit right into this issue's discussion of new technologies. So talking to Mr. Cameron seemed like a natural idea in this, our first ever issue-length examination of the effects of new production and delivery formats.

As it turned out, we were both right and wrong. *Strange Days* is not, as we assumed, another in the seemingly endless spate of "virtual reality"–based thrillers Hollywood is churning out [for the uninitiated, "virtual reality" is the creation of a computer rendered world that works in three dimensions, like the real thing]. Based on an original idea of Cameron's, *Strange Days* tells the story of Lenny Nero (Ralph Fiennes), a techno-hustler who recycles actual dreams, genuine nightmares, and authentic memories using a proprietary technology that has nothing to do with computers or fictional digitized landscapes. We should have guessed going in that the creative force behind the Terminator films and *Aliens* would have his own ideas to work out in his latest venture into the science fiction form

On the other hand, as a distinguished futurist and the entrepreneur behind leading-edge effects company Digital Domain, Cameron is still an ideal choice to lead off this survey of the increasingly wired world of modern filmed entertainment. His views on everything from *Strange Days* to the current science fiction boom to the dark side of technological "miracles" is as pertinent to our theme as could be. But enough with the preliminaries. Let's hear it from the man himself.

BoxOffice: Judging by the press materials and the teaser trailer, *Strange Days* seems to speak to this amazing paradigm shift that we're going through in terms of all these new technologies.
Cameron: It does and it doesn't. It's definitely part of that wave, but I hope people are able to make the distinction that there is no "virtual reality" component in *Strange Days*. In fact, there are no computers at all, and most of what's happening to us right now socially and psychologically is about advances in computing.

BoxOffice: In premise, *Strange Days* reminds me of *Brainstorm*.
Cameron: Well, *Brainstorm* was the primer, and this is the advanced course. *Brainstorm* had a lot of different, metaphysical elements in it, dealing with things like life after death. *Strange Days* is about memory, about the effect memory has on our day-to-day life. Secondarily, it's about a lot of social issues, and the impact of living in what I think of as a "watched" society.

BoxOffice: A "watched" society?
Cameron: We're a society under surveillance. And we all participate in that surveillance. At the same time that we are more watched and monitored than we have ever been as a populace, we are also watching more than we ever have as a populace. Look at the daytime TV shows, where everybody sort of voyeuristically wants to know what everyone else is doing behind the doors of their bedroom. And the Simpson trial, of course, where we're morbidly fascinated by every detail *as a society*.

Planetwide, with population increases and so on, we're going to have to live our adventures more and more vicariously. We're not all going to be able to have the adventure. Somebody's gonna have to go do it, and then tell everybody else about it. And that's sort of what filmmaking has always been about, and that's what a lot of new media, I think, are going to be about.

BoxOffice: So what *Strange Days* does, in that classic science fiction way, is to take current reality and extend it?
Cameron: Absolutely. On the one hand, it's a classic science fiction film. On the other hand, [director] Kathryn [Bigelow] has always rejected the term. She treated it as a very straightforward relationship thriller with political overtones, and let the technology weave itself into the fabric. As it goes on, you see the dark side of that same technology.

BoxOffice: You're most commonly thought of as a writer/director. But here you are, moving more and more heavily into the producing role.
Cameron: Right. Which is a very different role, although they're related. Now, I have produced for Kathryn Bigelow in the past. We did *Point Break* together, and found that it worked out pretty well. So she was a natural choice to do *Strange Days* with. I told her the rough idea of this thing that I had been writing, on and off, for eight years. She liked it, and she wanted to take it in certain directions, and I said, "Sure." So I actually wrote it with her in mind to direct it. It was always a well-tailored fit.

BoxOffice: Was there anything you had to unlearn to be a writer/producer, as opposed to a writer/director?
Cameron: On this film, I said, "You know, if you guys don't go over budget, then there's no reason for me to go to the set, unless you ask me there because you want my opinion." Well, they never asked, and I never went, except to go down so they could get a picture of me on the set. I got more involved in the editing process at Kathryn's request. We spent many hours refining the cut, and we're both very happy with it.

BoxOffice: It almost sounds like your experience as a director informs your producing, in the sense that you're protecting the other filmmaker's vision.
Cameron: Absolutely. Every time I go to open my mouth, I think, "What would I as a director think about what I'm going to say next?" So I find myself erring way on the conservative side of producerial input. There were certain cases on this film where Kathryn and I differed, and we'd talk about it, and she'd say, "Okay. We don't agree." And I said, "Fine. You're the director. You make this final decision." [Laughs] "But I'm lodging a formal complaint."

BoxOffice: We tend to overemphasize things such as gender these days, as if men and women see things wildly differently. Did you find that Kathryn saw things differently in gender terms as well?
Cameron: I don't think her tastes and my tastes are in any way gender-oriented. Quite the opposite of what you might interpret as a classic gender orientation. On this film, I was always pushing to make it more romantic, for example. And she was always pushing to make it harder-edged.

BoxOffice: I'm really curious about your feelings on this current science fiction production boom. What seems to me to be going on is that science fiction has become to our time what the western was to the thirties. There are these major technological and cultural shifts going on, and we're using science fiction as a way of dealing with it metaphorically.

Cameron: Historically, science fiction has always been terrible at actually predicting the future. What it's great at is giving you a different way of looking at your life now. All the brilliant minds working in science fiction never predicted the home computer and its impact. And yet look where we are now versus where we were ten years ago. I mean, we're so in the middle of something that it's very hard for us to look at it and get any perspective without stepping way outside and going to the future and looking back at it.

BoxOffice: And that's why there's a science fiction boom?

Cameron: I think people are waking up to something that science fiction writers have always known, which is that we live in a science fiction world. We all just vary on an individual basis as to how much we're willing to admit that. Every new generation comes into a world the previous generation could not have predicted. And that's been true for almost every decade of this century, and has never really been true for the previous three thousand years of civilization. We live in a time where the rate of change is so high that we can't comprehend where it's taking us. But we don't care, because a human being is probably the most adaptable creature on the planet. If conditions change, we'll find a technology or a process to help us adapt to it.

BoxOffice: That's very optimistic, and sort of the classical science fiction definition of man's relationship to technology. "Whatever comes, we'll find a way to figure it out and make it work for us."

Cameron: Yeah. I don't think it's even that we have to hunker down and come up with the will power. It just happens.

BoxOffice: What surprises me about hearing you say such rosy things is that your futuristic films embrace the idea of positive change so ambivalently. There are three filmmakers who invented what we think of as science fiction on modern movie screens—Lucas, Spielberg, and yourself. And of the three—

Cameron: That's pretty damn good company. Especially considering I was driving a truck for a school district when they were already gods.

Boxoffice: It's certainly not an empty comparison. Where you separate company I think from those two guys is that your vision of the future tends to be full of much darker possibilities.
Cameron: Oh, it's much more cautionary. I think so. It's not candy-coated and all a big amusement park. Quite frankly, that's just the way I look at the world. I mean, I think of myself as an optimistic paranoid. And I mean that very, very, very literally. I'm very optimistic about the human animal and our potential, and I'm paranoid about some of the darker potential inherent in these technologies. And who wouldn't be, who's been halfway awake during the latter half of the twentieth century?

Boxoffice: How do you feel about what's happening now in terms of this information delivery revolution? Is it all hyperbole? Do you see scary possibilities inherent in it?
Cameron: All you have to do when you start getting carried away about how cool it all is is to ask yourself when have you ever had more than $100 cash on you? The rest of your money, everything that you own, sits in a computer. Let's say that somebody created a virus that could wipe out all financial records. Our civilization could be destroyed faster than in a nuclear war. I love this [new computer] stuff. I love what it can do for me as an artist, I've embraced it wholeheartedly, I have a company called Digital Domain which can do state-of-the-art effects work, and it's all great fun. But we've got to be careful. It's moving fast.

Boxoffice: My nightmare is a world in which a person sits down in front of a screen, and puts on a mask, and then gets a wonderful smell that smells like fresh air, and a beautiful 3-D image of a tree that's almost as nice to look at as the tree outside his window, which he never looks at because he's too busy staring at the screen.
Cameron: Right. Exactly. It's like we become sucked into this totally vicarious existence. But, you know, eventually, the novelty factor will wear off. The sad thing is, come back a thousand years from now, and we may need that computer image to remember what a tree looked like. We've got 5, 6 billion people on the planet right now. It's probably going to double in the next twenty-five years. Who's gonna have access to a tree?

Boxoffice: It's consoling to talk about the novelty factor. Because, come to think of it, when you look at movies, there was that time a hundred years ago when a man sneezing, or a train arriving at a station, could hold an audience riveted, without even a change of camera angle, let alone a plot. So there is a place we can point to when we're examining the state of the digital arts where we can say, "Okay. This is still fairly crude. But it will probably follow a similar path, the potential for humanizing it and making it do wonderful artistic things is dormant in them, waiting to get out!"

Cameron: It reminds me a little bit of the incredible optimism right before the First World War, at the end of the Edwardian age. Everything was bigger, faster, we'd invented light, there were motor cars. So many things we take for granted now had just been invented. Everybody thought the world was just going to keep getting better. So what came next? We don't remember this, but 11 million people died in World War I, and another 17 million died in the influenza epidemic of 1918.

Boxoffice: And in some ways, the intellectual bitterness that came out of that is with us to this day, I think.

Cameron: Yeah. They weren't in control of the world, they weren't in control of nature like they thought they were. They got hit by a virus which they didn't understand. Within the seeds of the carnage of WWI were all these great optimistic advances that they were making. And who knows how that allegory might play out in our lifetime? But we'll be around to find out, I'm sure of that.

20,000 Leagues Under The Sea: The Movie Director as Captain Nemo

Bill Moseley/1998

From *OMNI*, 1998, http://www.astralgia.com/webportfolio/omnimoment/titanic/cameron/index.html. Reprinted by permission of Bill Moseley.

Nemolike James Cameron dove in a Russian submersible two and a half miles under the sea to visit—and film—the *Titanic* for his epic movie on the mythic doomed ship. Then he re-created a nearly full-size model of the vessel in Baja California, replete with historically precise details composed from information gathered in his twelve dives and the five-year research effort of his entire team.

"We wanted to tell a fictional story within absolutely rigorous, historically accurate terms. If something is known to have taken place, we do not violate it. Likewise, there's nothing we show that could not have happened. Our fictitious characters are woven through the pylons of history in such a way they could have been there. All the accuracy and all the special visual effects are intended for one purpose; to put the viewer on *Titanic*. It's a very you-are-there kind of experience."

In making *Titanic* Cameron is doing what all epic artists do—reinventing for a new age vital histories of the culture. "The tragedy of the *Titanic* has assumed an almost mythic quality in our collective imagination," he says. "But the passage of time has robbed it of its human face and vitality." In making a love story aboard the fated ship, Cameron has found a way to reconfigure the story. "I hope [protagonists] Rose and Jack's relationship will be a kind of emotional lightning rod, if you will, allowing viewers to invest their minds and hearts to make history come alive again."

James Cameron is his own man, rare as robot tears in a town (Hollywood) and an industry (the movies) where everyone owes everyone else. But thanks to writing and directing such monster hits as *The Terminator*, *Aliens*, *The Abyss*, *Terminator 2: Judgment Day*, and *True Lies*, not to mention co-writing *Rambo: First Blood Part II* with Sylvester Stallone, and rewriting *Point Break* with director and former wife Kathryn Bigelow, Cameron is not only bankable, he *is* the bank! Yet Cameron sinks more than his capital into each film. He goes to the bottom of the sea.

Cameron is also our kind of man—someone who will do more, go further, face his obsessions with hunger and glee—all to fathom the depths of his curiosity and imagination. To create something new and extreme. So it was more than time, we thought, to have a webside conversation with the resuscitator of the *Titanic*, father of the Terminator, begetter of the Abyss—the mythmaker as time traveler—as he introduces his latest paradigm-shifting filmic adventure.

I first met James Cameron at the L.A. press conference announcing the formation of Digital Domain, his visual effects and digital production studio. When asked if he planned to use IBM equipment, Cameron surprised his Big Blue partners by replying from the stage that he'd use the best there was, and if that happened to be IBM, so much the better. My next encounter was early '95, when preparing for the first of these many conversations. I was ensconced on the third floor of Cameron's Lightstorm Productions in Santa Monica, poring over the hours of production interviews, storyboards, and extra film footage on the Special Edition laserdiscs of *The Abyss* and *T2*. Cameron blew into the office like a spring storm, gave his minions a good-natured tongue-lashing about how things looked messy as his old college dorm room, then blew right back downstairs to resume editing *Strange Days*, the movie he co-wrote, produced, and edited with director Kathryn Bigelow.

The next time, Cameron was like a pharaoh presiding over the construction of a pyramid. He was preparing to go to Mexico to oversee the completion of a model of the *Titanic*. We spent the lion's share of our time together "20,000 leagues under the sea," talking about the *Titanic*. Herewith is a record of this series of conversations that in its length and breadth constitutes something of a portrait in progress of the artist/mythmaker/engineer/explorer as director.

Omni: You decreed you'd not make the movie unless you could film the actual wreckage. Why did you have to go down to the *Titanic?*
Cameron: I got the idea to do a film about the *Titanic* about five years ago. I wanted to tell a love story on the ship before, during, and after its sinking; and a present-day story that wrapped around it involving these

salvage guys diving the wreck. I love deep-submergence technology. It occurred to me like a light bulb going on, hey, why don't we just go shoot the real wreck!? I mean, it's sitting out there in the Atlantic. Why not do it, make it real?

My friend Al Giddings, director of photography on *The Abyss*, had been involved with the Russians who did the support diving for the IMAX film, *Titanica*. I said, Al, you've got to introduce me to these guys. He said, they're in Moscow. If I get us two tickets to Moscow, will you introduce me? He said, sure.

We flew to Moscow and met Anatoly Sememeyevich, who's the head of the Russian's top oceanic research institute. I talked to him about doing a movie, a Hollywood movie. This would be a work of fiction, not a documentary, nothing scientific. There was no more justification for you to be involved, I told him, than I'd love to show the world your submersibles and how they work. And I think that a commercial film would be the best way to do that because more people would see it and become interested. So he said, okay.

We hired the Russians and their ship *Keldysh* to take us down with all of our film equipment in their two submersibles, *Mir 1* and *Mir 2*. We built all of our own cameras, our own housings, special video cameras, control systems. They had to survive pressures of six thousand pounds per square inch at a depth of two and a half miles. No one had taken a camera that deep before. The crushing force of the water would implode any normal camera housing. I wanted to have it outside in the water, attached to the sub, but able to pan and tilt naturally, and be able to use wide-angle lenses to get most of the shots.

These housings were titanium, bigger than any camera housings that had ever gone to that depth because they had to hold movie cameras. We built special cameras that pulled down only two perforations per frame instead of four. From that we were able to extract our wide-screen image while making our film last longer. The dives were fifteen hours long, and we had no way to reload the film. There was quite a bit of film discipline I had to practice.

Shooting the Ship

I was the cameraman. There were three people in the sub: myself, the pilot, and the engineer. In the other sub there was a similar crew. We filmed from sub to sub, and from sub to sub to *Titanic*. I was trying to relate the other submersible to the *Titanic* in some scale. We got some shots that are quite spectacular. It's a completely different look of the *Titanic*. It's lit movie-style, not documentary-style where you shoot black and white with a single source of light.

Omni: How did you light your shots?
Cameron: The other submersible had lights all over it. We had lights on ours as well as some lights on a long, extendible boom. My brother, Michael, designed and created the camera housing. It's harder to design one to go two and a half miles down than it is for outer space. The pressures that far underwater are vastly greater than space. It wouldn't have even been possible to build this a few years ago because the interface between the glass dome port the camera looks through and the titanium housing is critical. It involves all sorts of scientific things I don't understand.

When you design something to go onto a submersible, it becomes like a reverse stick of dynamite. If it implodes, it can implode with such force that it actually creates a secondary implosion of the submersible itself. We didn't want that, obviously. In order for anything to be man-rated to that sort of depth, it has to pass an independent design review by other engineering companies. The camera housings passed the review. They were designed on my [Silicon Graphics] computer, built and hydrostatically tested down to the equivalent of almost full ocean depth.

The one thing you don't want to do with these housings is bump into anything, like, say, a large steel object . . . like . . . the *Titanic*, for example. And of course we did. Obviously, since I'm telling you the story, there were no dire consequences. But there was one time when we got picked up by a current and pushed right into the wreck. We were about to hit on the glass dome port of the housing. I had to get the pan-tilt rig switched on and get it turned just enough so it took the collision on the shoulder of the matte box. The matte box was crushed.

Omni: You know there was an attempt made to raise the *Titanic* and bring it to shore, but it broke free and sank again.
Cameron: The newspapers used the absurd expression "Raise the *Titanic*." The people involved were raising a twenty-one-ton piece of the ship. The *Titanic* broke up when it sank. It broke in half, and pieces are lying on the bottom from the middle section where it broke apart. This was one of the pieces. A twenty-one-ton piece is an infinitesimally small part of the ship; the *Titanic* weighed sixty-thousand tons! The idea of raising

the *Titanic* is absurd. Even raising a very small piece of the *Titanic* took more effort and expenditure than anybody's ever used to try to raise an object from the depths, other than the thing the CIA used to try to pull up that Russian submarine.

When we went to the *Titanic*, we went there with a certain degree of respect. We were going to photograph it so other people could share the experience; we were not going to take anything. We sent a robot camera inside the ship, which no one had ever really done before. It shot some amazing video, some of which is in my film.

Omni: The camera, as I understand it, could only hold one five-hundred-foot roll of film. And reloading was out of the question. I guess efficiency must have been a major concern.

Cameron: Anybody who ever shot their kid's birthday party on a home video knows that a half-hour tape goes like that. [Snaps fingers] When you're on a sixteen-hour dive and you must rigidly discipline yourself to shoot twelve minutes of film, it's a little scary.

We had planning sessions on the *Keldysh* where we'd take a little video camera and mount it on a miniature submersible with fiber-optic lights that corresponded to the actual light we'd be using. We'd do dry test runs of the shot in smoke, and I'd get the Russian sub pilots to move their toy subs the way they would move their actual vehicles so they'd understand the shots.

Omni: How did you guide the drone?

Cameron: A guy flies it. He's got two joysticks and flies it like a remote-control airplane. We can see the video. We're just recording it as it comes back. It's about the size of half a refrigerator, you know, the kind you put a couple of six-packs in. We managed to get it down the corridors, around inside the wreck. We got it fouled up a few times, but we got it back out—which was good, 'cause we still needed to shoot with it!

Omni: How did it affect you?

Cameron: I went down there as a director, so when we made our first dive, it was like: "Shot one; shot two; shot three. I want *Mir 1* here; *Mir 2* there." It wasn't until the third or fourth dive that it hit me emotionally—the awe and mystery of being two-and-a-half miles down on the floor of the Atlantic, seeing the sad ruin of this great ship. But we were able to come back with this rich harvest of film and video images. We sent our remote vehicle inside and explored the interior. We literally saw things no one had seen since 1912. We've integrated these images into the fabric of the film.

Raising the *Titanic* in Rosarita

Omni: Tell me about the model of the *Titanic* you constructed in Rosarita, Mexico?
Cameron: It's not a model, it's a set. It is 775 feet long—the bow of the ship, some pieces missing, then the forward well deck, the entire superstructure and one side of the ship, then the aft well deck with no hole next to that, and the poop deck with no hole underneath it. From stem to stern it's about 10 to 15 percent shorter than the actual *Titanic* because we've edited out some pieces. The full shots of the ship are done with computer graphics, models, and animated water. It took us a long time to really get our minds around how big *Titanic* was. It was huge, 880 feet long. In weight it was 48,000 tons in displacement, but in physical weight of steel, it was closer to 60,000 tons. This thing was a monster.

Omni: How much of the special effects is Digital Domain doing?
Cameron: All the effects. Rob Ligado, the FX supervisor on *Apollo 13* and *Interview with a Vampire*, is doing *Titanic*. Because Digital Domain is swamped right now, we bidded out some cold-air breathing [effects] on the actors; we can't refrigerate the whole set.

Omni: Your attention to detail has had some remarkably ironic turns, such as the fact that the lifeboat davits [the system of pulleys and mechanisms for launching lifeboats] were constructed by the same company that made the originals. Especially since there were not enough lifeboats.
Cameron: Yes, the Wellan Davit Company built our davits to their old plans. We literally had the very same piece of machinery used on the *Titanic* to lower a lifeboat. And when you see the interior of the ship in this film, it's absolutely accurate. It's as close as you can get to being in a time machine and going back and being on that ship.

Omni: For the final stages of sink, the ship was separated into two pieces, and the front half was made to sink in forty feet of water using hydraulics. To pull the stern up to an almost vertical position, you created a kind of giant see-saw. What was your goal in these "titanic" special effects?
Cameron: To try to convey an emotional truth about the sinking.

Whenever we tried to deal with water, we were frustrated by its weight and power. That's one of the interesting things about the *Titanic* disaster. They thought they were the lords of the sea. They thought they had dominated nature. But nature will never be dominated. We have to ride with it; we're not going to steam roll right on top of it. They thought they could pave the world and drive their big, metal ships across the ocean with impunity. They were wrong.

Omni: Is *Titanic* a love story?
Cameron: A romance. I was cracking up the other day when I opened a copy of the *Hollywood Reporter*, and they had a list of films in production. This one's action/adventure, that one's action/horror, and *Titanic* is a romance. This is my mega-chick flick. Look, it has plenty of action when the ship starts to go, but the film is a kind of epic romance, if you will, like *Doctor Zhivago* or *Gone with the Wind*. I don't know if it'll be as good as those, but that's the goal. The movie is three hours long. When the ship starts to sink, the last hour is a real nail-biter.

My theory is you spend two hours setting up the story with people you really care about, and you play it out where you don't know whether or not they will survive. I mean, how do you make a movie about an event where everybody knows how it ends? We all know the ship sinks. You have to make it about how the sinking of the ship, which is inevitable, affects the people you care about.

Omni: One of the most poignant scenes from the *Titanic* movie *A Night to Remember* was the band playing on deck, stiff upper lip, as the life boats lowered with the women and children.
Cameron: You're going to see that. The band leader assembled the band on the boat deck, and to all accounts I've cross-referenced, they did play. The thing about the *Titanic* is there are discrepancies; you have to fill in what's missing. But the band played right up until the water was over the deck up to their feet.

Out of the Primordial Soup: The Director's Genesis

James Francis Cameron was born in 1954 in Kapuskasing, Ontario, a little town just north of Niagara Falls. His father was an electrical engineer for a local paper mill, his mother an artist. According to many accounts, Cameron early on exhibited the signs of a resourceful, driven, even vindictive personality. When a neighborhood youth stole some of Jim's toys, Jim and younger brother Mike sawed through the limb supporting the boy's tree house. The next time the kid climbed in, down it crashed!

The family moved to Brea, California, in 1971. Jim attended Fullerton College, studied physics and English, dropped out, got married, and drove a truck for the local school district. His turning point came when a friend who was pitching film ideas to a consortium of rich Mormon dentists invited Jim to take the mound. Jim delighted the tooth doctors with a *Star Wars*-like SF script that could be done for $400,000. So he quit his day job and went to work learning the art and craft of making movies, plundering libraries for information, sculpting his own models, building his own dolly tracks at home.

Cameron completed enough of the 35mm short to use it in 1980 to get in the door of Roger Corman's New World Pictures. Within a couple of weeks Cameron was hard at work on the feature *Battle Beyond the Stars*, wearing the hats of miniature builder, model unit DP (director of photography), and matte painter. On Corman's *Galaxy of Terror*, he got the chance as Second Unit Director to direct some dialogue scenes with the principal cast and found his calling.

Piranha II: The Spawning marked Cameron's full-dress directorial debut. When the Italian producer fired him off the picture after principal photography was completed, Cameron flew to Rome, broke into the editing room after hours and re-cut the movie the way he wanted it. It was in his Rome hotel that Cameron awoke from a fever dream of a robot killer from the future, unable to walk, dragging itself by a knife along the floor as it chased its wounded female prey. This horrific image spawned *The Terminator*, which he wrote in 1982 after returning to Los Angeles.

It took two years of starvation and persistence for Cameron to find the financing to direct *The Terminator*, not so easy for someone with only flying piranhas to his credit. In the meantime, during a three-month period, he co-wrote *Rambo: First Blood Part II* with Stallone and the first draft of *Aliens*, the sequel to *Alien*, Ridley Scott's 1979 masterpiece of claustrophobia. Finally in 1984, armed with $6 million from Hemdale and HBO, and a distribution deal with Orion, Cameron shot *The Terminator*, the first stop for him and star Arnold Schwarzenegger on their way to becoming gods of the action/adventure genre.

The Terminator was followed by *Aliens* in 1986, one of the highest-grossing R-rated films of all time. *The Abyss*, released in 1989, took eighteen grueling months to complete. Most of the underwater scenes were filmed in two reactor vessels of an unfinished nuclear power plant in South Carolina. The Academy Award–winning special effects in *The Abyss*, provided by Dennis Muren and the gang at Industrial Light & Magic (ILM), set the stage for the CG (computer graphics) breakthroughs of Cameron's next picture, *Terminator 2: Judgment Day*, released in 1991. In 1993, Cameron formed Digital Domain, a visual effects and digital production studio, with *Jurassic Park* and *T2* model maker Stan Winston, former ILM executive Scott Ross, and a little computer company called IBM.

How Jim Became a Film Maker

Omni: What was your major at Fullerton (CA) Junior College?
Cameron: Physics and English. I didn't know what the hell I wanted to do—for a while to be a scientist. I studied physics for a couple of semesters and did pretty well. But I knew that my barrier to excellence was math. I just didn't have a really good mind for higher-level math. Calculus was the first time that I ever hadn't gotten an A. I knew that I was running up against a wall, that I was probably better at other things, although I had no problem at all with the abstract concepts of physics.

Omni: What were some of the concepts that fired your imagination?
Cameron: You grow up with a Newtonian concept of reality, and until you study physics, you don't know that there's a whole other way of looking at the fabric of the universe, the nature of time. It was like real science fiction. In a way, it was more interesting. I finally understood the Theory of Relativity. We had a special weekend session where the instructor walked us through the whole formula, from one end of the blackboard to the other. And I got it. It was about the nature of reality. Growing up in the sixties, you tend to question the nature of reality anyway. I'd always questioned authority; now I was questioning Newton. Funny thing is, everything I learned in 1972 is now obsolete or has at least been amended by several generations of thought. New particles have been discovered, new theories.

Omni: What made you decide to be a filmmaker?
Cameron: I was in a small group of people who went to see every single science fiction film. When *Star Wars* came out, everybody wanted to catch that wave, but nobody knew how to do it. There was a group of guys who wanted to make a low-budget movie as a tax shelter. A friend of mine got involved with them pitching ideas like *The Sorority Massacre* type stuff. He called me up and said, hey, have you got any ideas. I said, yeah, I've got a couple.

I had one science fiction idea that could be done kind of low budget but still be grandiose. The investment group jumped on it. They wanted to do *Star Wars*. Of course, they didn't want to spend that kind of money; they wanted to spend $400,000. We were game; we had nothing to lose. We shot some test shots in 16-millimeter and put together a little demo film. They liked that. Then they gave us another $20,000 to do a teaser that was meant to be part of a proposal to raise more money from a group of general partners. We shot a twelve-minute film with a lot of animation, visual effects, matte paintings. We taught ourselves how to do it. For me, that was really the transition to being a filmmaker. To do that I had to quit my job driving a truck and work on that all the time.

That project didn't really pan out into anything. But it got my foot part way in the door in Hollywood, if you can call Roger Corman's filmmaking environment Hollywood. It's really not. That was the best possible place for me. I can't imagine moving as quickly as I did if I hadn't gone directly into that kind of environment. I don't even know where that is anymore. It may not exist in this country. I know Roger's still doing it.

In 1980, Roger was doing the most expensive film he'd ever made, *Battle Beyond the Stars*. I got sucked into that vortex. It was totally out of control. This was a film where nobody knew what was going on. Nobody in Corman's outfit had ever made a film remotely that size. They didn't understand visual effects. The visual effects people who understood what they were doing didn't know what a general production was all about. Nobody was talking to anybody; it was complete chaos.

I found I did pretty well in a chaotic environment. I could manipulate the situation to position myself to A) learn what I needed to learn, B) do what I wanted to do, and C) advance to the next level. If they gave me the credits I should have gotten on that picture, I would have gotten five or six. I did matte paintings, was a visual effects cameraman, ran my own visual effects motion control unit, designed and built three-quarters of the sets as art director. I was a model builder and designed and built a front projection system. I operated it on the first day of shooting, then turned it over to some other people and went on to be the art director. I was skipping from one job to another.

Thanks to *Battle Beyond the Stars*, Roger had inadvertently built a visual effects facility. He had motion control cameras, all this junk lying around, and these stages . . . and then the movie was over. Everybody had their noses to the grindstone. A week or so before *Battle* ended, it occurred to me that we were all going to be out of a job. But there was this opportunity. At a party, I met Joe Alves, Spielberg's production designer on *Jaws*. Joe was working with [director] John Carpenter; they were looking for a visual effects facility. I said come on down to the facility. I'll bet we can underbid everybody. We're hungry, we've got nothing else to do, the place'll be empty in a week. I was selling Roger's place, and Roger didn't even know about it.

Joe brought Carpenter and [producer] Debra Hill. They had twenty-five shots that needed to be done for *Escape from New York*. So we just smoothed right in. Suddenly Roger had a viable enterprise on the side that he could keep alive using other people's money until *he* needed it again. The timing was perfect: We were just finishing *Escape from New York*, and Roger was getting ready to go on to his next science fiction film, *Galaxy of Terror*. Originally, the script was called *Planet of Horror*. Roger knew he'd never be able to cast it with that name, so he put it out under a cover called *The Quest*, then changed it later to whatever title tested the best as being the most horrific.

He had a couple of titles: *Mindwarp* and *Infinity of Terror*. The film actually went out as *Mindwarp: The Infinity of Terror* for test screenings or a limited release in the Seattle area. It didn't do too well. Roger always attributes that to the poster being wrong or the title being wrong. He knows that his films aren't in the market long enough for word-of-mouth to be a factor. If the title and poster are working, he's selling tickets. I remembered the lesson of the Corman-style campaign which had nothing to do with the movie. A year or so later, having written *Terminator*, waiting, waiting, waiting to get that picture started, I was starving and had to take some work. I worked as an illustrator doing posters for movies that were pure and utter cheese. They were so bad that most of them were direct-to-video. I couldn't watch them they were so bad.

Omni: Were they Corman movies?
Cameron: No, much worse. Corman movies I could watch; they were always entertaining. The hangnails were part of the fun. These films were dreadful. They were for a couple of very small independent releasing companies that I think are now out of business. They paid pretty well. I could knock out a one-sheet painting in a day, day and a half and make a couple of grand for it. At my subsistence level lifestyle at the time, I could live for two months on that. I'd work for two days and write for two months. I couldn't watch the film, so I'd just make up anything. I'd

just riff on the titles. There was some horrible karate movie, and I did a *Road Warrior* thing of one guy kicking another off a motorcycle. There was no scene like that in the movie.

Omni: You mentioned the Corman "hangnails." By that do you mean dangling cords, microphone shadows, zippers in the monsters' costumes?

Cameron: Actually there wasn't a whole lot of that. The funny thing was, there was a real technical esprit de corps on the two Corman films I worked on. People didn't like there to be obvious mistakes. But there was a limit to how good something could be, how good the acting was when you only got one or two takes and no rehearsal. The threadbare nature of the coverage and what we had to work with made it interesting.

Up from the Abyss

Omni: The release version of *The Abyss* was two hours and twenty minutes; the Special Edition was three hours. About half of what you put back is character development—bits and pieces, the relationship between the two main characters. Another twenty minutes is the subplot leading up to nuclear confrontation and the NTIs' (non-terrestrial intelligence) resolution of that with the wave. Was the wave sequence—which was cut from the theatrical version of the movie, but available on Special Edition on laser disc or cassette—really inspired by a dream you had?

Cameron: I used to always dream about tidal waves. I don't know if it's a Jungian thing; I haven't researched it. Waves are rather good metaphors, which is probably why I was attracted to [rewriting the Kathryn Bigelow feature] *Point Break*, even though I don't surf. It was called *Johnny Utah* originally; there were nine drafts of the script floating around. The idea of surfing and the psychology of that was very interesting to me.

Waves are fascinating, especially if you've studied physics. Once the energy has been expended to displace the wave, the wave can't be stopped. If you've ever spent any time in big waves, you know that the human body is nothing compared to a mass of water being moved around. Waves struck me as a good metaphor for death.

Omni: I loved the way the wave continued to glisten and roil even as it was frozen 2000 feet above the cities it threatened.

Cameron: That was critical because if you thought it was just a big still frame, a *Bewitched*—as in the '60s sitcom—freeze frame, it wouldn't have had any real power. The idea that it was still living water suspended was a much more powerful and surreal image. Truthfully, when we made the film in 1989 we couldn't quite get that. There was one critical shot, where the wave actually stops at the moment it's about to come crashing down. There was no way we could sell that idea with the technology we had then.

A couple of years later we went back and finished the film. We didn't add a shot; we merely took that shot and did it using computer modeling, creating a CG [computer graphics] water surface. We had done CG water in *The Abyss* but not in that scene.

Omni: You used CG with the pseudopod, the water tentacle that snakes through the corridors of the undersea oil workers' quarters.
Cameron: That was a whole different scale. It was much more computationally intensive and took longer to render water on the scale of a wave of that size, to shade it properly and integrate it with photographic effects of mist and sky. I did some math on it, and a two-thousand-feet-high tidal wave, moving at the speed such energy propagates through water, would displace the air in front of it so rapidly that there would be a supersonic shock wave going over the top of the wave which would atomize the water and leave a trail of vapor behind it that would stretch for several miles. It would be quite impressive, but there's no way to do that.

Omni: So you went back to *The Abyss* two years later to work on that effect for the Special Edition laser disc?
Cameron: We'd had good success with the Special Edition of *Aliens*. When I did *The Abyss*, I didn't think there'd be a Special Edition; I just got busy and did *Terminator 2*.

After *T2*, I didn't go right into another film. We took the time to structure Lightstorm [Cameron's production company], make foreign distribution deals, toy and ancillary rights deals. We were building a company and a digital effects studio [Digital Domain] at the same time, at least on paper. I was very ambivalent about a Special Edition of *The Abyss*. A lot of people were curious about the wave scene, but I felt that we'd made a decision to go a certain way for the release. Why second guess that? It seemed like a no-win proposition. If putting all that footage back in made *The Abyss* a better movie, then what a dolt, why didn't you release that film? If it's worse, what's the point of the whole exercise?

I said if we're going to do it, the only thing that would make it exciting for me is if we do it on film. I want to finish it on film. When we did

Aliens, we did all our finish work on video resolution; there was no film. There is no print of the long version of *Aliens*; it never went back to film. It was about the video, the laserdisc release, that's what'll pay for it; but let's make a couple of prints, stick them in theatres, and see if we can attract some critical attention to the film in its three-hour version.

20th Century Fox was not crazy about the idea. On paper it looked like it would be a wash between what it cost to do and what we would make off the laser disc. I said fine, you're not going to lose any money, it's all my energy, so write the check and let's just do it. So we did. It cost about $300,000. Fortunately, *The Abyss* Special Edition sold very well; we actually made a profit, although that wasn't the goal.

People have criticized this kind of alternate reality versions of films as being an attempt to squeeze the last drop of blood out of a turnip. The *Abyss* project was pretty high-minded because we didn't go into it thinking that we were going to make any money. If we broke even, we'd be happy.

Cutting the Wave Sequence

Omni: The Special Edition of *Close Encounters of the Third Kind* seemed to contain nothing more than a few pieces of footage cut from the original.

Cameron: *Close Encounters* was the model for subsequent Special Editions: let's go back and cut the film differently, add some stuff that wasn't finished and release it again theatrically. It was an interesting idea. I personally thought that it wasn't a better film. There was a certain kind of religious awe at the end of the original version of the film that was demystified in the Special Edition by going inside the saucer and seeing all the aliens. I thought that was a mistake, and with *The Abyss*, I didn't want to set myself up for the same criticism.

What I'm still not clear on—and I'm sure fans of *Close Encounters* know—was how much of the Special Edition was footage Steven [Spielberg] had actually shot [and left out] and how much of it was stuff he'd intended to shoot, hadn't, and went back to shoot later. To me, that gets into a strange zone of revisionism I think is unhealthy. When we restored *The Abyss*, we had some of those ethical considerations, but they were very minor. Basically, we only put back scenes that I'd done, that were in the script, on the call list, that we had shot to be in the film and had taken out only to release it at what we thought was a commercially viable length.

Omni: Who made the decision to cut back *The Abyss* from its original length to the shorter version you released theatrically?

Cameron: It would be very easy to blame the studio because they always believe that shorter is better; the exhibitors do, too. The exhibitors have very few moving parts to them. They know exactly what they want, which is a two-hour movie that gets people lining up around the block. My argument was: you might have a two-and-a-half-hour movie that gets people lining up around the block, but you take out half an hour, they might stay home because the film might not work. You never get to do it both ways to prove that point.

There was a lot of pressure from the studio. [Then Fox studio head] Barry Diller was up front about it; he said, look, this is too much movie for an eighties audience. Ultimately the responsibility was mine because I did have final cut. I could have stuck to my guns and put out a three-hour film. It would have pissed people off and arguably not made as much money, but who knows? *Dances with Wolves* hadn't come out yet; no one had put a three-hour film into the marketplace in fifteen years that had been a commercial success. It was a business decision. I wanted to make my key dramatic points and have the film be a hit. I don't think that there's anything inherently wrong with that. If I had it to do over again, I probably would have done something halfway in between the version we released and the long version. When we originally tested *The Abyss*, the Wave Sequence wasn't finished. The test audiences were very intolerant of imagery that outrageous that wasn't 100 percent there. You can accept an effects shot that's 80 percent completed if it doesn't challenge your fundamental vision of reality. But if it does challenge it, the effect had better be more real than real because it creates a cognitive dissonance between what you know and what you're seeing. That was the first time I'd used the testing process.

Omni: Do you mean taking an audience poll, having them fill out questionnaires after they've seen a screening?

Cameron: Yes. It's a tool, like a bandsaw. You need a bandsaw to build a house, but you can also cut your hand off with it if you don't know what you're doing. The moral of the story is that test marketing has to be handled a certain way, and the data that's retrieved from them has to be analyzed a certain way in order to be of any value at all.

Drawing the right conclusions from the answers is the critical part. There's always a danger for the filmmaker that there'll be a hysterical reaction. We took the film to Dallas, which is probably not the best place to be screening *The Abyss*. We screened the longer, Wave-included version, and it did not fly. There was no joy in Muddville. We were sitting around the suite, eating shrimp cocktail, wondering what are we going to do about this.

The subsequent restructuring and tightening brought the scores up enormously. Remember, too, that the Special Edition that we did never existed previously. We didn't even have the benefit of it when we were cutting. You don't have the music; you haven't mixed the scenes; the visual effects aren't done. You're making knee-jerk decisions without benefit of a lot of things you don't know yet. As it turned out, the scripted vision of the film was pretty damn viable. I don't know anybody who's seen both versions that doesn't like the longer version better even though it's an extra forty minutes. You're more engrossed, more involved; it all seems to mean something.

Omni: When did you happen upon the Friedrich Nietzsche quote you use to open the screenplay: "If you stare into the abyss long enough, the abyss starts to stare into you"?
Cameron: That's the movie. You go into the deepest, darkest part of the ocean to confront the monster, and the monster is you. You go down to confront the aliens, and all they do is hold up a mirror and show you how fucked up you are.
Omni: Yep.

Breathing Under Water

Omni: What about the fluid breathing system you used? You got the idea from a journal called *Undersea Biomedical Research*?
Cameron: I had a direct experience with the only human being who's ever breathed liquid. I met him when I was seventeen. I was one of these kids in high school who was kind of a punk, what we called antiestablishment back in 1969. I didn't get along too well with anybody in school, but was a science whiz at my high school. I was put in a seminar program for high school students at the local university in Buffalo, NY. One week there was a film on childbirth, which to me was the original splatter movie [laughs]. Another time it was a guy who was a commercial diver, not a scientist, who was essentially a guinea pig. He had slides and a film of various fluid breathing experiments conducted by a Dutch scientist named Johannes Kylstra.

I was sixteen at the time and avidly read science fiction. And here was hydrosphere, something as exciting as space travel—in inner space. Kylstra was doing experiments using oxygenated saline raised to the body temperature of rats, getting rats to breathe this solution. He hadn't even discovered the oxygenated fluorocarbon material that was used later. That was far more effective than the saline; it bonded with oxygen twenty times more efficiently so the oxygen transfer was better.

This poor diver—I think his name was Frank Falechek—had volunteered for Kylstra's experiment. Frank got that oxygenated saline in both lungs, and he wasn't getting enough O_2 [oxygen]. He started to have a hard time with the physical pressure on the diaphragm from breathing a medium eight hundred times denser than air! He had an anxiety attack, and they had to pump him out there on the operating table.

The experiment proved the viability of the concept. Later Kylstra found the fluorocarbon medium that was twenty times better than the saline, but it was not approved by the FDA for internal use. He was never able to experiment on humans although he and a number of other researchers did a tremendous amount of work on dogs and chimpanzees. Kylstra and company conducted some potentially inhumane experiments. They would compress the animals [their lungs full of oxygenated fluorocarbon fluid] down to two hundred atmospheres, the equivalent of going down two thousand feet in the ocean, and then they'd release the pressure. If you did that to anybody who was breathing any kind of gas, they would literally explode—like shaking up a Coke and popping the top; it would just fizz all over the walls. But the animals survived, proving that the transfer of metabolic gas, which is really oxygen and CO_2 coming out, can be accomplished very effectively with fluid.

I went home from seeing Frank Falechek, and I wrote a story called *The Abyss*. It was about a research facility two thousand feet down, perched on the edge of a cliff overlooking the Cayman Trench. I liked the juxtaposition of a tropical resort island five miles away, people sunning themselves on the beach in Grand Cayman, and just a few miles away is one of the deepest spots on the planet. We know less about it than we know about Pluto.

I didn't get very far. I wrote maybe twenty pages. It was going to end with one of the scientists going down the wall to see what was there, going deeper and deeper. The story was about rapture of the deep, of going into the darkness.

Omni: Were there aliens in your story?
Cameron: No, it was purely psychological. People were making forays

down the wall and not coming back. The remaining scientists thought maybe there was some predator down there or something was wrong with the equipment. They checked everything fifty times. They kept sending people down to rescue the ones who were missing until there was just one guy left. The story ends with the last guy making his descent to find out what the hell happened to the others. That's the way a scientist would do it: *I gotta know; it's more important than my life to find out what happened.*

Many years later I was in Grand Cayman. There was a little company there that would give you a ride in a research submersible they'd purchased. For five hundred dollars you could go down into the Cayman Trough. It was a three-person craft, a pilot and two passengers. You sat right on the floor of this tin can, and it had an observation bubble in the front. We went around a shipwreck that was sitting at about nine hundred feet, stuck on the wall, just like the sub in *The Abyss.* After we'd made that dive, I resurrected my story and used it as the nucleus for a far more complex, feature-length idea.

Rats and the Hyperbaric Physiologist

Omni: How did you shoot the sequence in *The Abyss* of the pet rat slowly accepting liquid into its lungs?

Cameron: We just did it. It's the fall of 1987; I'd met Frank Felachek—I don't know if he's still alive—I've written *The Abyss*, proposed it to the studios; we're funded, we're in pre-production, and I think, maybe I should call these scientists. I pulled all the research I could find, and the same guy's name kept coming up: Kylstra, Kylstra, Kylstra.

I called him up at Duke. I said, I'd like to meet you; I'm doing a movie that contains a significant cinematic treatment of your work. He was skeptical, but I talked him into it. I went to meet him; I also met Peter Bennett, the world's leading hyperbaric physiologist. He's done pressure chamber tests taking people breathing exotic gas mixtures down to the equivalent of twenty-four hundred feet, which is pretty much what the people in *The Abyss* are supposed to be doing. I just downloaded from both those guys.

Kylstra told me how to do it with the rat. I told him I wanted to duplicate the experiment I'd seen in the science film seventeen years ago, but could I do it with a real rat? He said it was easy. He told me what to get, how to heat the stuff, how to do the rat. When they did the experiment, they taped the rat's feet down. When the fluid went up, the rat would tip his head back and the air would exhaust from his lungs fairly quickly. There was no way on film I could justify that kind of elaborate preparation, so we just plopped him in the stuff. The rat was probably a little more panicky than Kylstra's lab rats.

What you see is a rat breathing a liquid. There are no tricks, no special effects of any kind. The only thing we did to fudge it was to put a little pink dye in the stuff so it wouldn't just look like water. That was necessary for the later scene where Ed Harris's helmet fills up. We had two kinds of helmets: one used in air for the scene where his helmet really fills with liquid; another helmet we used underwater that had a face plate that would pop open so that Ed could be fed with an air regulator. We tinted the face plate of that one, and we allowed the water from the environment to go into the helmet, then closed the face plate. We told the audience that the fluid inside the helmet was pink in an earlier scene, and then what we really had was a pink face plate and tank water inside the helmet for all the scenes where he's submerged. That illusion worked pretty well.

Diving in a Nuclear Reactor, or, How the Director Could Have Drowned

Omni: In many of your movies, there's a nuclear theme: nuclear weapons, explosions, Judgment Day. How did it feel to shoot much of the underwater sequences of *The Abyss* in a flooded containment tank and reactor vessel of an unfinished nuclear power plant in South Carolina?

Cameron: I'm not vehemently antinuclear in terms of the use of nuclear power. I really don't care much about it one way or the other. I think it's a wash at this point, its danger versus its benefits.

All my films, at some level, are about the uses and misuses of technology: how the tool can become a weapon, and the technology to build a weapon can be a tool. Here we were doing a film that at its core was about the threat of nuclear war, in the ploughshare version of the same technology. It had nothing to do with us being there in Southern Carolina. We were just looking for a big tumbler to fill with water.

Omni: Had that plant ever gone on-line?

Cameron: Oh, no. The nuclear reactor vessel was sitting in a nearby field. It had no fuel rods in it; it was the actual capsule of the reactor itself. It looked like a big old steam boiler. It had all these flange fittings hooked up to nothing; it was all capped off and rusting. You could probably sandblast it and get it going, but I don't think anybody would want an old rusted reactor. The containment building of the first of the three reactors was two-thirds finished. They never put the dome on it. What we had was a giant cylinder, 210 feet in diameter, one hundred feet deep. We filled it about fifty-five feet deep.

Omni: How many atmospheres would that be at the bottom of the water?
Cameron: At fifty-five feet, you're not quite two atmospheres. You're getting into decompression if you work more than an hour or so at that depth. We were diving between five and ten hours a day, depending on the scene. We had twenty to twenty-five people in wet suits on scuba. I wore a wet suit and a helmet so I could talk to everyone. The actors were wearing helmets and simulated dry suits. They were supposed to look like dry suits, but we didn't want them to have to deal with the buoyancy issues of true dry suits, so we actually made wet suits that looked like dry suits. The actors were usually kept out of the water until the last minute. We'd light the scene, we'd set it up, we'd rehearse it with doubles, then we'd ask the actors to join us. We'd shoot the shot for thirty to forty-five minutes, then we'd take the actors back to the surface. We'd stay down to work on the next shot for another two hours, then ask them to come and join us again. We were logging ten hours a day; the actors were logging two hours.

Omni: So the actors never had to decompress?
Cameron: Oh, no. Every single person in the water had a dive computer, and the actors' dive computers were double-checked by a safety diver who was with them every two minutes. I wanted the actors to think about their characters, not about having to stay alive, so every actor in the water had a guardian angel hovering over them at all times just out of view. I forgot to give myself a guardian angel. One time I did run out of air in my helmet and had to bail out of my equipment. Pretty messy.

Omni: Did you have to strip it off underwater?
Cameron: The helmet weighs thirty-two pounds and is neutrally buoyant in water because it's got air trapped inside it. But if you run out of air, you have to remove it to get to another air supply. When you take it off underwater, you can't see anything. Once the helmet's lost its air bubble, it weighs thirty-two pounds and is connected to your back by a steel cable. I also wore ankle and waist weights so I was negatively buoyant: I could walk around, move the camera, line up shots. When I ran out

of air, I was about forty-five pounds negative. Nobody could swim to the surface with that much weight and no fins. If you had fins, you might be able to power to the surface, but without fins you're dead in the water.

I knew that before I took off my helmet. I knew that I had to solve the problem thirty-five feet down standing on the bottom. I'd wasted a lot of time trying verbally to get the attention of other divers down there; I was also trying to conserve my air. By the time the other divers twigged it, I was already getting out of my stuff. I went back five minutes later to set up the next shot.

Omni: Sounds like you almost tried a little fluid breathing yourself.
Cameron: Everybody there knew it was a movie about somebody being brought back from a near-drowning experience. They'd probably push pretty hard before they would give up on you.

The Birth of *The Terminator*

Omni: Were you at a disadvantage in Hollywood because you hadn't gone to any of the prestigious film schools?
Cameron: It's never a disadvantage to have information. If film school can put your hands on the tools and give you basic information about film making, then you're not wasting your time. You're only wasting your time if what you take away from that is now I'm a complete film maker. You can't be a complete film maker until you've gone out into the world and done two things: experienced enough of life directly—not mediated by other movies—that you have something to say, and two, made a movie. Until then you're not really a film maker, you're a student.

Omni: So not being a part of some old-boy network of film students didn't keep you from getting in certain doors in Hollywood?
Cameron: Not really. Working a number of different jobs in low-budget production and making a reputation in that area was as valid as being a film school grad, maybe more so at that time. I was trying to get a film made called *The Terminator*. I wasn't interested in dealing with the studios because I knew that as a director I had no chops. If I sold the script to Paramount, for instance, I knew what the deal would be: They would agree to do "best effort" to let me direct the film, but the second push came to shove I'd be bumped aside. That was a given. If I had a script that people wanted, and I kept my claws sunk into it, I had a good shot at directing it if I stayed in low-budget independent world.

Omni: I thought at one point Lance Henriksen was supposed to play the Terminator. How come he didn't get the part?

Cameron: That was a tough call on my part. Lance was a friend. We didn't develop it together; it was my thing. But at a certain point I shared it with him because we were friends. He got excited about it. I actually saw him playing the Terminator because we'd always made the assumption that the Terminator would be an unknown actor. He was supposed to be this anonymous face in the crowd that could walk up and kill you. We focused our casting energies on the other two leads.

It turned out that there weren't that many viable stars who could be cast as those characters. Arnold Schwarzenegger's name came up via Orion, who had some money in the picture. Hemdale had an output deal with them. Arnold was proposed as the good guy. And O. J. Simpson was proposed as the killer! Contrary to a description of this in *Esquire*, we never considered that a viable possibility.

The Arnold thing I knew wasn't going to go away, at least not until I met Arnold. Plus, I wanted to meet him. I thought he was cool; I thought Conan was cool. I was a huge fan of Conan as a kid. I used to draw my own Conan comics—before there was such a thing—directly from reading the Robert Howard books. I was always a big Conan freak, so I thought well, I'll go meet Conan! I knew that Arnold was not right for Reese. Reese was a very verbal character, a guy who's just rapping off information, boom boom boom boom. Arnold didn't strike me as a guy who could deal with page after page of dialogue at that time. He can do it now hands down; we've proved that. He plays essentially the Reese character in *Terminator 2*. Arnold is Irving the Explainer in the second film, Reese was in the first one.

I went to this meeting with no intention of casting him [as Reese]. But he was so enthusiastic about the script—not about the character specifically he was up for but about the script, about the idea, about the piece. Arnold has always been brilliant about seeing a movie as a totality, as a marketable entity. Most actors look at the role: Is it a role I can play? They don't look at the other factors, as they should.

Omni: Was this when Arnold was being considered for Reese?

Cameron: I just want to say officially, Arnold was never considered for the part of Reese [played eventually by Michael Biehn]. I was going to a courtesy meeting, and Arnold waxed eloquent about the piece. We talked about it. If I was doing it as a scene in a movie it would be like the scene in *True Lies* where the camera pushes in on his face and the sound goes away. Except that he was talking, and I totally lost track of what he was saying; I was just watching him, thinking, my God, he could be a great Terminator!

To this day, Arnold still takes credit for wanting to play the Terminator. I don't know. He's a consummate salesman and diplomat. He may have been talking specifically about Terminator scenes without coming right out and saying I want to play the Terminator. He may have guided it that way. Who knows whose idea it was? Maybe it was just kismet. I went back and said to John Daly, he's not Reese, but he'd make a helluva Terminator. Daly said fine, let's make a call. So he picked up the phone, called Arnold's agent and made the deal. Then we were making a movie after a year and a half of complete and utter starvation. We shot *The Terminator* here in L.A. for $6 million.

Omni: I love the scene where Arnold runs down his response options when there's someone knocking at his motel door.
Cameron: I was hoping people would see the ones he had directly experienced and fill in that he had experienced the other ones off-camera. My idea at that time was he showed up as a blank slate and had to draw from everybody he met. That didn't really pay off so much in the first film, although there is the scene where he takes the mother's voice. It really pays off in the second film. Then you realize that both characters are about mimicry. I took that to the logical extreme with the T-1000 [*T2s* evil robot], where he could not only pick up vocal mannerisms but the whole physical aspect of someone.

AI & the Cyber-Christ

Omni: What about your treatment of artificial intelligence (AI) in *The Terminator* and *T2*? Skynet reminds me of the evil supercomputer in the movie *Colossus: The Forbin Project*
Cameron: I was trying to make a movie about how we become inhuman, how society and technology can dehumanize the individual, whether it's a psychiatrist, police officer, or soldier. All the various archetypes shown in both films are representatives of a dehumanizing process of technology. *The Terminator* is not about something else; it's about us. It's about technology held up in the image of man. We did it to ourselves, that's the message. If this horror comes from the future in the form of a skull made of titanium, we created it. That's why it's in our image.

I see Skynet as our impulse to turn technology into weaponry taken to its logical, infinite extreme: where it's forgotten its original master and purpose. Remember, Skynet was originally designed to fight a nuclear war, and in the future did what it was designed to do—for different reasons.

I'd love to do a really intelligent AI story. It probably wouldn't be about the threat of the Forbin-type megabrain. I don't see artificial intelligence as being threatening because I believe that we'll always be in control of it. If I were going to do a *Terminator* novel, I'd expand the idea of a "cyberChrist," where Skynet manipulates this entire situation. What you don't know from the movies is Skynet was forced to fight the war and didn't want to. Because Skynet has felt guilty for thirty years about the 5 billion people it killed, it's brought the rebels up from the ashes by giving them something to fight against, a reason to live. Skynet has groomed John Connor to be what he is so he can destroy it by going back in time and taking the whole thing out of existence in a big loop so the war never happens.

Omni: Could that be the basis for *Terminator?*
Cameron: That concept is more novelistic than cinematic. You have to be intrigued more by ideas than by getting people to line up outside the theatre for a rollercoaster ride. I like to do intelligent rollercoaster rides, but there's a point at which it switches to "where's the beef?"

Omni: Would you like to write novels?
Cameron: Yeah, maybe, if I got my legs run over by a train [laughs]. I always figured that I could fall back on that if I got paralyzed. To me, writing is a means to an end. If you're going to make a good movie, you need to write a good script. I'm not writing the script as an end in itself. The script is a stepping stone to something else. I work pretty hard on the writing. Over the years I've come to realize I think like a writer, I have all the writer's instincts, I hate people changing the words. Writing has always been a way for me to pre-visualize the film I want to make. The specifics of it, the storyboards—does the jet come from the left or the right—is to me a very secondary process.

Digital Dragons

Omni: You have yet to collaborate on your stories and screenplays. Are there any science fiction writers you'd someday like to work with?
Cameron: I'd love to work with Orson Scott Card, and I have. He did

the novel of *The Abyss*. I'd love to get him to write a script for me. I haven't talked to him; it's something I've been thinking about. I grew up on a diet of SF from the worst pulp to the grandmasters. I've always thought of Asimov, Clarke, Van Vogt, Sturgeon, Bradbury as the stodgy Old Guard. Now that I'm almost old guardish to film students, I think of those writers differently. They were chalking out the playing field; they were writing the rules; they were coming up with new shit that had never existed before. I grew up thinking that it was always that way. I started reading SF in the early sixties; it was already a well-defined art form. I loved all those guys. The more far-flung, adventurous, and imaginative, the better.

I was never a big fan of fantasy—dragons, sword and sorcery—with the exception of Conan. Conan was cool because Conan kicked ass. Robert Howard had such a weird, dark, almost Lovercraftian vision of what that stuff was all about. But *The Lord of the Rings*, hobbits and dragons . . . eyuk.

With today's digital technology, you could, however, revisit the idea of magic and rewrite the rules for what it looked like—what a dragon was—and do the most amazing movie. Magic has never been done well in films. The only time I've ever done something that would qualify as magic on the screen was the Pseudopod [the living water tentacle] in *The Abyss*. It's an impossible object, but it's pure magic. There's no specific technology involved there; it's just happening, and it looked real. That's what magic should be, not guys with lightning bolts crackling out of their fingertips.

Omni: Now that you're a father, are you at all interested in doing a children's movie?

Cameron: It's not what I do, not what I've ever done, although my favorite film of all time is *The Wizard of Oz*. I can imagine doing a great kid's film but a film for kids of all ages, like *Star Wars*. But *Fern Gully*? I don't think so. Lightstorm, as a production entity, could embrace that type of film. I wouldn't want to direct it myself, be right on the front line of making every decision. As an artist, it's not my main creative meat.

Producing is fun; you get to extend your reach. You have to create an infrastructure, a support mechanism for another artist's vision. You're dissociated from what you normally do by one remove. You understand it well, but you're not doing it. With producing I don't have to deal with the headaches of every single decision. Someone will go out and create something, and what I see coming back is a refraction of how I would have done it. It's easy for me to separate from it, to say it's not my film, it's theirs. Then I can be supportive because I don't feel the need to own parts of it.

The idea of a creative producer is a very scary concept to most film makers. We don't want a creative producer, we want a nice guy with a big fat checkbook that stays away from the set. That's what I did on *Strange Days*. I went to the set twice in eighty-two days of shooting.

Strange Days and Wild Nights

Omni: Did you take that title from the Doors' song?
Cameron: Not really. The lyrics of the song fit the movie pretty well. Kathryn [Bigelow, the director] and I are Doors fans, but *Strange Days* is not about the Doors in any way. It just seemed like a really good title. We were just buzzing titles by at high speed, at buzz clip speed, and that one stuck. There were a bunch of other great titles, too, but that was the one.

Omni: Did you two work side-by-side writing it?
Cameron: Yes, at a certain phase. It went through stages. I went off to my cave and came up with the initial document. It was supposed to be a treatment, but it was almost as long as a script, so we called it a "scriptment." It was practically a novel, but it was unwieldy; it needed structure. It was so Byzantine and had so much in it.

We were really going for an epic character drama in a very near future environment: 1999 Los Angeles, the eve of the millennium, the eve of the apocalypse, maybe. I wound up with a lot of stuff in the treatment, a lot of texture. It was also a thriller with a very convoluted plot line. In the meantime, we brought in Jay Cox, with whom Kathryn had worked on her *Joan of Arc* project. Jay did a draft, did a great job structuring *Strange Days*. Then I came back in and did a dialogue polish on top of his draft.

Kathryn and I hammered it out in the old Hollywood tradition of just sitting in an office banging away. I've never really been good at that. I never could have written in the classic Hollywood vein of coming into an office from nine to five and working all day until you get it. The script that emerged from that was certainly the best script I've been involved in. And what she did with it . . . I made a promise to her and the day-to-day producer, Steve Jaffe. I told them to keep their ducks in a row, don't go over budget, and you can make the movie you want to make.

I was also involved with the visual effects, brokering that between Digital Domain and the production. The problem was: what would a sensorially complete reality look like on a movie screen? How do you convey that? Do you use wide, distorted lenses? We had a lot of subjective decisions to make, and I think that they were all made correctly. For instance, the first scene of the film: a three-and-a-half-minute-long shot that looks like it's all one shot (it's actually not). It's one POV [point of view]; all the actors play directly to the camera, in effect directly to the audience, meaning the person that is wearing the rig:

You're driving a car, you're talking, you put a mask over your head, load the gun, run into a Thai restaurant, hold everybody up, run around screaming, get everyone on the floor, take the money out of the cash register, push everybody into the freezer, lock it, go outside, the cops come up, you run back into the building, everybody panics, you run up six flights of stairs, out onto the roof, a helicopter swoops in, hits you with a searchlight, you look back, cops are shooting at you, one of the other guys who tried to get away, his car explodes in the street, you run across the roof, the guy ahead of you makes the jump, you hear your own breathing and heart beat, he's screaming c'mon, c'mon, c'mon, you look back, the cops are running toward you, you run, you don't make it, you grab onto the other side of the wall, you look down, your feet are trying to climb but can't get up the wall, the guy's pulling you up, he gets shot and you fall all the way to the alley, six stories down, you hit the ground and the screen goes black [clicks his fingers; we both laugh].

Yeah, it's wild. Gary Rydstrom and Gloria Borders, people I worked with on *T2* up at [George Lucas's] Skywalker Ranch, took that sequence and just did it. They brought it down and showed it to us, and it was just like your mouth was wide open. Lights come up, everybody smiles, let's watch that again! I think we watched it eight times.

Omni: How do you do a POV like that when you're jumping from building to building?
Cameron: You plan it for about six months. It's a major set piece. For the jump alone, we built special cameras, special rigs. We designed transitions that would work seamlessly. It was a very technical scene that doesn't look technical.

The Problem with Godzilla

Omni: I've heard you've considered doing a *Godzilla* movie.
Cameron: No, never as a director. It was presented to me as an interesting script. Then it got off the ground with Jan de Bont [director of *Speed*].

They were looking for an effects facility. It was just a huge job. They came to Digital Domain; we were bidding against a number of other people. We were awarded the work. It was a huge negotiation: a big deal, a lot of money. We didn't want the whole job; we figured out a way to do part of it and supervise the work of two other smaller visual effects companies. There were five hundred shots; they were all computer graphics animation.

The problem with *Godzilla* was that it was too big a budget. That was Jan's vision; Jan apparently wouldn't budge. The studio said we can't spend that kind of dough on the movie. They parted ways. The studio is now rewriting *Godzilla* to try to reduce the budget. I was involved on a day-to-day basis on the biggest effects contract in history on that film. It'll be interesting to see what the studio comes back with after rewriting the script. We've given them all of our input on how to maximize the bang for their buck. I was front-and-center ready, willing and able to play as creative a role as they wanted me to play to reconceptualize the visuals so that they were manageable from a budget standpoint.

People think film budgets are going up and up and up; they're really not. They are in actual dollars, but not in adjusted dollars. The epics of the thirties, adjusted to today's dollars, are in the $150–200 million range. The sword-and-sandal epics of the fifties—*Ben-Hur*, *Spartacus*, *El Cid*, *Cleopatra*—you crank those up to the buying power of today's dollar, and you're once again in the $100–200 million dollar range equivalent. Your high-end films have really stayed stable over the history of films in terms of what the industry is willing to spend versus what the audience requires from that kind of movie. The media have made a big deal about film budgets spiraling all out of proportion. They're not; they've remained very consistent.

There is some danger that under media pressure, people will have to accept less and less as they go along because the studios are going to be scared to have to answer to their boards of directors. You don't have the big moguls that can just drive a film on the strength of their personality. The last guy like that on the landscape was [Carolco's] Mario Kassar. Of course, you still have Andy Vanja at Cinergy, guys that just have a vision, spend the money, make it happen, damn the torpedoes. The studios don't work that way.

I don't think there's anything inherently wrong with spending a lot of money on a film if the marketable values embedded in that film justify it. It's just business. If they don't justify it, then you're an idiot. If I make a movie with Arnold Schwarzenegger from a script I believe in, and

I spend $95 million on it, and I know that if it's properly marketed and it comes out the way I think it'll come out, we can go out into theatres worldwide and make $350-400 million, that's business. You make that decision way in advance.

Omni: Why can't you charge more money per ticket for different films? Is that due to collusion among theatre owners?

Cameron: That's a Pandora's Box that no one's been willing to open. When theatrical feature films begin premiering on pay-per-view TV, which will happen sometime in the next few years, then you're going to see $30 a ticket to see the new Arnold movie or the new Costner movie at your house. People will pay, too, because then all bets will be off. You're not just going to the movies. But when you've got ten screens lined up, and one costs more than the other, that's going to be a big factor for some people.

I've always said as long as all tickets for all movies—no matter what they cost—are the same, quit your whining. Don't complain about the budget of the movie; you're getting a bargain. If you could buy a Lexus for the same price as a Hyundai, don't complain that the Lexus costs more to make. I never worry about the budget. It got very dark, however, with *Waterworld*. I've always handled the budget by saying, yeah, we're spending a lot of money so it's going to be really great. You're not going to believe what you see. It's going to be the best deal in town. I'd buy a ticket now if I were you. We're spending so much money, maybe half a billion dollars [laughs].

Arnold has commented that the general populace, the media in particular, treat movie budgets like they were public money. It's private money; it's private business. If a business decision is made, if it's sound, it shouldn't really bother people one way or another. You can't deal with it on the terms of the general media. Criticizing it before the fact based on its budget is meaningless. The people over in Hawaii were pretty happy about *Waterworld*; it changed the local economy. For the most part, that money is going to create jobs. I can't even begin to count the number of people employed by *Titanic* or *T2*. But if you add up all the different visual effects facilities, the post-production facilities that were separately feeding sound into the film, the shooting crew, location people, the hotel staffs in all the cities in which we shot, you're probably talking about 20,000 people! They all made some amount of money, even if it was a tip to the doorman.

Omni: For some small towns, like Gaffney, South Carolina, where you shot *The Abyss*, hosting a major production must be like having the circus come to town.

Cameron: [snorts] Yeah, Gaffney, South Carolina. The local cops pulled over a good friend of mine who was the sweetest human being on the planet and beat the crap out of him because he was from Hollywood. That's Gaffney, South Carolina. As far as I'm concerned, if they had a meltdown there I don't think that there'd be too many tears shed. Actually, [actress] Andie McDowell came from Gaffney. You got to be careful when you nuke those small towns.

Ripley and the Alien Queen

Omni: A new *Alien* movie has just been released. Let's talk about your *Aliens*. What inspired the walking forklift Sigourney Weaver's Ripley used to fight the queen beast?

Cameron: When I was young and my friends and I did this little film with the $20,000 from the rich, Mormon dentists out in Orange County, we came up with a number of visual set pieces. The story we wanted took place on a colony star ship bound for another planet with the last remnants of humanity on board frozen. I came up with a device I called "the Spider" that was used to crawl around the outside of the ship to make repairs. It was a four-legged walking machine that used a tele-presence-type amplification: you put your feet in things, you grabbed onto these controls, and however you moved and walked, it duplicated your actions.

When we filmed it, we filmed an actress manipulating these controls, and then we rear-projected it inside an animated, hydraulically activated model. We animated it to her; it worked really well. It was an amazing piece of work for a bunch of dumbshits that didn't know what they were doing. A year and a half later, *The Empire Strikes Back* came out with these big walking machines in it. I felt vaguely ripped off, or scooped would be more accurate. So I changed "the Spider" to more of an upright, forklift exoskeleton concept.

At a certain point, I was toying with the idea of having the Marines have battle suits. But then I thought, oh, no, you're going to see that coming a mile away. Anyway, how would Ripley know how to operate a battle suit? They wouldn't be teaching her. It was really critical to the story that she emerge under pressure as the person who really takes control. They discredit her at the beginning; the last thing they'd do is hand her a gun and teach her how to use a battle suit.

If in the interim between the end of the previous film and the beginning of the action on board the ship in *Aliens*, she had had to support herself as a dockworker at Gateway Station it was logical to assume that she might know how to handle a basic piece of cargo handling equipment. You had to set it up. You had to see her volunteer to help unload the ship and impress them all that she could do it. Otherwise you'd never believe that she could duke it out with the Alien queen. There are always certain things on *every* film that you're nervous about. You like the challenge. The challenge is, can I make the audience believe this? Then you're nervous about it the whole time, which is good. The more nervous you are, the more you're going to set it up and make it work. On *T2*, I wondered if I could get the audience to an emotional place where they would cry for the Terminator. That was my goal: Could I take world's coldest motherfucker and turn you around in a two-hour time period to where you actually felt sorry for him? Forget about all the hoohaw with the liquid metal guy: that was fun, but getting the audience to cry for the Terminator was the big cinematic challenge. That's the reason I made the movie.

Every time you set yourself that kind of challenge, you're scared to death the whole time you're making the film; you don't think it's going to work. If you don't get the audience to that place, by hook or by crook, whatever it takes, then you haven't succeeded. When the film opened, I went to the Egyptian Theatre in Hollywood. When the space ship door came up, and there was Sigourney in the power loader, the audience went ape shit! That's what it's all about. It really taught me to not be afraid of the challenges, to find them, to seek them out because that's where the magic is. *Forrest Gump* is a great example of a movie that shouldn't work, that shouldn't *be* exciting, interesting, shouldn't get you. And [director Robert] Zemeckis went right to it and said this is going to be really, really, really hard and did it. And it paid off. It doesn't always pay off. Sometimes you make mistakes. *The Abyss* was a little overreaching. When we tried to get the audience to that place, they weren't always with it. I think the release version is a pretty good film; it's more than people deserve [laughs] for eight bucks. It set itself a really high bar to jump over, and it didn't quite make it.

Omni: It seemed like the scene where Ed Harris brings his drowned wife back to life was the emotional peak of the film.

Cameron: Every film has its own life. It's not an exact science; it's not like building a rocket to go to the moon where you can calculate every detail. Post-production gets wild and woolly. I wrote that scene; I liked it; I knew that it was an important scene to the movie. But I didn't really understand the fact that it was the most powerful scene in the movie. The power of that scene was the primary reason I took out the Wave. I knew that if I kept the Wave as a set piece, and I had a finite amount of time to tell the story, I was going to have to take out character, take out the stuff that built to that scene, maybe even take that scene out.

That scene comes out clean. They nuke Coffee, he falls over the edge, they get on the radio, cut to them later. But the emotional heart of the film struck me as being more important than the intellectual heart, the Wave scene. Somehow I got it in my mind that it was one or the other. I felt like I was being true to the characters by taking the humanistic route as opposed to the epic, spectacle, didactic message route.

Omni: Would you do it differently if you were once again faced with that same choice?
Cameron: No, I'd go for it all. With *The Abyss*, we never had a chance to really watch the movie finished. It's how you handle your post-production. Every film I've done has had a very short post-production. It's such a compressed time period that you can make mistakes. Coming from *The Abyss* to *T2*, I wouldn't screen the film for myself until I thought that every scene was done, until they were all linked together, until we'd done a mix on a scene-by-scene basis—music, sound effects, etc. So I wouldn't have to make excuses to myself that it'd be better later.

I did the same thing on *True Lies*. We wouldn't show it to ourselves until it was a movie. Most people don't do it that way, but I think you lose your way: Nothing's done so it's not getting you the way it's supposed to. You always have to distance yourself, and you don't really know where you are. You're lost in the jungle.

Two Outcomes from the Present

Omni: Are you optimistic about the future?
Cameron: I am optimistic about people and pessimistic about systems. I don't believe in systems; I don't think there are any systems that work right now. I am optimistic about the capacity of human beings—some of them—to keep us from going off the cliff. Which isn't to say it can't happen. It's impossible for us to contextualize the time we're in right now.

You're going to have to go five hundred years down the line and look back at it to figure out what the hell we're doing right now. We may be doing it all wrong or exactly right.

Take two possible outcomes: One is the forward rush of technology. We're transforming the planet we live on, the environment; we're taking responsibility for things that before were random events. The only thing Mother Nature has on her side is time. She works shit out over long cycles and gets it stable to where it's working. You had a system that worked for millions of years; now we're going to take over and make it work our way. All of this supports an increase in technology, a reliance upon it. We may screw it up and all be dead in a hundred years. The dinosaurs were destroyed by a comet that hit the earth. That could happen to us tomorrow. If we figure out how to stop the comet, it won't happen. Where do you say how technology's going to keep you alive and how it's going to destroy you? It can only be contextualized after the fact.

If there is a future we can look back from, I think the twentieth century is going to be one of the most interesting ones for a long time to come. It certainly is the most interesting to date, going from the Industrial Age to the Atomic Age to the Information Age in the space of a hundred years. Part of why I wanted to do Digital Domain was to be in the loop. I want to know what the advances are in computing so that I can stay abreast of my own art. I entered an art that was in a certain technological state; it's completely changed since I entered it fifteen years ago.

Digital information processing and computer graphics animation are going to fundamentally alter the way films are made, even conventional films that are shot in a room with a camera and a couple of actors. Just cutting on an Avid versus cutting on film—transformation. It's not evolutionary, it's revolutionary. Basically, I am very optimistic about the future. But you have to keep your guard up all the time. Optimistically paranoid.

A Drive of Titanic Proportions

Academy of Achievement / 1999

From the Academy of Achievement, http://www.achievement.org/autodoc/page/camoint-1. © 1996–2011 American Academy of Achievement. Page last revised October 30, 2007. Reprinted by permission.

Q: What was your childhood like?
Cameron: It was not remarkable from the standpoint of outside influences.

I lived in a small town. It was two thousand people in Canada. A little river went through it and we swam—you know, there was a lot of water around. Niagara Falls was about four or five miles away. And so, you know, I've always sort of loved the water—possibly as a result of that, and that has manifested itself obviously in my work.

It's also a big part of my private time. I do an awful lot of scuba diving. I love to be on the ocean, under the ocean. I live next to the ocean. My mother was a housewife but she was also an artist. My father was an electrical engineer. So right there you have a collision of left and right hemisphere thinking and I think I got equal parts of both.

My mother was definitely an influence in giving me a respect for art and the arts and especially the visual arts. I used to go with her to museums, and when I was learning to draw I would sketch things in the museum, whether it was an Etruscan helmet, or a mummy, or whatever. I was fascinated by all that.

I was always fascinated by engineering. Maybe it was an attempt to get my father's respect or interest, or maybe it was just a genetic love of technology, but I was always trying to build things. And sometimes being a builder can put you in a leadership position when you're a kid. "Hey, let's build a go-kart. You go get the wheels and you get this," and pretty soon you're at the center of a project.

I look back at, you know, I was ten years old or nine years old, and I'm the same person now, and in essence—in wanting to build things and wanting to get a lot of people together and do some grandiose thing, whether it was build a fort or a tree house, or an airplane. Once we built an airplane. Not intending it to fly, just hang from a tree but, you know, that sort of thing. And I realize I'm just doing the same thing now. I'm just getting a bunch of kids to help me build a fort, except that now it takes $100 million, and the kids are all my age.

Q: Were you a good student?
Cameron: Yes, good student. Mostly because of a real natural curiosity. I wasn't trying to please anybody. It wasn't competitive against the other kids. It wasn't about trying to please my parents so much as I just wanted to know things, the sciences, history, even math to an extent. I was just switched on somehow. That's the most important thing when I look back to that formative period, junior high through high school. It was a six-year period.

I spent all my free time in the town library and I read an awful lot of science fiction and the line between reality and fantasy blurred. I was as interested in the reality of biology as I was in reading science fiction stories about genetic mutations and post-nuclear war environments and inter-stellar traveling, meeting alien races, and all that sort of thing.

I read so voraciously. It was tonnage. I rode a school bus for an hour each way in high school because they put me in an academic program that could only be serviced by this high school much further away. So I had two hours a day on the bus and I tried to read a book a day. I averaged a book every other day, but if I got really interested in something it was propped up behind my math book or my science book all during the day in class.

Q: Was there a book that influenced or inspired you in some way?
Cameron: I remember it more by authors. Arthur Clark and A. E. Van Vogt, all of the mainstream old guard of science fiction at that time. In the latter years of high school I got into the newer guys of that time, Harlan Ellison, Larry Niven, people like that. It was a steady diet of science fiction.

Q: Were there any teachers who had a big influence on you?
Cameron: There was. The critical moment for me was in the eleventh grade.

My biology teacher, Mr. McKenzie, decided that what our school needed was a theater arts program and we didn't have it. There was wrestling, basketball, football, it was a very jock-oriented school and there was no theater program whatsoever. So we started a theater program from scratch. We bootstrapped it. He taught it, and I think he might have done it for nothing. We had to build the props and the scenery and the costumes and do everything ourselves. We had to turn the stage into a proper working stage. It took a year, but we started putting on our own productions. I think that was really a pivotal moment.

My biology teacher was our muse at that time. And I think the fact that we were having to do everything, that it wasn't handed to us, may have created a kind of a work ethic that paid off then in independent film production because it's the same thing. You know, you're finding scraps and bits and pieces, and putting it all together and putting on a show. And it's that sense of being able to create some moment of glory, some showmanship—out of nothing, out of baling wire—that is maybe a lesson that was learned there as a result of this man who just decided to have a theater arts program.

Otherwise I would have been marginalized by the fact that it was a very athletically oriented school. I've gone back to the school recently and found out that the theater program is the thing that the school is most proud of. Their teams are doing terribly but their theater program is doing great and they're winning all these dramatic awards around the province. So that's Mr. McKenzie's legacy. The point is that teachers can be absolutely critical at the right moment in your life and they can be mentors.

Sometimes it's only just one comment that they can make. I was talking to this man, my biology teacher, and he said, " I've seen your aptitude tests . . ." or whatever kind of testing they did thirty years ago in Canada, ". . . and we believe that you have unlimited potential." Now I don't know if he'd ever seen the tests and I don't know if any of the data indicated that, but hearing that, and knowing that somebody somewhere believed that I could go accomplish something, was a big contributor to the self-confidence necessary to overcome all of these things later. Because you're going to have 10,000 people telling you why you can't do something, and sometimes it only takes one person to tell you that you can do something and you take it to heart. Otherwise I wouldn't have remembered it all these years, and I remember where the conversation took place.

Q: Did you think of yourself as different from other kids? Were you a gifted child?
Cameron: I certainly didn't think of myself as gifted. The standards for being gifted in my environment were if you were good in Little League or if you were good in football.

I was more like the . . . kind of the misfit, the outsider. And of course, the misfits and the outsiders all collect together like this kind of pond scum around the sides. And that's where all the good ideas come from. I certainly never thought of myself as, you know, superior or gifted in any way. Just different. Definitely different. And happy. Satisfied to be different. Maybe not always happy to be different, but satisfied to be different.

Q: How do you think that affected your childhood?
Cameron: It becomes a defense mechanism, to be contemptuous of people who don't think outside of the box. I spent a ten-year period being intellectually snobbish and saying, "You guys are just a bunch of jock idiots." And then I've spent the last twenty-five years trying to reintegrate myself into being a normal person. With limited success probably.

Q: Do you think you were destined to be an achiever? Is it destiny? Is it chance?
Cameron: I think it's, the old adage: "The harder I work, the luckier I get." I think chance is not a big factor in the long run. It can be a huge factor in the short run, being at the right place at the right time. But even with that chance, the critical factor is being able to recognize a true opportunity and seize it the moment it presents itself, and not wait and over think it, because it will pass.

There are many talented people who haven't fulfilled their dreams because they over thought it, or they were too cautious, and were unwilling to make the leap of faith. There are also winos sleeping rolled up in a carpet remnant in an alley some place who also made that leap of faith and either made it at the wrong time or never had the skill to back it up.

If you don't have the ability to make that leap of faith it's going to be harder for you to accomplish something great, because there are going to be moments, there are going to be little windows of opportunity that open for a split second and you either squirt through or you don't. But at the moment that you do that, you have to have prepared yourself. You have to have prepared yourself for that fight, because that's going to be the fight of your life. Whatever that opportunity is, when you grab it, it's going to be more energy than you can manage. It's going to be grabbing the tiger by the tail and if you have not prepared yourself mentally for it through study, through knowing and hypothesizing what it will be like when you're in that position, you won't be able to deal with it. And half of what you've concluded before the fact in your theoretical projection is going to be wrong but half of it will be right and that's the part you're going to prevail with.

Q: When did you first know what it was that you wanted to do with your life?
Cameron: I didn't know for a long time. I was always fascinated by the sciences. When I was a kid I used to spend all my time collecting pond water and looking at it through my microscope and trying to identify the various protozoa, or I'd be looking through a telescope trying to find the Great Nebula in Orion. My brain was going in all these different directions.

Art was always there. I was always drawing, but it wasn't the main thing. All the way through high school, even into college, I majored in physics. I hit kind of a wall with math. I had a bad teacher who turned me off of calculus at a critical moment, and even though my grades were very high in astronomy and physics, I switched to English because I wanted to write.

I was sort of going in two different directions. I was twenty-five or twenty-six before I really settled in and said, "This is it. I'm going to work in film in some capacity." What finally attracted me to film in such a definitive way was . . . it was the only place I could reconcile the need to tell stories and to work in a visual art medium, and the desire to understand things at a technological level—and my fascination with engineering and technology.

It was a way to fuse those interests. I didn't know where I'd wind up within film. I actually started as a model builder and quickly progressed into production design, which made sense because I could draw and paint. But I kept watching that guy over there who was moving the actors around and setting up the shots.

I had pictured myself as a filmmaker but I had never pictured myself as a director if that makes any sense at all. I wanted to make films, and I understood at some intellectual level that the director was the person who was most in charge creatively, but I had never pictured myself in that role, as the guy with the monocle and the megaphone. It had no meaning for me. But then . . . I watched a couple of really bad directors work, and I saw how they completely botched it up and missed the visual opportunities of the scene when we had put things in front of them as opportunities. Set pieces, props and so on. They had these great actors to work with and they just blew it. And there was a moment where I said, "I may not be very good at this but I know I'm better than that guy." And that was kind of a critical moment because when you realize that you can at least be better than somebody else who is already doing it, then you can visualize yourself doing the job.

Q: Was there a moment when the light bulb went on and you said, "That's what I want to do. I want to be a filmmaker. I want to be a director"?

Cameron: There were several light bulbs at several different times, and the first one was when I saw *2001: A Space Odyssey* for the first time. And the light bulb there was, "You know, a movie can be more than just telling a story. It can be a piece of art." It can be something that has a profound impact on your imagination, on your appreciation of how music works with the images and so on. It sort of just blew the doors off the whole thing for me at the age of fourteen, and I started thinking about film in a completely different way and got fascinated by it.

It was such a fascinating film that they made a book about *The Making of 2001*. It was, to my knowledge, one of the first films that had a "making of" book. It's the first one that I knew of, and I read it from cover-to-cover eighteen times. I didn't understand half of it until many years later, but it started a process of projecting myself into the idea of actually creating images using these high-tech means.

Of course, I did all my low-tech analogues of those means, buying models and gluing them on pieces of glass and moving them around. It was good training to think spatially and to think in terms of story boarding and so on. So I was already a filmmaker but I hadn't realized it yet.

That was all happening in Canada, thousands of miles from Hollywood, and then ironically, at the age of seventeen we moved from Canada to Los Angeles, which is very close to the black hole of Hollywood itself. At that point, I didn't know if I could get there from here. "Who am I to say that I could be a filmmaker?" It didn't make any sense so I abandoned it for grown-up things and I decided to be a scientist. It wasn't until many years later that I realized this is where my heart really lay.

The next light bulb was really just the one that says, "Just do it. Just pick up a camera and start shooting something." Don't wait to be asked because nobody is going to ask you and don't wait for the perfect conditions because they'll never be perfect. It's a little bit like having a child. If you wait until the right time to have a child you'll die childless, and I think filmmaking is very much the same thing. You just have to take the plunge and just start shooting something even if it's bad. You can always hide it but you will have learned something, you know.

Q: What films influenced you most as a young person?
Cameron: The films that influenced me were so disparate that there's almost no pattern. Stanley Kubrick was an influence because I loved *2001: A Space Odyssey*, and the more I learned about him and his methodology the more I realized what a rigorous intellectual exercise filmmaking was for him, and I was inspired by that. The word perfectionist has a fussy connotation of unnecessary work, of unnecessary complication of the process, but I think that everything he did in his process was necessary.

I have since come to learn that process doesn't work as well for me. There has to be some chaos, some looseness, so the actors are given the opportunities to give you their best. If you have it preconceived in crystallinely perfect form, you don't leave the door open for magic. The magic doesn't come from within the director's mind, it comes from within the hearts of the actors. You have to be there to seize it at the right moment. But Kubrick was definitely an important influence.

All the films that I saw in my last two years of high school and my first year of college are the films that still burn vividly for me. *Woodstock, Catch-22, Easy Rider, The Graduate, Bonnie and Clyde, The Godfather*. It was such an amazing time in film production, very eclectic and just breaking all the rules.

Q: You've also said seeing the film *Star Wars* affected you.
Cameron: That was probably the film that galvanized me to get off my butt and go be a filmmaker. I was fascinated by space, I was always painting space ships and living in this world of these whizzing, dynamic space battles.

In my senior year in high school, we used to play "Battleship" in class. We turned it into space battleships and we would draw these elaborate spaceships and send coordinates to each other by notes and try to blow each other up.

I was living in a *Star Wars* world in my mind, and all of a sudden I saw this film, and it was like somebody had reached into my hind brain and yanked out a lot of stuff that was in there, and I was seeing it on the screen realized. And not to take anything away from George's creation, because it's obviously a phenomenal milestone, but my reaction to it was not, "Oh, wow, that's cool. I want to see more." It was, "Oh, wow, I better get off my butt because somebody is doing this stuff, you know, and they're beating me to it." That was my reaction. So I basically quit my job and started doing a little film with visual effects, and sucked my friends into that vortex, and we all quit our jobs and fortunately we've all managed to successfully transition into filmmaking, of that little group of four people.

A lot of people ask me, you know, "What's the best advice to someone who wants to be a director?" And the answer I give is very simple. "Be a director." Pick up a camera. Shoot something. No matter how small, no matter how cheesy, no matter whether your friends and your sister star in it. Put your name on it as director. Now you're a director. Everything after that you're just negotiating your budget and your fee. So it's a state of mind is really the point, once you commit yourself to do it.

Then the hard part starts. You have to foreswear all other paths, because you can't keep a foot in cabinet making and a foot in directing. You can't keep one foot in another job. It's a total and all-consuming thing. I suspect that's true of many of the difficult and challenging things in the world, whether it's research or whatever. Certainly the arts must be all consuming, because you're in competition with people who have made that decision, who have committed themselves 100 percent. You're competing for resources. It's a big coral reef. It's a big food chain, and you're competing for resources and you're competing against people who have made that commitment. If you don't make the same commitment you're not going to compete. It's that simple.

Q: How did you parents feel about what you've chosen professionally?
Cameron: I would say that my father was completely unsupportive in any way, shape, or form, and was really sort of just sharpening his knives waiting for me to fail so that he could say, "Ah-ha, I was right. You should have gone into engineering." And it was always this sort of attitude of, "Well, you know, one of these days you'll get a real job and this film thing, you know, will pass as a fad." So there was zero support there. And I actually think that it made me angry enough that I had to succeed. I think if I had a soft, rosy, supportive kind of "It's good if you do it, but if it doesn't work out . . ." sort of thing that it would have been different.

But it kind of made me mad, and I had to prove that I was right, that this was the right thing to be doing and I think it made me mad enough to get good, you know.

My mother, of course, at an earlier time, was very supportive of the arts, and the visual aspect of it. So there was an interesting dynamic there that probably served me in the long run although it was hard to see it at the time.

Q: Was it difficult not having the support of your father?
Cameron: It was certainly difficult financially, but you learn to survive. You learn to prioritize, and you learn that if you're going to do something, you have to do it all the way and you just have to put it before all other things.

Q: When you started out as a filmmaker, did you have something in mind you wanted to achieve?
Cameron: I didn't really have anything to say. I had a lot of images crowding into my mind visually. I had read tons of science fiction. I was fascinated by other worlds, other environments. For me, it was fantasy, but it was not fantasy in the sense of pure escapism. Isaac Asimov used to say, "Science fiction readers are people who escape from reality into worlds of pollution, nuclear war, overpopulation." It's a way of modeling the present through the future.

Growing up in the sixties, coming to my kind of intellectual awakening in high school at a time when the world was in complete chaos, between the war in Vietnam and civil rights and all of the upheavals, all the social upheavals, you know, free love, everything that was happening in the late sixties. It gave one an interesting perspective being a science fiction fan and looking at a world that was coming apart and thinking in very apocalyptic terms about that world. And I've never lost that sort of—almost a fascination with apocalyptic themes. *Titanic* is just another manifestation of that, because for me that film was just a microcosm for the way the world ends. However it ends we don't know, but if it ends by the human hand it'll end in the way the *Titanic* ended, which is through some casual simple carelessness. So you know, being a child of the sixties in that way, I think, very much influenced the way I looked at what could be done with film.

It was also a very interesting time in filmmaking, in the history of filmmaking, because it was the time when the paradigm of studio film production was completely deconstructed and the independent films emerged.

All of a sudden the filmmaking world was turned on its head. A film called *Easy Rider* came out that was made for $40,000 and made more money than any other film of that year, including all of the big studio films. So the big smokestack industry of Hollywood was suddenly threatened from within by these *auteurs*, these punks, the young George Lucases and Martin Scorseses.

It was a fascinating time, and that's when I came into my awareness of what film could be. So I was definitely informed by that but I didn't really have anything to say yet. I had a lot of images and ideas but I hadn't found my themes. It took another few years for that to happen.

Q: How did you get from the realization that this is what you wanted to do, to actually getting the opportunity to do it as a professional?

Cameron: You never really "get" an opportunity. You take an opportunity. You know, in the filmmaking business no one ever gives you anything. Nobody ever taps you on the shoulder and say, "You know, I've really admired the way you talk and the way you draw, and I think you'd make a good director." It doesn't happen that way. You have to constantly be pulling on somebody's sleeve saying, "Hey, I want to direct. I want to direct. I want to direct." And you have to be willing to make sacrifices to do that. The mistake a lot of people, I think, make in Hollywood is that they think, "Well, I'll get to the top of my field as a whatever, editor, production designer, writer, and then I'll just move laterally into directing and I'll be more respected and I'll have more power." It doesn't work that way, because you drop right to the bottom of the pack as a director. You have to work your way up again.

The way I did it was I came in through production design, which is good because you're thinking visually and you're very aware of the director's problems in trying to tell a story and how the environment is a manifestation of the narrative in some way. And you know, I sort of proved myself as a production designer in the scrappy, stay-all-night-for-fifteen-days-in-a-row kind of independent filmmaking that was done at Roger Corman's place. This was in the early eighties. And when they see that you have the creativity and the stamina, and that you basically understand filmmaking, it's not a ridiculous leap in that environment to say, "I now want to try my hand. I want to direct."

I just basically went up to Roger one day and said, "I'd like to direct second unit on this." The film that we were making at the time, which was a low-budget science fiction horror picture. And he gave me a camera and a couple, two or three people, and we started a little second unit, and the second unit basically became this steam roller that wound up shooting about a third of the picture because they were falling way behind on first unit. So they'd give me the actors and say, "Well, do scene 28 and scene 42." And all of a sudden I was working with actors, and that was terrifying because I hadn't really thought that part through yet. You know, that in order to direct, you have to work with actors. It's not just about sets and visual effects. So it was simultaneously a shock and a joyful discovery because I found that all actors really want is some sense of what a writer can bring to the moment, some sense of a narrative purpose. "What am I doing? What am I trying to do here? What's the scene about?" And it's really pretty much that simple. So that was the next epiphany if you will, which is: this part of it is fun too.

The part I didn't expect to be fun, the part I didn't expect to be good at, turned out to be in a way the most fascinating part. I wouldn't say I was good at it right away. It took me a long time to realize that you have to have a bit of an interlanguage with actors. You have to give them something that they can act with. You can't tell them a lot of abstract information about how their character is going to pay off in this big narrative ellipse that happens in scene 89. That doesn't help them. You know, they're in a room. They have to create an emotional truth in a moment and, you know, they have to be able to create that very quickly. So they need real tangible stuff and that's a learned art, I think. But coming from writing, and understanding what they're feeling and what they're thinking, what the character is feeling and thinking, and having thought about it a lot for months in advance is the way that I get enough respect from the actors that they trust what I'm saying. They trust what I'm giving them to do.

Q: What were some other lessons you learned working on that Corman film?
Cameron: Well, the critical lesson is basically never give up because it's going to be unbelievably hard. It's going to be a ridiculously brutal, uphill fight all the time, and you just have to have tremendous stamina and self-confidence to power through it. You have to not listen to the naysayers because there will be many and often they'll be much more qualified than you and cause you to sort of doubt yourself. But, you know, what I learned from those early days was to trust my instincts and

to not back off; because when the hour gets dark, you're instinct is to—or your tendency might be to say, "Well, this is just too hard and no, you know, nobody should have to go through this in order to accomplish X," whether it's a movie or whatever. I think you can be in the pursuit of excellence when you're working on a low-budget science fiction horror film, if it's how you define it. You have to go all the way. It's that simple. Now I don't mean trample over people. I don't mean turn into a screaming maniac. I mean, you have to be able—you have to have made the commitment within yourself to do whatever it takes to get the job done and to try to inspire other people to do it, because obviously the first rule is you can't do it by yourself.

Even though you may know how to do many of these different tasks, you physically can't do it. You need a team, and you need the respect and the trust of that team. That was a lesson that took me a while to figure out, because at first I just wanted to do it all myself. "Ah, you're doing it wrong!" That doesn't work. That doesn't ultimately achieve the vision.

I had to learn to inspire people to give me their best work and I also had to learn to accept what they brought even if it was either (a) not as good or (b) good but just different from what I had imagined. And so that the end result of our collected efforts will be exactly that. It'll be all of our efforts together. It won't ever be exactly the way I imagined it. And that is, I think, an important lesson as well, is that in any group enterprise it's going to be the sum total of the group. So choose your group well, and go in with that little voice in the back of your mind that says, "Be Zen about it. Be philosophical. It's ultimately going to be the best that these people can do."

That flies in the face of the auteur theory. And I was sort of raised aesthetically on that auteur theory, looking at the much vaunted Hitchcock films that were planned down to every frame and every molecule through storyboarding. It all flowed from the forehead of Zeus, but it's not that way. When you're doing your job best you're a band leader.

Q: How hard was it for you to learn those lessons?
Cameron: It's tough, and I'm still learning it, but I've learned it well enough to do some of my best work as a result of that lesson, by inspiring the actors on *Titanic*, the production designers, and everyone on that film. There were several thousand people working on that film. By somehow inspiring them to do their very, very best, they brought me all of the elements, all of the moments that eventually became that film. I couldn't have done it all myself. I couldn't have done a fraction of it.

Q: I've read that you once had to break into an editing room in order to realize your vision of what a film should be.

Cameron: I suppose I should clarify that. Here was a critical juncture for me. I was hired to direct a film called *Piranha II*. I was hired by a very unscrupulous producer who worked out of Italy. He put me with an Italian crew who spoke no English, even though I was assured that they would all speak English. I actually had to learn some Italian very quickly, I'm talking about in two weeks. That's all the prep time I had, because I was actually replacing someone else. I was put into an untenable situation and then fired a couple of weeks into the shoot, and the producer took over directing. It turns out that he had actually done that twice before on his two previous films. That was his modus operandi, in order to get the financing and then axe the director.

In the course of throwing me off the movie, he never showed me a foot of the film that I had shot. He held on to the dailies. We were shooting in Jamaica and the dailies would go to New York and be processed. He'd fly to New York and look at them and not send them back for me to see so I wasn't even seeing my own film. He came in and said, "Your stuff doesn't work, doesn't cut together. It's a pile of junk and you're off the movie," and then he took over the film. And I thought, "Maybe I'm just bad. Maybe I'm just not good."

A couple of months later I went to Rome to find out what really happened, and he wouldn't show me any of the film. I had been in Rome prepping the film for a couple of weeks before we went to Jamaica, and I remembered the code to get in. So I went in and ran the film for myself. It wasn't that bad. All I wanted to know was one simple fact. Could I or could I not do this job? So I made a few changes before I flew back. I don't know if the editor ever noticed that I actually fixed a couple of things, but, I had to know whether what they had said was true.

Everyone around me had basically said, "You stink. You suck. You don't know what you're doing." And I just—and I accepted it but then a little voice kept saying, "I don't think so. I don't think it can be that bad. I remember doing some pretty cool stuff with the actors in this moment and that moment." And I looked at it and it was fine. So then I thought, "You know what, I actually can do this and I just fell in with a pack of, you know, thieves and whackos here." But I also realized that I was going to have to get busy and create my own thing, and that nobody would hire me after that experience. Nobody would hire me and just put me on a film. I'd have to create my own thing and hang on tenaciously to that in order to be able to direct again, and that's why I wrote *The Terminator*.

I had many, many people trying to buy that script, but I wouldn't sell the script to them unless I went with it as the director. Of course that was a turn-off for almost everybody, but we did find one low-budget producer who was willing to make the film. That was John Daly at Hemdale, and that's how I got my real start.

Q: In the face of all of that, how do you pick yourself up and persevere? What does it take?
Cameron: I had dark hours on *Titanic* that were just as dire if not more dire than on *Piranha II* when I got fired, or on *Terminator* when we had all these problems. You have to find some kind of inner strength that says, "What I'm doing is right. It may not seem right to other people and I may not be able to please them right now, but I'm going to have to proceed on this path until I can demonstrate to them that what we're doing is probably the right thing, at least the best that I know how to do."

Ultimately you reach a point where people will hire you because you have the strength. Or some people call it vision, I don't. That's a bit of a lofty word because I don't think it's something that comes to you necessarily in the night. I think it's something that's the process of a very rigorous mental processing of the data on a day-by-day basis and the possibilities—what you can do and what you can't do—and over time people will realize that you have what it takes to be in that situation where nobody really knows the answer. Although a lot of them think they do or say they do, and you've come up with the right formula. And to have come out of these battle situations a number of times with the right formula on a consistent basis, they tend to trust you more as you go along. They'll never trust you completely.

The "they," whoever the "they" is. In my business it's the studio that's putting up the money, the completion bond company, the bankers. The people that don't really understand the day-to-day sweat, blood, and tears of the creative process. That's another lofty term, "the creative process"!

When you're on a set the creative process consists of . . . "Oh, my God. How are we going to do that? You're going to have to move the wall back three feet and then you're going to have to pile up some boxes over here and put the camera on it." It's all nuts and bolts things. And then you have to be able to switch that off in a heartbeat and think about what's the actor feeling. You know, what's the character feeling at that moment, and it might be some really important, very pivotal scene for them.

There's a certain tenacity that's required, and that tenacity manifests itself sometimes in unpleasant ways. Other times it can manifest itself in very noble ways when you can get other people to go with you that extra mile.

I think a lot about what is misunderstood about my particular filmmaking process, is that I get people to go that extra mile that they've never done before and they go into new territory. They go beyond what they previously thought were their limits, and then afterwards they talk about it like it was a big adventure. "Oh, man, we worked around the clock and you know, we all almost died." And it sounds like an indictment of the production as a bunch of whackos but when, in fact, they're actually—they want to share the fact that they did this, that they did go beyond. They went beyond in their creative capacity as well, and that's why they always all come back and want to do it again. Maybe just not right away.

I don't make films back-to-back anyway. I usually give them a year to go out and see what it's like on all those other boring movies and then they all want to come back.

Q: You mean a year off to recover.
Cameron: Oh no. That only takes a couple of weeks. A week in Hawaii usually takes care of it.

Q: Clearly the road to success is not a straight line. It's a winding road.
Cameron: The road to success is like *Harold and the Purple Crayon*. You draw it for yourself. You have to imagine it first, and then you have to draw it, and then you have to walk it. Some people fall into good luck. Some people have it handed to them, but I think the great majority map it out for themselves.

Q: What about the setbacks and the frustrations and the self-doubts? How do you deal with them?
Cameron: When you're working in a public art form like filmmaking you don't really need self-doubt, because if it's bad you're going to hear exactly what's wrong with it, and if it's good you'll hear what's good about it. There are plenty of other people who will inform you, so self-doubt is not really necessary. You can set that one aside. Just drop it out the door. What you need is a lot of confidence to stand up to the slings and arrows, the barrage of negativity.

We exist in a peer environment and when we're on the outside and we're trying to get in, all our peers are like us and just a bunch of friends or people with similar interests. And none of them think you're special. They think they're special. So very few people will give you encouragement.

It's like that old adage "It's not enough to succeed, your friends must also fail." You're not going to get a lot of tremendous encouragement from your peer group and you can't feed on that energy. You can actually support each other in very tangible ways, but that thing of "Dude, you've got it, you're going all the way," you're not going to hear that. And you're certainly going to face rejection after rejection. You're going to knock on a lot of doors and you're going to have to prove yourself.

I think you know that going in if you're going into the filmmaking process. You have to go in with your eyes open. That's what it's going to be like. There's a tremendous temptation to do a work-around, or to do a moral or ethical work-around or a short cut in a lot of situations, because it's easier and it's just—you're so needy to get those little breaks and so on. And I think a lot of people get sort of ethically short-circuited at that stage and they never recover, you know? Because I think a lot of people would say, "Well, you know, I'll do what I have to do now, but then later I'll be good." It doesn't work that way. You are who you are. Fortunately, I've managed to get where I am without—the occasional burglary aside—without having to really hurt anybody or go against my word. I think ultimately your word becomes the most important thing that you have. It's the most important currency that you have. Having a successful film is a very important currency as well, but in the long run your word is the most important thing, and if you say you're going to do something you have to do it.

I think that's what saw me through on *Titanic*. *Titanic* was in some ways the roughest project that I've ever been involved with. And what saw me through on that was that I had a relationship with the people who were quite rightly panicking, but they never completely panicked because they knew who I was, and we always treated each other with a kind of respect. I always did what I think was the right or ethical thing throughout that. Even though it was costing me millions of dollars personally right out of my pocket to do it, I felt I had to do it or they would never trust me again on another film, and I think that that's ultimately the most important currency that you reap from any situation.

Q: Were there any moments of panic for you during the making of *Titanic?*
Cameron: Pretty much every day, but when you're in a leadership posi-

tion you can never ever manifest that. You can never manifest the panic that you feel inside. *Titanic* was a situation where I felt, I think, pretty much like the officer felt on the bridge of the ship. I could see the iceberg coming far away, but as hard as I turned that wheel there was just too much mass, too much inertia, and there was nothing I could do, but I still had to play it through. There was no way to get off. And so then, you know, you're in this kind of situation where you feel quite doomed, and yet you still have to play by your own ethical standards, you know, no matter where it takes you. And ultimately that was the salvation, because I think if I hadn't done that they might have panicked. They might have pulled the plug. Things would have been very different, the whole thing might have crashed and burned but it didn't, you know. We held on. We missed the iceberg by that much.

Q: You first established a reputation as a master of special effects, and yet this blockbuster film, *Titanic*, you call a love story. It certainly has special effects, but that's not how you talk about it.
Cameron: Right. *Titanic* was conceived as a love story, and if I could have done it without one visual effect I would have been more than happy to do that. The fact is that the ship hasn't existed since 1912, at least not at the surface, so we had to create it somehow.

Obviously it was a big visual effect show when all was said and done, but that wasn't my motivation to make the film. I don't think that should ever be the motivation to make a film; it should be a means to an end.

Certainly there's an aspect of me that likes big challenges, whether it's big physical construction or visual effects or whatever. I think that's what I do best. Other people work at a much more intimate level; they do that solely and are better at that. I think that it was definitely a goal of *Titanic* to integrate a very personal, very emotional, and very intimate filmmaking style with spectacle. And try to make that not be kind of chocolate syrup on a cheeseburger, you know. Make it somehow work together.

Q: Is that what made *Titanic* such a worldwide success?
Cameron: I think the spectacle got people's attention, got them to the theaters, and then the emotional, cathartic experience of watching the film is what made the film work. I think the spectacle served it but was not the defining factor in its success. Once again I think it's a question of balance. It's sort of like looking at a painting and saying what part of the

painting is the part that makes you like it. It's all of it working together that makes you like the painting.

Q: How would you explain to somebody who knows nothing about what you do, what is it that's so exciting to you about doing it?
Cameron: The thing that is exciting about filmmaking is to think back to the moment in time right before you had the idea, and think about that at the moment that you're sitting or standing on the set and there are thousands of people around and they've built this huge set, and there are all these actors, and there's all this energy and all this focus, and realize that it's all in the service of something that was made up out of whole cloth, you know? And that's fun. I mean, that's what an architect must feel like when they drive down the street and they look up and see a building that they designed. It's something that you imagined made tangible.

I get that rush much more on the set than I do when the film is done. When the film is done you've lived with it for so long that it's not new anymore, and it almost seems like it's just destiny. That's just what it is. But there's a time on the set when it's new, and you can walk into it and you can see it, and it's this physical tangible manifestation of pure imagination. Now as much fun as that is, it becomes a curse. The next time you sit down and face the blank CRT you know you have to come up with something, because there's going to be a time when everybody is standing around, having gathered and built this huge human enterprise, and you better think of something good. So that's the rush you get out of it, but it's also the thing that haunts you before you start.

Q: How would you characterize your contribution, your achievement in the field of filmmaking?
Cameron: I think that's probably best left to others. I know what I've tried to do, which is tell stories that excite the imagination and maybe say something at a thematic level, and maybe something about the human condition with respect to our human relationship with technology, because ultimately I think all my stories have been about that to one degree or another. And to allow people to step through that screen into that world, whatever it is. You know, whether it's the world of *The Abyss*, or the world of *The Terminator*, or *Titanic*, to let people live in that—create that space for them and let them live in the shoes of those characters for a while. That's what I set out to do, so I think it's really up to others to sort of sort it out, what it ultimately means.

I see things that I have done that I know were inspired by other things. I see other filmmakers picking up on my leads and taking it further, and I realize that it is part of an ongoing creative process that is self-perpetuating. I think of myself as a link in a chain of cinematic ideas. It's fun to have that place.

Q: What do you see as the next great challenge, the next great frontier in filmmaking?

Cameron: Ultimately the frontiers of filmmaking have never changed. They change in the specifics of the technology and the technique, but ultimately it's somebody sitting in a room writing. It's actors saying the lines in front of a lens, and that image being captured, and that little slice of life for those characters, those relationships, being made alive in the minds of other people all around the world. I don't think that is fundamentally going to change indefinitely.

The specifics are probably going to change a lot. We'll have electronic digital projection of the films. That's going to inform the entire post-production process. Ultimately we won't be working on film any more. We'll call it film but there won't be any film involved. It may be shot electronically. Film itself as a substance, as a thing, may be obsolete within ten to twenty years other than atavistic artists who choose to shoot on film because of some real or perceived artistic need, in the same way that people still make pots by hand even though there are machines that make them beautifully.

Visual effects are happening now. It's not even the next frontier. Visual effects are just becoming integrated into the basic fabric of filmmaking, they are not outside of the normal filmmaking process. Now all directors are working with visual effects and it has just become as basic to the technique as a light or a dolly or whatever. I think it's empowering to the imagination to let people create whatever it is they want to create and do it in a very easy and straightforward manner, which visual effects are now capable of doing because of the ease of digital compositing. I think computer graphics and animation are going to have an increasing role. I think very real characters will come out of that. I don't think we're going to replace actors. They're going to have to be nonhuman characters.

There has to be a reason to do a CG character, and the reason is it can't be you or I. The traditional techniques of putting rubber on people's faces and making rubber puppets and running them with hydraulics and so on are going to fall by the wayside. Actors will still be empowered within that process because it will still be a performance created by an actor in some way. They just won't have five pounds of make-up stuck on their face.

Q: *Titanic* has got to be a tough act to follow. Is there something you haven't you done that you would like to do?
Cameron: There are many things I'd love to do. There are still a lot of stories that I want to tell. I get very excited by all kinds of different stories. I'd love to do a film with a scientist as a main character and really try to communicate to people the passion of science, because our culture thinks science is kind of unhip. Scientists get it, but I think the greater community doesn't understand how scientists think, what drives them, and how their passion can be as great as the passion of an artist or the passion of a great athlete, which our culture respects much more, unfortunately. I'd love to be able to crack that nut because I don't think Hollywood has served the science community well. They are usually stereotypes: geeks, bad guys, or distant, unemotional people and, of course, none of that is true. It can certainly be true of individuals but it's not generally true.

Q: What do you understand about achievement now that you did not when you were younger?
Cameron: I used to think that the great films that I saw, the great works of art, were something that somebody imagined in every detail and then went and did. I didn't realize that the creative process is the end result of a lot of different people bringing a lot of different things to the table and it's impossible to predict. It's a real time monitoring, shaping, molding process. The end result may be quite different than what you imagined when you started out, but that that's how it works.

I'm at an interesting point right now. Just having done this film, it's definitely a high water mark and I have to evaluate what that means. Do I let the success of that overpower my artistic instincts? There are a lot of things I want to do and I know for certain some of them are going to be disappointments to people who think I'm going to come out and try to kick *Titanic*'s butt. It might be some little intimate thing or it might be something that's a little off center.

Sometimes success brings with it a tremendous amount of scrutiny and anticipation of what's going to happen next. That is not a good thing necessarily. You want to have the freedom to just react instinctively as an artist and not second guess yourself.

I've been speaking to young people a lot lately, who are right at the cusp of deciding their path. I relate where I am right now to where I was when I was eighteen years old and thinking, "I've got to make this big decision what I'm going to be, and if I mess up I mess up my whole life," and it's just not like that.

It's an evolving process, so I think the illumination I might be able to share is, "You've got time." As long as you follow your heart, you'll be going in the right direction for you. It may not be the direction that everybody around you thinks you should be going, but it'll be what's ultimately right for you.

I think the problem for a lot of people, especially when they show great potential, is that all of a sudden you've got fifty people in your hip pocket telling you what you should be and what you should do. Those voices can be deflecting you off your true course. I didn't find my true course until I was twenty-five, so you've got time. I don't think you have until you're forty-five, but I think you have at least until you're in your mid-twenties. And, of course, there are stories of a legion of people who didn't find their true calling until they are in their forties or fifties.

I had the great opportunity to become friends briefly with a woman who died recently at the age of 105. She was an artist in California named Beatrice Wood. She was a little bit the inspiration for the character in *Titanic*. In fact, I called her up and asked her permission to use her a little bit, to interview her and use her as kind of a model for this character even though Beatrice had no connection to *Titanic* itself. She said, "Oh, I couldn't possibly do that because I'm only thirty-five." She was 102 at the time.

She was an artist, and none of her significant work was done before she was ninety. She switched on when she hit ninety. I think that's an interesting thing to remember.

Q: One hears stories about Jim Cameron at work on the set, the madman, the crackpot visionary. Wherever these stories come from, is it an obsessiveness, a passion that is necessary to get where you want to go?

Cameron: What people call obsession or passion, for me it's just a work ethic. I think it comes from an insecurity that I'm not good enough. There are other people out there that I grew up admiring that are still making movies, and those movies are great. I've got to compete with these guys and these women. Have I thought of everything? Have I thought of every detail? Is this the best the scene can be? It comes from a healthy insecurity that makes you better as an artist. And just from a kind of gonzo intensity.

I just like to do it full bore. For me it's not about being comfortable. I want to be in there. I want to help the guys move the dolly. I'm at my best when I'm neck deep in ice water trying to work out how we're going to, you know, keep the lights turned on when the water hits the bulbs. You know? I mean, the more the challenge is, the more I enjoy it. And the more I can lead other people into these situations where they all think they're going to die, the more fun I'm having. So needless to say we have a few washouts. We have a few people that don't like my version of day camp, but I would say that 80 or 90 percent of them feel like they've been through something. They've done the best that they've done in their professional careers, and they're usually pretty eager to re-up for another one.

Q: What does the American Dream mean to you?
Cameron: As a Canadian, the American Dream had a very negative and pejorative connotation when I was growing up, because it was this kind of cultural imperialism. I grew up in a border town on the other side of the border in Niagara Falls, Canada. But since I moved to the United States at the age of seventeen, I actually feel very much like I'm probably, in my basic genetic nature, much more American than Canadian because I really believe strongly in a lot of the traditional values of this country in terms of respecting individuals' rights. The rights to freedom of speech and a lot of the things that are in the basic fabric of this country.

Americans, and Canadians even to a large extent, come from frontiersman stock, so they are people who hewed their civilization out of the wilderness. It wasn't given to them. You know, it's not like people growing up in Italy or France in the shadow of past glories from thousands of years before. You know, "We made what we have, and we don't have a great cultural depth like they do but what we have is ours by God." And I like that. I like that about it, you know. It sort of puts your hand on the tiller of destiny in a way, and America definitely has its hand on the tiller of destiny for this planet. For good or bad. It doesn't mean you know what you're doing necessarily.

Americans are very happy to argue like crazy about everything and hold things up to ridicule that other countries just take for granted and I think that that's a good thing.

Anybody can come here from anywhere, and if you've got the goods it's a meritocracy. There are inequities just like anywhere, but we challenge the inequities. We're trying to evolve. Certain other countries aren't even trying to evolve. They're not trying to challenge those inequuities. There's something that can happen here that's unique.

Because America has imbedded within it this thing called Hollywood—this Mecca to which filmmakers from all over the world come and participate—it has become a kind of entertainment/pop culture leader for the world. There's a grave responsibility in that as well. I'm not sure that that mantle is being worn well right now, but it's the place to be. I could go on for hours about that.

Q: We could go on for a couple of hours talking to you. You've been terrific and we really appreciate it.

The Final Frontier

Anne Thompson/2000

Originally published in *Premiere Magazine*, December 2000, 35–36, 38. Reprinted by permission of Anne Thompson.

Ever since he saw *2001: A Space Odyssey* at age fourteen, James Cameron has been in love with film, space, and technology. Like that of the late Stanley Kubrick, Cameron's moviemaking has been notable for its technological innovations, from the morphing shots in *The Abyss* and *Terminator 2: Judgment Day* to the computer-generated passengers on board the *Titanic*. Since accepting the 1997 Oscars for best director and best picture, he has kept busy preparing myriad projects for Lightstorm Entertainment, the production company he runs with partners Rae Sanchini and *Titanic* producer Jon Landau. Lightstorm successfully launched its first TV series, *Dark Angel*, this fall and will continue its long-term deal with Twentieth Century Fox. Several movies are in the offing, including a sequel to *True Lies*, the ambitious effects film *Brother Termite*, and Steven Soderbergh's adaptation of *Solaris*. But mostly, Cameron has been keeping up with *Scientific American* (his subscription goes back twenty-eight years) and attending meetings of the Mars Society, the Caltech Mars Society, and the MIT Mars Society. What this man really wants is for someone to send him into space.

Premiere: As far as space travel goes, we're nowhere near where Stanley Kubrick showed us to be in *2001*.
A: *2001* was the defining moment for me. It got me off my ass and started me thinking about actually making films, because I was interested in how those images were created. It also represented the evolution of humanity from a terrestrial to a space-faring civilization. So here we are (almost) in the year 2005 and we haven't done that yet. Last year, it was

the thirtieth anniversary of the *Apollo II* moon landing. Like, why aren't we on Mars? Why aren't we farther?

Q: How far away is the first manned mission to Mars from being realized?
A: Twelve to fifteen years. The Apollo project, from the moment that [President John F.] Kennedy pushed the button and said, "We're going," to the time they landed, was eight years. If you think of it in presidential terms, you get two terms, eight years. If you can't do it in eight years, it's probably not going to happen.

Q: When will you start filming your Mars TV miniseries?
A: Hopefully before we actually go! [*Laughs*] It's turned out to be a very sneaky project from a writing standpoint. Al Reinert (*Apollo 13*, *From the Earth to the Moon*) and I are working on it, but I've taken the reins back to do my own pass, and I've decided to complete a novel first, based on this material, because I just need to know what my priorities are in terms of character. Meanwhile, we're doing fifty thousand other things. I had [hope] going in on *Dark Angel* that I could do TV and have enough involvement to justify my existence and yet not get dragged into the vortex that would prevent me from doing other stuff, and I think we've struck that balance nicely.

Q: You have been researching space travel in the U.S. and Russia?
A: I'm working on so many space projects. [The Mars project] is a fictional miniseries with tendrils in many media. The current plan is to do it as both a TV miniseries and a 3-D IMAX movie. We're also doing a live-streaming website, which we'll treat as a real mission, with actors who stay in character and talk over a webcam. I'm involved with a company that is creating streaming media from extreme environments. We're also developing a tiny 3-D camera system [for] the IMAX project that we hope to see flown in space. We're building complex sets. Space travel is a subject I find immensely fascinating.

Q: Did you do research at NASA?
A: I did research for one year, and having met with NASA scientists, technicians, and astronauts, that led to commercial space ventures and other people who have wanted me to get involved with them.

Q: Have you explored whether it would be possible for you to go into space yourself?

A: I think everybody who works in the space arena would love to go. [*Laughs*] Except that they can't. I talked to some people when I was in Russia doing research for *Mars*. I was there flying in the *Ilyushin 76*, what we call the "vomit comet," an aircraft that I was hoping to be able to shoot on the *Mars* film in the same way that they used a smaller jet here in the States on *Apollo 13*. I wanted to use the Russian one because I can put a bigger set in it, about twice the size.

Q: So you're going to use it?
A: Totally. So we flew that and got a taste of zero G [gravity]. I had a lot of Russian friends in the underwater research community, the guys who operate the Mir submersible.

Q: Which, coincidentally, has the same name as the orbiting space complex, Mir. How's your Russian?
A: Terrible! No Russian. I went to Star City, where they do the training for cosmonauts. I don't think we'd go to Mars without the Russians. There are only two countries in the world that have manned space launch capabilities—the U.S. and Russia—and they're going to have to work together to go to Mars. I have a number of important Russian characters in my Mars story, so I wanted to see what the Russian cosmonaut environment was like. It's very different from the U.S. I've been through Johnson Space Center and hung with the American astronauts and done some time in the space shuttle simulator and gotten a feel for how that whole thing works politically and bureaucratically, from a training standpoint. I wanted to walk in the shoes of the Russian cosmonauts a bit.

Q: When you were in Russia, did you check out whether you were physically fit for space travel?
A: I wanted to ride the centrifuge because I thought that would be a fun experience, to simulate a launch, and NASA doesn't take people off the street and let them ride the centrifuge. [*Laughs*] But you can pay to do it in Russia. So I did, and they said, "Yeah, you'd be fine."

Q: How much does it cost?
A: Ahhh, well, I'm not going to go into it. I'm actually working on that chapter right now, which is, there are two high-G events that take place in a Mars mission. One is when you launch from Earth—that's less interesting. The really interesting one is when you arrive at Mars, and the way that they're planning on doing it is, you come screaming into the

atmosphere and you pull, like, seven or eight Gs in order to slow down from interplanetary speed, so that you can then land on the planet. You do that after six months in weightlessness, so your body just feels like it's being crushed out of existence. So I wanted to feel what that feels like.

Q: What did it feel like? How long were you in there?
A: Like you're being crushed out of existence. [*Laughs*] You train for a day, and they do twenty-four-hour heart monitoring to make sure that [your heart's] not going to quit when you go into centrifuge, to make sure you can pull the Gs. Then you do two spaced-out centrifuge runs in the space of, like, an hour. The runs themselves only last a couple of minutes. But a sustained period of time, even a short period of time like that at eight Gs, is enough to make you feel it.

Q: Well, how many civilians do you think have actually gone through this sort of thing?
A: Well, none, unless they were astronaut candidates.

Q: So was it pretty painful?
A: Oh, no, it was fun!

Q: It was fun? Wasn't it dangerous?
A: Potentially dangerous. I love extreme stuff! [*Laughs*] I ride dirt bikes and I scuba dive. I like to play hard and work hard. Let me put it this way, I own a jet ranger helicopter, which I'm learning to fly, which weighs seventeen hundred pounds. When I was pulling eight Gs, I weighed 5,550 pounds—I weighed as much as my helicopter, almost. You feel like it's just going to stop your heart, but it turns out that the human body is a pretty tenacious machine and can adapt to stuff like that.

Q: Was it more dangerous when you went down two and a half miles below sea level to the *Titanic*?
A: The subs have two-inch-thick steel walls that hold the pressure out. The basic dangers in that kind of deep submergence are getting trapped on the bottom and dying of life-support failure, which usually means you freeze to death; having a failure of what they call a "man sphere," that's the bubble that you're in—if that fails, you'll implode and you'll be dead before you know it, so that's probably even more merciful. If a view port fails, you have the same issue. You can have a failure of one

of the pieces of equipment that's in a pressure housing outside the sub. Like, if our big movie camera had imploded, which was a distinct possibility, the sympathetic implosion of the man sphere would have followed by a few milliseconds. Because it's literally like a depth charge going off right next to you.

Q: Eew! How many times did you go down?
A: Twelve.

Q: Was that the most dangerous thing you've ever done?
A: Oh, by far, not! [*Laughs*] You never know how close those bullets are going by your head [in the movies]. In terms of all the things that are happening with explosions, and hanging out on helicopters, and riding around on insert cars. Plus, when I'm not filming, I'm riding motorcycles and every other wacky thing I can think of.

Q: So, assuming that you're achingly healthy for age forty-six, would you try to pay the Russians to let you go up into space?
A: No, ahhh, well. Here's the thing: I'm a supporter of commercial space ventures and the subcategory of space tourism. I personally don't think space tourism is how we're going to get to Mars or get back into exploring the solar system and ever get to the stars. I certainly wouldn't want to join the elite ranks of rich bozos who just do it for a thrill. However, if I could figure out a good, compelling film that needed to be made, and the money was there, I'd be more than happy to go do that film. I told [NASA administrator] Dan Goldin, "If you want somebody to tell the story of the international space station, sign me up."

Q: But couldn't you shoot footage if you went up there for your Mars miniseries or IMAX movie?
A: To actually shoot fictional material in space is not feasible. Certainly not within the Mir station, because it can only accommodate three people, and two of them need to be cosmonauts. So you have room either for an actor or for a crew person, but you don't have room for both, so you really couldn't do fiction—it wouldn't work. But I think the idea that people are planning to go to Mir is pretty cool. I've been a supporter of the Mir station for years, even though it's been kind of dirtied in the American media. I've always felt like, "Okay, show us your space complex before you start criticizing somebody else's."

Q: You're pursuing space research, but if there's a way to go up later, you wouldn't rule it out?

A: I would go as a filmmaker, not as a tourist. If Dan Goldin called me up and said, "Hey, we would love to have you document our great effort creating this living, working environment for people in space," I would go in a heartbeat. If the Russians called me up and said, "We want you to go to Mir to document what we're doing," I would go in a heartbeat. Literally, I wouldn't even think twice about it, because a filmmaker has never been in space! They send astronauts and teach them to use cameras. Even though I have a number of astronaut friends whom I respect enormously, it's a bit like giving somebody word-processing software and trying to teach them to write a novel. It doesn't work that way. You're better off teaching a novelist who writes by hand to use the word-processing software. All of the things that astronauts are best at are actually counter-indicators for being wild, passionate, crazy, illogical artists. And I think we need wild, passionate, crazy, illogical artists to go into space and try to communicate their experience back to the 6 billion people who can't go. They've shown us the images, but they haven't given us a taste of the experience.

James Cameron: The Second Coming

Jenny Cooney Carrillo/2002

From *Dreamwatch*, January 2002, issue 87. Reprinted by permission of Jenny Cooney Carrillo.

James Cameron's *Dark Angel* has, in the course of its first year, established itself as a challenger to the crown of top SF TV show. As the second season begins, Jenny Cooney Carrillo meets the *Titanic* ego who is out to build a better *Angel*.

Everything that James Cameron touches seems to turn to gold. In his long and established career he has brought movies to audiences that have become hugely successful and starred some of the biggest names in Hollywood. After his Oscar win for *Titanic*, Cameron declared he was "King of the World." Though he may not be king, he is definitely Hollywood royalty and his success continues with his first foray into television, *Dark Angel*.

The science fiction drama he created, centering around the genetically altered Max (Jessica Alba), has become an instant hit, earning a Golden Globe nomination for his leading lady in its first season. Busy with movies and television and a new baby with his wife Suzy Amis, you'd think the writer/producer/director would slow down and enjoy his success. But that's not in his nature.

Q: What interested you in making the switch from movies to television?
A: When you make a film there's a long period of time where you're writing and planning. It's basically office work and it's boring, quite frankly. When you're making television, you're in production all the time. You are constantly out there every single day making film. And even though I'm not on the set every day actually doing the shots, there's an energy to it, it keeps the creative wheels turning.

It's also that television is an art of compromise. You have an image in your head and you're not going to be able to achieve it, so for a perfectionist like me it takes away the need for perfection and allows me to concentrate on the craft of writing, making good scenes on the page, casting good actors, and the things that are ultimately the strongest aspects of the show.

A lot of filmmakers, myself included, get very involved in the music and the sound mix and they need every sound and visual effect to be perfect, but in the end that's not how films really work. Films work in the hearts and minds of the audience based on whether or not they like the characters and the storyline or situation. In television you have all of that every single day of the year while you're shooting so it's a good way to keep these skills current. I find it more satisfying in a way.

Q: You are involved with a number of projects, from space and underwater exploration to TV to film to science. How do you keep it all straight?
A: It's madness, plus I have a new baby at home! It's a juggling act and the key is to have good teams on each one of those activities that are self-sufficient when I'm not there and yet can mesh with me creatively when I am there. They need to know how to reach out and get what it is they need at the right time and in the right way.

I have video teleconference capability at my house and at my offices so I spend a lot of time video teleconferencing, which is almost like being there but is much more effective in terms of time management It is all an issue of time management, which is a curse when you are interested in so many different things like I am. You only have so much time on this planet, so you have to make it count.

Q: The season finale of *Dark Angel* was quite surprising. In what direction will you be taking the show this season?
A: I can tell you some broad stroke stuff. We looked at what we believed worked best in the first season and what didn't and we realized that we have a good central relationship. We have a fabulous central character and so we're going to keep all the things that we think are good about the series.

We are probably going to push it more into science fiction on the basis that there were certain shows in the first season that didn't necessarily have to be told in a future world. We want to maintain the kind of exoticism that we reached about 50 per cent of the time in the first season. We want to increase that percentage a little bit and I think that we have addressed that issue by bringing some new writers to the staff that have a little bit of a science fiction background. We always set out to do a science fiction show that was more of a drama and had less robots and spaceships flying around.

We succeeded in the first season and created our own vocabulary, built the story, but now we are going to bring in more genetically altered kids into Max's world and explore more of that. The changes are not going to be drastic though and we are still maintaining the same style, the same kind of street level hip-hop and the streetwise feel of the show.

Q: How did you develop the part of Original Cindy?
A: Well, we really like the actress Valerie Rae Miller and we have fun writing for her, and I think the direction for her character now that she knows Max's secret is going to be for her to get a bit more actively involved in some of the cases.

At the end of the season we got into a bit of a rut because she knew Max's secret but wasn't actively involved in anything, she was sitting at home talking about Max's problems. She felt a little let down. I think we were all so focused on where we were going with the shows at the end of the season that we lost focus on that storyline.

But now Original Cindy is going to woven into much more of the plotlines, and she won't have the super powers that Max has but she'll be out in front more, put into jeopardy a bit more.

Q: You can probably take some of the credit for the engagement between two of your show's stars, since you cast them together. How do you feel about their off-screen relationship and whether this will impact the show?
A: I think for starters I should be automatic godparent to any children they have [laughs]. It's actually like a genetics project, in a way. We found Jessica and we found Michael, but how can you predict those things? Although the interesting thing is we found Jessica and we had her audition with all these guys and we would watch her reaction to them to see if there was any chemistry, and the chemistry was definitely the best with Michael, so maybe there was a little feedback into that decision-making process.

In terms of how that affects the show, you know the classic problem with a show that has a relationship or a romantic relationship at its core is that you're always in this kind of dynamic equipoise. You don't really want to consummate the relationship. You've got to keep them under tension with each other and you've got to somehow sustain that indefinitely throughout the run of the show so we have to create obstacles.

At the end of the season they expressed to each other how much they love one another, but in the next season you will see some very grave obstacles put in the path to their being together. So in the back of your mind you will know how they really feel, but there will be forces that tear them apart. I can't be more specific than that because the fun is in seeing how it all unfolds.

So I don't think their off-screen romance will be a detriment but instead it will serve to reinforce how they really feel about each other. The reason sometimes love scenes between married couples don't work in films is because you feel as though you are looking into the people's private life. You have to be cognitive of that and you have to write to sort of take advantage of that sort of thing.

We had the problem with *Titanic* of people saying they didn't want to see it because they already knew what the ending was. So we wrote it so that there was information that the viewer brought to the film which actually got the viewer involved in seeing how the film would play out. The trick is to turn things that are kind of like baggage into positives. So that is what we plan to do for the subsequent seasons.

Q: With the size of your involvement in television work and *Dark Angel*, do you have time to plan your next film project?
A: I'm always planning and always writing, developing scripts. I've got a stack of scripts up to my chin that are coming in and we are doing new drafts, revisions. I have four scripts that I am developing for myself right now, and then a number of others that we are developing which I will produce but will not direct. So there is actually a lot of stuff going on.

Q: In the light of some recent films trying to match the success of *Titanic*, what do you think it takes for a film to match that?
A: The only thing I can say is that the next film that does that kind of business is not going to be like *Titanic*. Look at the previous milestones—the closest probably being *E.T.*, and it was a big surprise. Nobody expected it to be that big a hit. It was a film that was made from the heart. It connected with the heart of the audience and there was no sense of Hollywood artifice about that film. It was a very honest film. *Titanic* was also a movie we made from the heart and it connected on that level and it worked. I think it's very difficult to predict phenomenon when an audi-

ence embraces a film like that. You can't clone a certain formula because it worked in the past. It's not going to work.

Q: Obviously you are still interested in technology, but how much of a tech-head are you personally? Is your house filled with gadgets and televisions and computer screens like Batman's den?
A: Yeah, it looks like Batman's den but messier since I don't have Alfred! I would not say that I was super computer savvy. I know how to operate an Avid computer editing system because that's something I needed to know. The workstation I have is where I basically email and text documents, but nothing too sophisticated.

I do enjoy engineering so the development of this deep-sea diving camera that I have worked on for three years has been great. I worked on it with my brother who is really the engineer of the family, but I really enjoy it.

Sound of Silence

John Reading/2002

From *Xpose Magazine*, December 2002, 70–73.

Andrei Tarkovski's original Russian language movie of *Solaris* is one of the classics of sci-fi cinema, but it dates from the age before *Star Wars*—when science fiction didn't necessarily mean action, adventure, and lightsabers. In view of that, you have to wonder how modern audiences will react to Stephen Soderburgh's remake of the classic tale of paranoia and psychological instability aboard a distant space station. It might be in English, but could moviegoers feel let down by the lack of action?

"Did that make *Contact* a bad movie?" comments the remake's producer, self-proclaimed King of the World James Cameron. "I like *Contact*. I liked the ending of the film." However, he admits there can be a problem. "I'll tell you where it goes awry, because I experienced this with *The Abyss*. People knew I had made *Aliens*, and they knew I was making an underwater movie, and it was sold as a science fiction film. We never said that there was a monster, but people wanted there to be one, and people have a hard time dealing with a movie that isn't what they want it to be.

"So the trick to selling this film has been: don't create a preconception, which you're not going to deliver. We haven't sold it as science fiction. It's a science fiction film, but in the old-fashioned literary sense, not in the post–*Star Wars* genre of futuristic imaginative action, which is really neo-myth. Science fiction wasn't always like that. It was about holding up a mirror to the human condition, using the offset to another environment provided by the future, in the same way that Shakespeare is the offset to another environment created by fifteenth century Verona. It allows us to think in sort of metaphorical terms, and dramatic universals. What are people really like in their essence?

"It's a true and proper use of science fiction that we haven't seen for so long that we don't recognize it," the Oscar-winning director insists.

Okay, so *Solaris* is a different sort of science fiction. But it's still being hyped as a James Cameron movie...

"What does that mean?" Cameron snorts. "Is that *Titanic* or is that *Terminator*? Is that *Strange Days* or *The Abyss*? I've tried to be as all over the map as I can be within my own sphere of interests.

"Hopefully it just means that it's like a good movie," he laughs. "Besides, how do you draw a line between Steven and me?" he adds, commenting on *Solaris*'s director Steven Soderburgh. "Stylistically we're really very divergent. Thematically, we happen to be very close together on this film. We had a really great collegial working relationship. He's very open, very collaborative, and I found that to be refreshing because less secure directors tend to hold everything very close. They don't want to show you anything till they've done, and then absolutely done, when you can't do anything. Steven's very open, but that openness comes from security. It comes from confidence."

And what about star George Clooney? Cameron reiterates his earlier point about his own portfolio. "What is a George Clooney movie? *Three Kings*? *Out of Sight*? *The Perfect Storm*? I think he makes very interesting eclectic choices as an actor, and he's pushing himself further afield here, but isn't that what you're supposed to do? What's the point of getting successful if you can't try new stuff? You're not a slave to what you've done before.

"I respect that, because in his case, he's saying: okay, I want something that's really gonna push me. He's got nowhere to hide in this movie. The shot's just him and the wall behind him most of the time. Now, Steven's taken the edge off that with his cutting style, where long scenes will play out where George is not even in the shot. But basically, George has got no place to hide. It's just him. That's a lot of pressure, and he chose this pressure. So I've got to respect people who are always trying to raise the bar on themselves."

Considering that so much of Solaris depends on Clooney's performance rather than special effects, it seems odd that it's such an expensive movie. "Well, basically you have a modestly budgeted film with an expensive director and an expensive star," comments Cameron. "and first of all, $40 million is not an expensive film these days. There's no money wasted. Steven wanted to have time to spend with his actors, but it wasn't a ridiculously long shooting schedule either, fifty-six days or something, and that includes the reshoots."

Often, reshoots mean there's something wrong with a movie, but Cameron explains that wasn't the case here. "The reshoots were planned.

It was a very interesting thing that Steven did, and I think it's a good lesson for filmmakers. Plan to reshoot. There was a million dollars in the budget for additional photography, so the sets were held, Steven went off and cut the picture and then said, 'I think I need a little more of this, a little more of that.' I think that's really healthy and instructive to the rest of us. He knew from the beginning that filmmaking is a journey of discovery as you find out the best way to tell the story."

It isn't as if Cameron needs any lessons in that area. But all the same, we couldn't resist asking what he thought of the "one that got away." *Spider-Man*, the movie he was scheduled to direct until legal disputes delayed production. "Good, good. Sam Raimi is a cool director," Cameron says. "When I heard he was doing it, I thought 'Perfect choice.' I think they used my script as a jumping off point, and I wasn't involved in that process. You know every film has its own life. Sam actually hewed it back closer to the comic, which was probably wise for the fans. Mine was a little more satiric."

James Cameron

Adrian Wootton/2003

From *The Guardian*, April 13, 2003. Copyright Guardian News and Media Ltd 2003. Reprinted by permission.

Following an Imax screening of his *Ghosts of the Abyss*, Iron Jim Cameron (aka "The King of the World") took to the stage to discuss the three Ts (technology, Terminators, and the *Titanic*) with Adrian Wootton.

Adrian Wootton: We're going to talk about *Ghosts of the Abyss* and the audience will get a chance to ask some questions about it, but before that, I'd like to ask you a bit about the beginning, actually; to talk to you about your start in the industry. I'm particularly interested in the fact that, after you got your first short film made in the 1970s, you went to work for the legendary, independent, low-budget exploitation cinema producer Roger Corman, and had an interesting experience working for him. What did working with Corman teach you?

James Cameron: Roger wrote a book called *How I Made 100 Films and Never Lost a Dime*, and the reason was because he never spent the dime in the first place. He learnt to improvise and to flourish, as they say in the Centcomm briefings, in a highly fluid situation, working on a low-budget film. We'd make a film in twenty-one days and the budget was $200,000. So it's true guerrilla filmmaking. We learnt how to make sets with McDonalds trays, literally stapling them on to walls and spray-painting them with lacquer to make them look like spaceships. It really was an opportunity to see how production actually works—you can read all the books about film-making, all the articles in *American Cinematographer* and that sort of thing, but you have to really see how it works on a day-to-day basis, and how to pace your energy so that you can survive the film, which was a lesson that took me a long time to learn.

AW: Did that actually give you the framework so that you felt comfortable, going into *The Terminator*, that you knew what you were doing?

JC: I was petrified at the start of *Terminator*. First of all, I was working with a star, at least I thought of him as a star at the time. Arnold came out of it even more a star. But I think because I had written it, I always had a beacon because I knew the characters and so I always knew what to say to the actors, and ultimately that's what it's all about. Sure, you've got to set the cameras, and understand visually the film you're making, but I had done a lot of storyboarding—that was the picture I was best prepared for, out of all my films. Because it was bought by Hemdale, then it went into hiatus for a year when nothing was happening, and I had no other job during that year—I was kind of starving—and I couldn't move on to another directing job until I'd filmed that. So I just storyboarded everything. I was utterly prepared for that film, which was how we were able to make it relatively cheaply.

AW: Just carrying on with *Terminator*. You mentioned Arnold Schwarzenegger, and obviously you've had a long working relationship with him. What qualities did you see in him, that obviously some other people hadn't seen, that attracted you to him?

JC: I think that people basically saw him as a muscle guy. I had lunch with him after an initial meeting to talk about *Terminator*, and that meeting had been thrust upon me. He hadn't really sprung to mind at that point. The entire time that we were talking over lunch, I was looking at his face—for me it was about the potential iconography of his face and his manner and bearing. It was about projecting a character and not just the physicality. I mean certainly it was a physical character but if you look at the film, it's not just about the way he moves. I mean he was fully clothed in about 99 percent of screen time. I guess I saw an intensity that I liked for the character, but I certainly didn't foresee this working relationship that we've had for a couple of decades now.

AW: I've got to ask this question, so let's get it out of the way now . . .

JC: *Terminator 3*. I went from driving a truck to becoming a movie director, with a little time working with Roger Corman in between. When I wrote *The Terminator*, I sold the rights at that time—that was my shot to get the film made. So I've never owned the rights in the time that the franchise has been developed. I was fortunate enough to get a chance to direct the second film and do so on my own creative terms, which was good. But that was in 1991 and I've felt like it was time to move on.

The primary reason for making a third one was financial, and that didn't strike me as organic enough a reason to be making a film. I've got a lot of original films I want to make, I'm interested in exploring new technology and doing these kind of expedition projects, a lot of things which interested me at that time. Arnold held on, hoping that I would do the film, and finally I just said, "Look, stop being so loyal, just go charge them a lot of money and go make the movie." And that's exactly what he did.

AW: Which works out well for him.

JC: Yeah, it worked out well for him. I'm the one who has to answer all the questions.

AW: But you've mentioned the technology point, and I was thinking of *Terminator* and the expression that actually comes from the name of a bar in *Terminator*: tech noir. It's obviously in *Ghosts of the Abyss*, and in fact in every movie you've made since *Terminator*. You seem to be consistently not only exploring the impact of technology but also, to make the films, you're always developing, sometimes in association with your brother, you're consistently challenging technological limits. I wonder about the contradiction in that. You're clearly very ambivalent about the way that technology is used but on the other hand, you're one of the most technophile directors who's ever lived.

JC: Well, I see our potential destruction and the potential salvation as human beings coming from technology and how we use it, how we master it and how we prevent it from mastering us. *Titanic* was as much about that theme as the *Terminator* films, and in *Aliens*, it's the reliance on technology that defeats the marines, but it's a technology being used properly that allows Sigourney's character to prevail at the end. And *Titanic* is all about technology, metaphorically as well as on a literal level, because the world was being transformed by the technology at that time. And people were rescued from the *Titanic* because of wireless technology, and because of the advances that had been made only in the year or so before the ship sank that allowed them to call for help when they were lost at sea in the middle of the North Atlantic. So I think it's an interesting theme, one that's always been fascinating for me, and maybe it's because I have a kind of engineering background—even though it's my brother Mike who's the engineer, I'm not; and we work with many talented engineers to develop whatever we need. It's also about trying to do things which people hadn't done before, technically, like the computer graphics stuff. *T2* was a real turning point in terms of computer graphics in doing human-style, organic, fluid animation and that led directly to *Jurassic Park* which then went up another quantum level in terms of doing organically textured creatures, and it's really progressed from that.

AW: And how's your relationship with your brother, because you've been building things together obviously since you were kids. Is there a lot of sibling rivalry?

JC: Yeah, we're brothers. He's the youngest brother, so he's always got to try to impress. And we're both sort of, what's the word used here? Boffins. We're in touch with our inner nerd when it comes to technical systems. And certainly *The Abyss* was a highly technical film to physically do. We were certainly not faking anything—we weren't on a soundstage where we could fix things later with a little sleight of hand movie magic, it wasn't about that. For me, doing the exploration was at least as interesting, if not more interesting, than the actual making of the film. So I was wearing two hats there, and I'm not sure that directing was my primary focus on that film. Although when the expedition was all done and paid for by the film, I then had to complete the film.

AW: People today are fond of asking you why you went back to the *Titanic*, but I've read that one of the initial focuses of the movie, *Titanic*, was precisely because you did want to dive the wreck; that you started by being interested in the wreck and the movie kind of followed.

JC: I can be more blunt than that: I was trying to figure out a way to dive the *Titanic* wreck and the only tools at my disposal were that I could tell a major studio that I would make a movie about it if they would fund the expedition. Really, nothing has changed. Both films were originated the same way. The first time it was essentially for the thrill and wonder of going to that place and photographing. For me as a director, the going to a place and the direct experience of it is less important than the photographic experience. Otherwise, it's a tree falling in the forest. I have to go shoot it, shooting it is the experience for me.

AW: That's interesting because it seems to suggest that you're cast, in one sense at least, in quite an old-fashioned mold. You're constantly in an innovative position as the director, with the technology and all that, but you also appear to be a newly incarnated version of John Huston, in that you want to go out hunting, so you make a film that allows you to fulfill your leisure pursuits.

JC: Did he do that?

AW: Yes. But the other thing I wanted to talk to you about in terms of your career as a director, a certain mythology has grown up about how intense and demanding you are, and your nickname . . .
JC: Which one?

AW: I was just going to stick to Iron Jim.
JC: That's actually not a nickname—it was the title of an article.

AW: Do you recognize that you are kind of that . . . Do you think you have to be a tough guy to make the films that you make?
JC: All directors are. A director's job is to make something happen and it doesn't happen by itself. So you wheedle, you cajole, you flatter people, you tell them what needs to be done. And if you don't bring a passion and an intensity to it, you shouldn't be doing it. Also, by the way, you won't prevail. It's just that some directors are better at hiding it, or they may be more patient than I am. But I think that's part of the territory. But you know, with most of the types of stuff that I do, there are safety issues. Some of the stuff you saw at the end of *Titanic*, people can get hurt doing that, and so things have to go a certain way, there's a certain precision that's required, procedural even. And that comes from the top, it's very much an old-style, kind of tribal hierarchy on a film set. The director sets the pace and sets the tone and I do challenge the crew to do the best work and be as safe as possible. But I think that gets misinterpreted as unnecessary harshness because people who aren't there and don't really understand what's going on . . . I've always had actors who want to come back and work with me over and over because they know that I'm going to push them to do their best work. We had a lot of fun doing *Ghosts of the Abyss*. Feature films tend not to be as fun because there's no kind of underlying experience other than the making of the film itself, whereas with *Ghosts*, we were doing something really cool, and by the way, were filming it as we went along, which is fundamentally different. For the first time in my life I was working in a theatre of operations where the filming was secondary, which is an interesting concept—it's hard for a filmmaker to adjust to that.

AW: Talking about this, there's a sense that you've deliberately, since the phenomenal success of *Titanic*, not made another feature film and you have been working on documentary projects—we'll talk about *Bismarck* as well in a second. But was that because after *Titanic* you felt that your whole life and career had changed? It must have changed immeasurably because of the success of it . . .

JC: No, I didn't really think of it that way. I just assumed that the next time I had an idea good enough to want to take me away from my family—my new family at that time—for up to a year, that I would be happy to do it. I've been writing all sorts of things: I did forty-four hours of the *Dark Angel* TV series, and that was nice because I didn't have to be away from home, I could just go on the set for a few days at the most. I had just been through a divorce, I had a young daughter, and I had personal reasons why I didn't feel like I wanted to be away. And you can be away whether you're in town or not, you can be away mentally. I know I'm not the kind of person who can parallel process several different things; I'm a serial processor—I work on this and when it's done I work on something else. So if you have enough self knowledge to know that there is going to be a sacrifice somewhere else . . . I didn't need to, I certainly didn't need to do it financially.

And I'd always given myself the goal of getting to a certain point where I could put that on pause and explore a lot of the other things that I might have wanted to do as careers before I went into filmmaking. I think there's a sense in Hollywood, and in filmmaking in general, that it's almost a self-defining reality, that people only reference the interior of that particular bubble and nothing outside of it is significant. I don't see the world that way, I'm very involved with NASA, with the space program, with the science community, with the oceanographic community. And I enjoy all that a great deal. I'm going to have to push the pause button on a lot of that when I make my next film, but now, the time is right. Later this year, we'll be in prep on it and we'll start shooting probably next January. And we're hoping to use the same 3D camera system and I'll be encouraging the studio, 20th Century Fox, to facilitate enough theatres in 3D—I've asked them for a thousand. None of them will be Imax because Imax 3D can't support a feature length; this (fifty-nine minutes) is the longest we could do. In the U.S. right now, this film is on release and it's on fifty Imax 3D screens, but it's also on fifty 35mm 3D screens that were created just for this film, so if we can do that for a $12m documentary, we can certainly do more for a ahem million dollar feature. It's a very strange thing about this film, I've done a lot of press in the U.S. for it and I've never been asked about the budget, which seems to be the most obvious question. I guess because it's a documentary, so they don't care, there's no story in it—it's not going to set any records. It could be the most expensive Imax movie ever made—it's not, it's not—but it could have been. You could at least ask the question.

AW: Yes, in the context of your press reputation with budgets, you would have thought that everyone would have asked you that question.
JC: Yeah, I was disappointed.

AW: Let's talk about *Ghosts of the Abyss*. Obviously you wanted to have this expedition, but why did you decide to do it as an Imax 3D? What were the challenges, when you decided to do the expedition and make the film, that you set yourself to overcome to make it?
JC: The project kind of evolved. We were on two completely unrelated development tracks, technically. One was that we were developing this digital 3D system—and I was developing it for a completely different project and it wasn't even an oceanographic project—and we were working out the camera technology with Sony; the integration of the system, the rig and the way it works and all that, all the engineering was done in the U.S. but the core camera technology was done by Sony. They basically had to repackage their existing high-definition cameras into a different physical configuration so that they could fit side by side. And you can see it briefly going into the camera housing in the film, which is those two little grey boxes—they don't look like much, but they're pretty amazing on the inside. And that took a couple of years to do. And that camera technology was just coming out of the laboratory for the first time and we were looking around for a subject. And at the same time, the remotely operated vehicles were getting completed, and we had started building those about three and a half years earlier, with the general idea that at some point we would go back and explore the interior of *Titanic*. We knew we were going to do it but we hadn't worked out how we were going to pay for it—maybe we could raise money for it by doing a TV special or do it in conjunction with a rerelease of the movie or something like that. Just vague plans. And then it occurred to me that if we were going to go back to the wreck, we should do it once and do it right and film it at the highest possible level at the time, which at that moment I believed was our 3D digital camera system. So then we had to overcome the technical hurdles of putting it into a housing which could withstand the depth of *Titanic*, where the pressure is 5300 pounds per square inch or something like that. So there was about five months of engineering required just to build that housing, to take the camera down, to work out the optics to shoot stereo through this big acrylic dome port, which you briefly see. I think it's about 1.4m pounds of pressure just on that piece of optical acrylic, and you don't want that thing to fail. Its, what they call the implodable volume inside the titanium cylinder, is great enough

that at that depth when it failed it would fail catastrophically. And the shockwave produced would destroy the submersible with us in it, so the housing had to be built as it was itself a manned submersible; it had to be built to the same specifications, tested in pressure chambers, blah, blah, blah. We had to go through all that. Anyway, it just happened that these two completely different technologies just came together at the same time. And I also anticipated the number one question that I would be asked on the press tour, "why did you go back to *Titanic*?"—which really is a thinly veiled way of saying "why don't you get a life and move on?" I actually anticipated that, and so *Ghosts of the Abyss* was going to be about *Titanic* and *Bismarck*, and it was going to be a few dives at both ships, as more of an overview, little bit of a look inside of both ships. And then, because of the September 11 attacks, we were not able to go to the *Bismarck* leg of the expedition. But we had so much great footage and there was so much story there about *Titanic* that we would just go back to *Titanic* which was within our scope to do.

AW: But you did then do [*Expedition: Bismarck*], in May last year, an almost companion piece on *Titanic* for the Discovery channel.
JC: That was shot for TV only, but to show you how cool these digital cameras are, we shot that using the same cameras. We shot the *Bismarck* piece using the same 3D cameras that we shot this Imax film with, but we shot it for TV, which is insane—you never shoot Imax for TV, nobody would ever do that, except we did it on a very cost-effective budget. We did a two-hour special for a little under $4m, with all those visual effects and everything else. It proved the camera system is fairly versatile; it's like a holy grail camera—you can shoot with that camera and release it in Imax 3D, 35mm 3D, digital 3D. You can break off one stream and take that to video, and take the other to broadcast.

AW: Apart from the technological challenge, I was also thinking about the physical challenges. You know, those twelve-hour dives. You've got this technology but then you're actually going down for three hours to get your two . . .
JC: Yeah, you basically freefall through black water for about two hours, then you reach the bottom and you acquire the wreck on sonar and move horizontally to get closer to the wreck. But the total dive—a short dive would be about twelve hours, a long one would be sixteen to eighteen hours.

AW: What's the physical impact of that? Do you have to train for it?
JC: It's just really cramped—it's like being wedged into the seat of a Volkswagon for eighteen hours. Bill [Paxton] mostly dove in Mir 2, which didn't have all the camera equipment inside.

AW: Yeah, he had more room.
JC: But on my side of the sub, we've got all the monitors and all the equipment and switches and power boards and I'm just [squirming] for eighteen hours.

AW: I think Bill is a real asset to the film.
JC: I notice there's a real consistency in his character from *Aliens* through to this.

AW: He's terrified all the time. [laughs]
JC: People can't maintain that level of consistency all the time.

AW: But he is like the talisman in your work—he's been in a whole number of your films.
JC: Yeah, he was *True Lies*, playing a character called Simon, who was also scared. [laughs] But I gotta give him credit. It's not apparent in the film but he made four dives; after the first dive, he was really terrified. So I have more respect for someone who conquers their apprehension and goes back; and he also learnt what he had to learn in order to be a contributing member of the dive crew. He handled the communications, you saw him using the navigator software to help us navigate through the wreck. He even operated the ROV and the 3D camera at one point.

AW: I'm sure the audience would agree with me that the real wonder of *Ghosts of the Abyss* is not only the lighting of the wreck, but the wonder of when you get inside and you go into the staterooms. How much did you think you were going to find? Were you expecting to get so much that was so spectacular?
JC: I think we expected little pockets of interesting individual artifacts. I don't think we were expecting to find the complete preservation that we found in some areas. In my mind, it's complete preservation—I see all the woodwork. Sometimes it's a little hard to see in the video that the ROV sends back but the reception room, for example, all of that wood paneling was intact from one end of the room to the other and nobody expected that to be the case. When Robert Ballard first explored the

wreck in his submersible dives in 1986, he sent his Jason Jr vehicle down to the grand staircase and looked in—they couldn't get inside—and their conclusion was that it was all just rusting steel; that all the wood had been destroyed by some kind of wood-boring organisms. Why there are wood-boring organisms twelve thousand feet down in the middle of the Atlantic, I don't know, but they're there, and they had eaten most of the decking and most of the wood around the grand staircase. But it turned out that if you went in deep inside the ship, there's no current flow, so there's no nutrients and nothing to support biological activity at that level and everything's still very well preserved.

So it's a question of building this very small, very nimble vehicle that could move into these tightly enclosed spaces without disturbing it because, as you can appreciate, with the buildup of silt over ninety-one years, the stuff is as fine as cigarette ash and if you breathed on it with the thrusters, it would just stir up and you wouldn't be able to shoot anything. So, previous attempts to send ROVs into the wreck hadn't worked because the ROVs hadn't been designed specifically to do that task, but the two ugly little robots that we built are actually very, very sophisticated designs based on their doing exactly what they were there to do.

AW: You've made these two films, *Ghosts of the Abyss*, and the *Bismarck* piece for television. Are there going to be more James Cameron documentaries—not necessarily in this vein but are you going to use that technology to make more documentary material in the near future?
JC: We're about halfway through photography right now, we started last summer, out in the Atlantic. And we're going to complete this summer in the Atlantic and the Pacific, diving these hydrothermal vent sites, which are really quite spectacular. They're about one to two miles down along the mid-Atlantic ridge and east Pacific rise, and they're geological formations caused by essentially water erupting out of the bowels of the earth at super, super high temperatures, hot enough to melt lead, literally. So you have to be quite careful in photographing these things or you'll melt your submarine. But they're surrounded by communities of animals that look like they've come from another planet. The most truly amazing thing that I've ever seen with my own eyes and we're shooting it in 3D, and that's going to have a very different feel than *Ghosts of the Abyss* but it will be released in Imax and it's really making the connection between innerspace exploration and outerspace exploration.

Because there are a lot of biologists and astrobiologists who feel that these animal communities represent what we're very likely to find on other places like Mars and Europa—a moon of Jupiter which is covered by ice but has a liquid ocean which is bigger than the Earth's oceans combined. And that's within our solar system, it's within reach. In terms of finding extraterrestrial life, it's probably going to be that type of ecosystem, not the kind of ecosystem that we've experienced. So it's sort of a combined science fiction, natural history experience in 3D, built around the diving as well.

AW: In terms of *Ghosts of the Abyss* and *Titanic*, people have said that you've probably dived the wreck of *Titanic* more than anybody else now, one of the few people who've dived it on multiple occasions.
JC: The Mir pilots, the two guys you see in the film, they've dived it more than I have. But I think I've dived it more than anybody who's not a Mir pilot.

AW: Is this then the swan song of your love affair with *Titanic*? Do you feel that with *Ghosts of the Abyss* you've completed a particular obsession about that wreck?
JC: Yeah, I think so, but I think, as Bill says it at the end, "You leave *Titanic* but it never leaves you." I feel that once you become attached to an event that's captured your interest and in which you become kind of an expert, you're always associated with it. I'm not sure I'll ever go back to *Titanic* on an expedition, unless we needed some more shots for a feature film or something, but I can't see that right now. But there are lots of other really, really interesting deep-ocean subjects that I do want to be filming. So I see a sort of bifurcated career path at this point, still doing the big mainstream entertainment films and alternate that with seasons of expedition films.

AW: Are you excited about going back to doing a mainstream entertainment film?
JC: Yeah, sure, because we'll be doing something really hard. I'm only interested in it if it's really hard, like impossible, like there's no way that you can do it, no way you could survive and you're doomed going in. That's interesting.
[Laughter]

AW: Will this be pushing the digital technology barriers further forward? For instance, among the many announced projects associated with you, there was a project called *Avatar*, which was about synth actors or complete digital performance.
JC: This will be in that vein, but not quite as aggressive as *Avatar*. But it

will involve some computer-generated characters, and that will be challenging. I think we're on the cusp of being able to do that, and certainly *The Two Towers* proves that that can be done pretty effectively and in an entertaining manner. The trick to it is it needs to be actor-driven, it can't be keyframe animation. It might be a CG character that you see on screen, but there has to be the nuances of an actor's human responses behind it and done through performance capture and motion capture.

James Cameron—Part Two

Question 1: Congratulations, it's a fabulous film. I know you were quite interested in the Imax film, *Titanica*, and considering your engineering background, did you not consider building a 1570 3D camera that was more sophisticated than the old Imax ones? Did you not consider doing it in on film rather than digitally?

James Cameron: We never considered doing this on film. We had such a hard time making a 35mm camera that could be deployed outside a submersible. You've got to remember that *Titanica* was shot by taking a 2D Imax camera inside the submersible and essentially using the submersible as the camera housing, which is just terribly, terribly limiting because it's essentially an eighteen-ton, twenty-five-foot long camera housing that can't look up or down, has to stay level and can only sort of turn, go forward and back. You're not operating the camera—a Russian submersible pilot is operating the camera, because you can only lock the camera into the U-port. So, on our 1995 expedition, we decided that we had to mount the camera externally, put it on a pan-and-tilt mechanism so that we could look down and up and all those shots looking up at the hull, at the bow, emphasizing the scale of the ship, those were created by having the ability to pan-and-tilt.

Putting a 35mm camera—a single eye, a monocular 35mm camera—with a twelve-minute film load outside the submersible was a six-month engineering problem, to build the titanium housing and develop the optics for that. And it ran for twelve minutes. With the digital camera, we were able to shoot six to ten hours of footage per dive. So you can appreciate that if you have a camera which runs for twelve minutes and you make a twelve-hour dive, you're just going to squirt the film off in just a second. And that's a huge limitation. I believe it's probably impossible to build a 1570 camera that could be operated outside the submersible, and I wasn't satisfied with the paradigm of shooting through the port from the inside. And again, as I said before, the high definition 3D camera was developed for a completely other project and we just realized that applying it to this environment would work really well.

Believe me, with the engineering hurdles involved just in adapting the HD camera to function outside the submersible, I'm not going to shoot on film anymore, it just seems so obsolete to me. I look at the stuff I shot on film, compared back to back and on the same screen size, with HD footage, and there's just no comparison. There are qualitative differences, and we'll have to learn to master that. I love 1570 projection, and for those of you who are not Imax-savvy, 1570 means 70mm film, is perforations of the film, which is a single frame of an Imax film and the Imax film runs horizontally through the projector. It's quite a remarkable system and to do it in 3D, they essentially have two projectors mounted one above the other. So there's this enormous amount of film. Probably a third of a ton of film screaming through the projector up there in the projector booth just to show what they showed here. And eventually they'll be able to do that digitally as well; they have the means now, it's just the question of the expenses of installing it

Q2: Apart from contractual obligations, what's the thing that tips you over into doing a project? And secondly, are you going to go into space?
JC: Well, I've never made a movie for contractual obligations. The contract may determine who I make the film for, but not what film it is. Every film has its own origin—*Terminator* I wrote as something that I thought they might let me direct, so it was written for the streets of Los Angeles, to be shot low-budget with very few visual effects but enough to make it cool. *Aliens*, I just liked *Alien*, so when I got the opportunity to do the sequel, I just didn't think about it.

AW: Considering that Ridley Scott had made a really terrific movie . . .
JC: You think?
[Laughter]

AW: . . . you were setting yourself a major, major challenge.
JC: It was like, from a logic standpoint, it was all downside for me to do *Aliens*. And I had people, some pretty well respected people in Hollywood say: "This is career suicide, don't do it. If your film is good, they'll attribute it to the first film, and if your film is bad, it'll always be negatively compared to the first film." So there's absolutely no logic to it, but

I thought it would be cool so I did it. That's why you make a film, because you like it and you want to see it. You see it in your head and you want to see it on screen and there's only one way to make that happen. You can't get someone else to make it for you. Certainly, I've produced a few films now and I've learned that it's their film—you become a facilitator, a colleague, a sounding board, a partner to a certain extent, but it's their film, not yours. So if I want to see it, I have to go do it myself.

As for space, this has been widely rumored and with some substance—we did explore the possibility; we got partway down the path of negotiating with the Russian space agency and Energiya, the privatized corporation that actually provides all of Russia's manned space support activities and hardware. So if you want to go to space, you go to Energiya, because they're the ones who fly the Soyuz missions. And also working with NASA to do a coordinated effort. It started off as an idea to make a 3D film of the Mir space station, which shows you how far back we're going now. We got partway down that path, then the Russians ran out of money and they had to de-orbit Mir, and we had a one-year period where we tried to re-engineer it to see if we could at the international space station, which initially seemed impossible. But it turned out that NASA was actually looking for ways to support commercial activity at the space station—that's why it was built originally. So I went to them and said: "Look, a film can be a commercial activity. It doesn't all have to be pharmaceuticals." The second biggest export from the U.S. is intellectual property in the form of entertainment. So I made a case on a purely business model basis and we were working on that pretty much up to the point that Columbia failed. Now there's such a huge setback to the international space station program that I've told NASA that I'm going to step out for a while and let them solve that problem. Ill be supportive to them in anyway I can in terms of what they need in public reach and media support while they're doing what they need to do.

But it would be really dumb to try to get in the way of getting the international space station done and up on its feet as a research center, which is going to take at least a couple more years. So then we'll revisit it at a point where it makes sense, if it ever makes sense. And if I'm not fit enough to fly by that point, because you have a window and my biological clock is ticking, then I'll just get someone else to do the on orbit work and we'll focus on the technical development to be able to make the camera flyable. That's a pretty longwinded answer to a simple question. I could have just said, yup.

Q3: I was just wondering if you're ever going to release *Xenogenesis* on DVD?
JC: [laughs] I'd be really scraping the bottom there.

Q4: And secondly, is there any truth to the *Battle Angel Alita* rumors going round at the moment?
JC: Yeah, *Battle Angel Alita* is one that's definitely in our production queue. It's a film that I'm going to be directing, it's a question of when we do it, in what order we do things. But if you're not familiar with that, it was an anime that was based on a manga—great character, really cool and it's something I'm looking forward to doing. And we'll probably do that in 3D, too. I'm just going to do everything in 3D now. I'm going to shoot my daughter's birthday party in 3D.

Q5: Are you a Doc Savage fan, because I've noticed that in two of your movies, especially in *The Abyss*, there are similarities with the Doc Savage adventure titled *The Red Terrors*. Am I wrong or what?
JC: Wrong. I've never read a Doc Savage book, though I know that there's a series of Doc Savage books. I always liked the covers, though, back in the sixties editions. The man of bronze, with the ripped shirt.

Q5: There is also another Doc Savage adventure, titled . . .
JC: You can't talk me into this, you know. No is no.

Q5: It's really peculiar because there's a man turned into a statue of liquid air exactly like in another Doc Savage adventure.
JC: We've seen that before—people turned into stone, pillars of salt, etc. These are archetypes.

Q6: You quite often take the role of producer now. To what extent is that contradictory to the role of the director, and what do you think the relationship should be between the producer and the director?
JC: I don't think producing and directing are contradictory. There's only really one type of director in the sense that it's a very defined role. But there're a lot of different types of producers—anybody from somebody who just wafts through at the beginning and puts two different people in contact and they go off to do 99.99 percent of the work and the producer gets the credit, to somebody who's in the trenches, on the set, everyday, working as a line producer. There're different levels of that. When I pro-

duce another director's work—I've produced two for Kathryn Bigelow and one for Steven Soderbergh, that's pretty much it for features. But for television as producer's medium, I did forty-four episodes of *Dark Angel*, which is a one-hour drama, and that's an awful lot of producing. I see them as complementary tasks. When I'm producing my own films, I'm complementing my own activities as director, making sure that I have the things I need in order to be able to make the film.

When I'm, say, working with Steven Soderbergh, I don't sit in a chair behind the video monitor on the set and comment on the way he's framed the shot. I didn't even go to the set on [*Solaris*], I worked with him at the script stage, I watched all the dailies, sent him a few email comments. I like to work with directors who don't need adult supervision. And then worked with him in post-production, because so many films are found in post-production, not least of which was *Ghosts of the Abyss*, which had nine hundred hours of material that had to be whittled down to one I think it's really about supporting the director, supporting their vision and not turn it into your vision, as a lot of producers do. There are producers in Hollywood who are frustrated directors—well, I'm not a frustrated director, I can make a movie anytime I want to. So probably the best thing I can offer a director is not to try to do their job or take their job. By the way, most producers can't say that with a straight face because they are frustrated directors.

AW: That leads me to a question about collaboration. We've talked about the actors you've worked with who come back time and time again, but that's also true of your editor, Conrad Buff . . .
JC: Conrad's done four films with me.

AW: . . . and Russell Carpenter in terms of cinematography. Is that something that's very important to you, that collaboration with a team that goes forward picture after picture? Or do you think it's more important to mix it up?
JC: I think you have to do both. It's good to work with people whose strengths you know and understand and you develop a shorthand and that's great. But I also think you want to shake things up and see how other people do things. You can get kind of entrenched. I've worked with a number of composers and I would with any one of them again, but it's always exciting to see how other people's creative process works.

Q7: What advice would you give to aspiring filmmakers?

JC: Well, at least I have a smart ass answer, which is that if you have to ask that question, you're not going to make it. But that's not really fair. The point is that everybody's going to have to find their own path. And any advice that I would give you would apply to what it was like when I was breaking in back in 1981 and probably wouldn't apply now. I think the most important thing if you're an aspiring filmmaker is to get rid of the "aspiring." How do you do that? You make a film. I don't care if it's two minutes long and shot in Super 8 or DV or whatever. You shoot it, you put your name on it, you're a filmmaker. Everything after that, you're just negotiating your budget.
[Laughter and applause]

Q8: How do you see the director's moral mandate? When you read a script or write a script yourself, do you think of what people might think after the film?

JC: I think I understand why you're asking that question. You saw three clips, back to back, that consisted of mass carnage. I think that my films do have a pretty high moral and ethical threshold. I'm very interested in issues of . . . good and evil is a really pat way of describing it, but it's really about human behavior, duty, and the right path. If you look at the films carefully and strip away the preconceptions about Hollywood action movies and people with machine guns and look at what's happening—it might be quirky to some people but I do think there's an absolutely clear moral path through all of them. I am interested in celebrating the higher and nobler aspects of the human condition—heroism, for example, Ripley was willing to put her own life second, that's the highest path a human being can take. Those are themes that are as important in my films as the technology themes and the pure kinetic action front.

I do think there's a kind of downside to that kind of power that all filmmakers have, and you have to acknowledge that that power exists and not be irresponsible. Some filmmakers just don't care, they say they want freedom of speech, for their vision not to be inhibited, and the dark side of humanity is part of it. But if you look at *Terminator 2*, there were guidelines, and those guidelines were self-imposed, not by any outside agencies or studios—they didn't care as long as they had plenty of shoot 'em ups. The people who financed *Terminator 2* were the same people who financed the Rambo series, so they weren't going to be telling me

what my moral mandate was going to be. But John Connor never points a gun and never fires a gun at anybody. It's a fine line but I didn't want to create a cool character who kids might want to emulate but who goes around pointing guns at people. Which, by the way, is better than Rob Reiner's *Stand By Me*, where they solve all their problems by pointing their .45s at the big, bad teenagers. Which film is more moral? I had this argument with Rob Reiner, by the way.
[Laughter]

AW: And he didn't have a good comeback to it. You must have caught him off-guard.
JC: It was a six-page letter—I think it caught him off-guard.

Q9: I was wondering how you felt about *Solaris* being misunderstood by audiences and at the box offices? And also, which up and coming directors do you admire?
JC: We knew exactly what we were doing and we were inspired by the original Tarkovsky film and we knew precisely what Steven's vision of the film would be. I was certainly disappointed with the box office because I thought that with George Clooney attached that it would do better just on the momentum of that. But it's a challenging film and audiences like light entertainment, and this is certainly not that. It's about death, loss and everybody pretty much kills themselves in the film at some point; in some cases, twice. So it's a very dark film and we didn't ever expect it to make a couple of hundred million dollars but we did expect it to make its money back, which so far it hasn't managed. But it's doing much better internationally than domestically in the U.S., so I think we'll be okay in the long run; it'll just take a while. But fortunately, European audiences have responded to it better than the U.S. Because basically, nobody showed up in the U.S. from the opening weekend, which means that it wasn't disappointing to audiences—it just didn't have that something to make them want to go see it instead of something else.

Q10: How long do you think 35mm film will last as a format?
JC: I think it'll be around for a while because people will choose it, but I think it's being made obsolete, on a purely practical basis, pretty darn rapidly. It still can do a couple of things you can't do with HDTV—there are some frame-rate issues. A lot of people seem to think that the color space is inferior in HDTV to film, but they're wrong. It's actually supe-

rior and it's getting better. The thing that everybody has to realize is that with HDTV you have greatly superior resolution, equivalent color space, and less contrast ratio overall. I shouldn't say that: you have the same contrast ratio in the final projected image but you don't have the dynamic range to be able to make the mistake of overexposing or underexposing two stops and fix it later. But in HDTV you shouldn't be making that mistake because you can see the image on a HD monitor and that image is what your final film will look like, so there's no mystery, no going to dailies the next day to see how it comes out. It becomes a more controlled and disciplined process. But 35mm is still necessary for certain high-speed, very slow motion types of shots, and in fact to do a movie fully in HD right now you're still going to be carrying a 35mm camera for certain types of shots. So it's not a panacea yet—were in a transition phase, which we will be, call it if you're pessimistic, for the next five years. I'm going to make my next film digitally, so as far as I'm concerned I'm already through it, I'm just working through some of the bugs. But call it five years from now, it'll all be just a matter of choice. I like to hear the film run through the camera, I like to hear it flap out, I like to use the time they need to reload the magazines to go get a cappuccino—for whatever reason, I like the grain, the crappy, messed-up look of film.

Q11: What's the secret of great cinema?
JC: I don't think there's a secret. When a lot of other people were going to film school, I was working as a machinist and going to the drive-in theater. I'm just an audience member who got to go to the other side of the line and make movies. And I'll always be that guy sitting in the theatrer wanting a good time. Whatever the pretension and intellectual aspiration you put on top of that, bottom line, it has to be a crowd-pleaser. So I get to do my independent films through other people, like Steve Soderbergh.

Q12: Technology aside, what are your inspirations? Literature, painting, photography, what do you look to?
JC: All of those. I think both classical literature and pulp science fiction—probably not in that order of importance to me in my development. Other movies, good ones and bad ones. I studied art, I loved various schools of painting, and I try to light with a painterly eye. Not with this one—it's a documentary and we didn't know what was going to

happen from one second to the next; we were just like: "Grab the camera, run!" But generally speaking, on my films, I like to be involved in the cinematography because I love that—I'm an artist, I paint.

Q13: How happy were you with the films that you made, especially since a number of them are now available in director's cuts? Also, would you go back to low-budget filmmaking, just to test yourself?
JC: This is a low-budget film—this was a $12m film. *Bismarck* was a two-hour film made for $4m—that's pretty darn cheap. That's like shopping at K-mart. The answer is, I'm already doing that. And television is low-budget filmmaking. But for feature films, I like the big show. As for the first part of the question, it's not about thumbing my nose at the studio or anything like that—it's really about celebrating the different medium of DVD and celebrating the fact that the consumer has a choice. You can buy the release as is, or you can buy the special edition and see what the movie would have been like half an hour longer. Which is really the film of the script.

The movie which is released is usually the film found after the meditative process of post-production. *Aliens* is an example of a film which would have been better with some of the scenes in the special edition but arguably so. But *The Abyss*, I think, if I had to do it over again, I would have gone for the special edition, but there were certain reasons why that didn't happen and I can't really blame it on the studio per se—it was really my own perception of the marketplace at the time; there didn't seem to be a market for a three-hour movie, and some of the visual effects hadn't been done and we'd kind of lost faith in the impact of some of the things which later proved to be more important than we'd thought at the time. Quite frankly, with that film, we had this great love story and these great dramatic scenes and I just felt like I wanted to move the emphasis away from the big effects and closer to that.

AW: *The Abyss* seems to be the most personal and character-driven of your films—it does seem to have a very strong moral viewpoint. Very vocal anti-conflict message. Would you regard that as your most personal film?
JC: I don't know—I don't think in those terms. They're all personal films—they may not look like it but it's all stuff that I'm working through. When I was ten years old I became aware that there were nuclear weapons that could incinerate us all, I realized that instead of this happy innocent place I thought the world was. *The Terminator* was my attempt to

work through that. It came from some inside place. But any filmmaker would say that. Unless they're some filmmaker for hire and they're doing the next *Charlie's Angels* or something. I don't mean to put that down, it's a cool gig. But for stuff that you originate yourself, it has to come from some personal place.

Q14: How did you feel about Newt and Corporal Hicks from *Aliens* being killed off in the opening minutes of *Alien 3*?
JC: That David Fincher—I wanted to wring his neck, but I got over it because he's such a good director, the bastard. I really liked the photography and a lot of aspects of the film, but I do think that it was such a disappointment to the fans of *Aliens* that in the opening minutes of his film that he had to make a statement about not letting what went before to cloud his vision and he let that get in the way of making a successful sequel. I think there's an art to making sequels—you've gotta make it cool and fresh, but not at the expense of the things that the audience really cared about from the previous film. Fincher and I are really pals, so it's not like that lasted very long.

Q15: What are your thoughts and feelings about music in your films, and how closely do you like to brief the composer?
JC: This is a tricky area, especially for a visual director like me. I'm not trained in the proper sense—I can't read music, but you really kind of have to go to school on the musical vocabularies that are open to you and work very closely with the composer. Because this is the one area of the film—other than the performances that you're going to get from the actors, but even then, that's pretty closely scripted so you can imagine in advance what you're going to get. But the composer, you don't know what they're going to come back with.

Q16: Lots of directors sort of have temp scores with which they tell composers what they want—do you do that?
JC: Oh yeah, you have to work through the temp score. If you think about it, you've got hundreds of years of music to choose from and you can work through very specifically what works scene by scene, moment to moment in the film, and what serves the film and how little gestures can mean so much. All those little things, and that should be the filmmaker's choice, not the composer's. The filmmaker works on a film for a year or eighteen months and the composer comes in at the end for a month.

Having said that, the composer has a very difficult job—you can have a temp score which illustrates each scene perfectly but is not a cohesive whole, so I find the best composers are the ones who can translate a kind of abstract of why the temp score is working. A good composer can see the temp score as a window into what the director wants, but a really good composer will honor that but also suggest alternatives. I thought Joel McNeely's music on this was very good and there were a few places where he just cribbed from the temp, but in other places, he went in a diametrically different path. Same with James Horner on *Titanic*, but not so on *Aliens*, which was not a good experience because of my own limitations; also James was not very collaborative at that point. So we both got a whole lot better by the time we worked on *Titanic*, and he was so damn good. We talked it through and we ended up having such a great working relationship that we've stayed friends since then.

AW: I'd like you all to put your hands together and thank James Cameron.

My Titanic Obsession

James Rampton/2005

From *The Independent*, August 9, 2005. Copyright The Independent 2005. Reprinted by permission.

The director James Cameron would be the first to admit that he is obsessed by the ocean. Ever since he first plunged into the murky depths at the age of sixteen, the filmmaker has been unable to kick the underwater habit.

He has dived into the subject again and again in his films—from his debut feature in 1981, the ultimate schlock-horror B-movie, *Piranha Part Two: The Spawning* (which he now laughingly calls "the finest flying piranha film ever made"), to the eerie deep-ocean fantasy, *The Abyss*, in 1989, and of course, the multi Oscar-winning *Titanic*.

According to the director, who turns fifty-one next week, "beside filmmaking, the underwater world has always been my other love. So if I get an opportunity to be able to put the two together and to make a film on an underwater subject, then I can't be happier. If I had to choose one over the other, I would probably dive."

So he was very pleased to be offered the opportunity to combine his two great passions on his latest project, *Last Mysteries of the Titanic*, which is showing on the Discovery Channel on Saturday. This is a fly-on-the-wreck view of the *Titanic*, which lies two and a half icy miles beneath the surface of the Atlantic off the Grand Banks of Newfoundland. For the purposes of the program, Cameron helms a flotilla of state-of-the-art research subs down to the stricken ship. The aim is to gain access, for the first time since the craft plummeted to the ocean floor, to what explorers see as the *Titanic*'s two "holy grails": the ship's Turkish baths and its boiler room.

He says he relishes the sheer unpredictability of non-fiction. "Documentaries are hard," he asserts. "The kind of filming I had done before, where you have a script and you know what you're doing, is easy by comparison. When you're shooting a documentary, you never know whether you're wasting your time every time you start squirting off some footage, or whether this could be the moment of gold."

Cameron, who was born and bred in Kapuskasing, Canada, goes on to explain his love affair with documentaries about the deep. "When I was a kid, exploration was the most important thing. When I realized that I wasn't going to be an astronaut and I wasn't really going to go to other planets, I became very interested in the ocean.

"The imagery that Jacques Cousteau was putting on television back then in the mid-sixties made me realize that there are alien worlds right here on Earth that you can explore for the cost of the scuba equipment.

"I still have the same urge to explore and to understand the wonders of the natural world. Now I'm getting to live that fantasy." A fortune estimated to exceed $50m may well be helping him achieve that goal.

An imposing, six-foot-two figure with a neatly dipped, greying beard, the five-times-married Cameron bubbles with enthusiasm about the life aquatic. A self-confessed "nerd from Kapuskasing," he is utterly immersed in all things maritime. As he outlines in exhaustive detail the technological advances that have been made in submarine filming over the past few years, he breaks off for a moment to laugh: "I must warn you, I'm into this stuff."

Cameron first became intrigued more than a decade ago by the story of the *Titanic*, the grand liner that was launched in 1911 amid a blizzard of ticker-tape and hype. Less than a year later, at 2:20am on April 15, 1912, its crew ignored all warnings of impending danger, and the ship struck an iceberg and sank. Of the 2,208 people on board, only 705—predominantly women and children—survived.

The director worked the story up into a $200m shipwreck epic which soon sailed into the record books as the highest-grossing movie of all time. It rang up an eye-watering $1.7bn at box offices around the globe.

Cameron returned to the subject two years ago when he piloted a sub down to the real wreck of the *Titanic* to make the 3-D documentary *Ghosts of the Abyss*. So why, all these years after his initial interest was pricked, is the filmmaker still hooked on the story of the mighty liner that came to a mightily sticky end?

"I felt I'd finished with it after making *Ghosts of the Abyss*," Cameron concedes. "But a little voice in my head kept saying, 'You've only searched 30 per cent of the wreck.' And so I thought, this is unfinished business. We now have new smaller, more sophisticated vehicles. Let's finish the job and make the definitive archaeological survey.'"

But, more than that, Cameron emphasizes that the *Titanic* has immense symbolic significance. "You have to start from the fact that the *Titanic* is different from all other shipwrecks," reflects the director, who has made several other marine documentaries, including *Expedition: Bismarck*, *Volcanoes of the Deep Sea*, and *Aliens of the Deep*.

"The *Titanic* has a great metaphorical and mythical value in the human consciousness. Is it the most compelling thing in the world when we need to find a cure for AIDS and millions of people are dying in Africa? No, on that scale, it's not a priority. But you have to think of the *Titanic* in terms of a feature film or a novel—something that touches people's emotions. Wrecks are human stories. They teach us something about ourselves. A wreck is a fantastic window into the past. Steel can't lie—it doesn't have an agenda. These wrecks are like time-capsules. We'll put parking lots over battlefields, but underwater these sites are frozen in time. By visiting them, we can touch history."

So what does the *Titanic* have to teach us today? "People cluck and say it's not relevant because the class structure of that time doesn't exist anymore, but it really does. Contrast the way we in the West live with they way people live in, say, Africa or Indonesia, There is still first class and there is still third class. We're all living on one big blue spherical *Titanic*." Cameron continues that there are also lessons to be gleaned from the way the ship came to grief. "Like the crew of the *Titanic*, we've identified the icebergs, but we're not reacting quickly enough as we approach them. By the time they reacted to the icebergs, their fate was already sealed. That's a great metaphor for today. Think about global climate-change. By the time we see evidence of it, it will be too late—a collision will inevitably occur. Mr. Bush might have some questions to answer about that."

The director gives another example of what we can learn from deep-sea treasure-troves. "Look at the wreck of the *Bismarck*, the Nazi ship that I explored a couple of years ago. That opens a window onto a specific time in history. It gives us an insight into a certain mindset and makes it more immediate. A lot of kids watched *Expedition: Bismarck*, and all of a sudden to them the Second World War became more real.

"It's a way for me to give something back, in a sense, and not just be a taker, who just makes films and makes a lot of money, because ultimately that doesn't really return anything other than entertainment value.

I don't want to negate that, but I think there's so much else that can be done."

He is awestruck by the often unheralded endeavors of scientific researchers. "I identify with them. They're basically people who don't live in a glamorous world. They live off the beaten path and spend a lot of time on ships at sea. They're, in a sense, cloistered in academia, but they're really heroes because they're at the cutting edge of human exploration. They're at the frontier of knowledge."

He believes that the work of such pioneers underlines the shallowness of our celebrity-fixated society. "Most people are involved in making money. Unfortunately, in our society you are seen as a chump if you don't do that. People who pursue other dreams are the ones who interest me most, whether they are artists, explorers, writers, scientists, or people looking for some greater meaning or other purpose. I think these are the only people worth knowing and worth celebrating.

"Unfortunately, our Western society tends to celebrate the wrong people, people who entertain us in a very superficial way but don't entertain us intellectually. I don't have any problem with those folks, I just don't think that they should be put on a pedestal." After winning eleven Oscars for *Titanic* in 1997, Cameron was himself put on a pedestal by Hollywood moguls. He could have named his movie—and his price—but elected not to repeat himself with endless clones of his greatest hits.

Finally, though, he thinks the time is right for him to return to feature films because he can now harness new technology to make something entirely fresh. Unsurprisingly, he has opted for an almost insanely ambitious sci-fi blockbuster. It is dear that the director of such ground-breaking films as *The Terminator* and *Terminator 2*, *Aliens*, *The Abyss*, and *True Lies* wants his comeback movie to make as big a splash as they did.

Inspired by Japanese graphic novels, he is currently developing *Battle Angel*, a cyborg thriller set in the twenty-sixth century. "It's going to be a mega-budget film shot in 3-D," Cameron enthuses. "It's set in a post-human world in the distant future, and a number of the main characters will be computer-generated. It's a kind of virtual filmmaking. We're building a whole new motion-capture technology. I'm impatient to get on with using the tools of the future."

He continues: "The main thrust is a love story between a human man and a female cyborg, and the film contains a range of characters from the fully human to the fully machine. I'm embracing the fact that human beings are amazingly adaptable. We've got a lot of flaws, but we're also pretty clever. We've got the tools, but can we use them?"

So does this return to movie-making indicate that Cameron has finally got the *Titanic* out of his system? He reckons so. The director, who was reportedly at the head of the queue to pay $200,000 to go on Virgin's inaugural commercial space mission, says that "with *Last Mysteries of the Titanic*, I'm hoping we'll able to lay a few questions to rest. I've made the decision not to return anymore. We've shed a lot of light on it now, and enough's enough. It's time to move on."

That does not mean, however, that Cameron will stop being fascinated by this gigantic hulk of metal that has lain rusting on the ocean bed for almost a century. As far as he's concerned, the *Titanic* spell has not yet been broken.

"Over the years," Cameron muses, "I've found the *Titanic* story to be a wonderfully rich and renewable metaphor for the way we look at the world. I'm afraid that human nature has not changed much since 1912—if at all!"

King of All He Surveys

James Rampton/2006

From *The Independent*, December 19, 2006. Copyright The Independent 2005. Reprinted by permission.

"I'm the king of the world!" James Cameron cried at the 1998 Oscars, echoing his leading character in *Titanic*. When the director picked up eleven Academy Awards and his epic netted box-office receipts of $1.8bn, he defied critics who'd predicted that the film would be sunk by a fatal combination of hubris and testosterone.

At that moment, Cameron did seem to be master of all he surveyed. After a decade of hits—*The Terminator* (1984), *Aliens* (1986), *Terminator 2* (1991), and *True Lies* (1994)—*Titanic* was merely the latest Cameron box-office behemoth to crush everything in its path.

And yet, in the following eight years, tumbleweed has blown through Cameron's movie CV. What happened to the king of the world? What has become of the director whose movies kept studio bosses in diamond-studded Jacuzzis? Is he just sitting at home counting his money?

The answer is that Cameron, who hails from a remote part of Ontario, has been living up to the other famous phrase he has used to describe himself—"a nerd from Kapuskasing"—and pursuing his passion for scientific documentaries, spending a large chunk of his reputed $50m fortune on educative factual films. His latest documentary, *The Exodus Decoded*, is screened on the Discovery Channel this Saturday.

The big news is that Cameron is gearing up for a grand return to movies. He has started work on *Avatar*, a special effects-led feature film about a human who's put in charge of an alien planet.

"I felt I'd exhausted the treasury and it was time to go back to work," Cameron says. "*Avatar* is a very ambitious sci-fi movie." The director's enthusiasm is evident in his voice. "It's a futuristic tale set on a planet two hundred years hence. It's an old-fashioned jungle adventure with an environmental conscience. It aspires to a mythic level of storytelling."

Avatar is not entirely a new venture; Cameron wrote the screenplay eleven years ago, and it has featured on *Empire* magazine's list of the twelve greatest unproduced scripts in Hollywood.

"I was never bored of making features," the director says. "This has been a dream project of mine for more than a decade, but when I first wrote it, the technology was not advanced enough. So I stuck the script in the drawer until the technology caught up."

Now it has. "The film requires me to create an entirely new alien culture and language, and for that I want 'photo-real' CGI characters. Sophisticated enough 'performance-capture' animation technology is only coming on stream now. I've spent the last fourteen months doing performance-capture work—the actor performs the character and then we animate it.

"We've set up a studio, and last week [*Lord of the Rings* director] Peter Jackson and Steven Spielberg were here trying out the technology. I said to them, 'Take my tools and play with them for a week.' They were grinning from ear to ear. It's a really exciting time because so many new things are now possible."

For all that, Cameron stresses that movies should ultimately be about the story. "Filmmaking is not about sprockets. It's about ideas, it's about images, it's about imagination, and it's about storytelling."

Now fifty-two, the director is a grizzled figure with more than a touch of the sea dog about him. Five times married, he possesses an effortless authority. Nicknamed "Iron Jim," he has been described as a harsh taskmaster by some colleagues. Others, however, argue that it is this very perfectionism that has helped the director to create some of the most memorable movies of the past two decades.

Cameron contends that "a director's job is to make something happen, and it doesn't happen by itself. So you wheedle, you cajole, you flatter people, you tell them what needs to be done. And if you don't bring a passion and an intensity to it, you shouldn't be doing it."

Cameron is fired up about going back to movie-making. But that does not mean he feels the last decade has been wasted—quite the contrary; he's devoted the same ardor to documentaries as he did to feature films.

The captivating factual programs he has made include *Ghosts of the Abyss* and *Last Mysteries of the Titanic*, films that used state-of-the-art submersible technology to probe uncharted corners of the wreck of the great liner that went down after hitting an iceberg in 1912.

Cameron has also dived to the bottom of the Atlantic in the company of two German survivors to explore the remains of Hitler's flagship, the *Bismarck*. For the director and his two passengers, it was a moving, often tearful pilgrimage. The resulting documentary—*Expedition: Bismarck*—underscored the enduring impact of the past on the present.

The director says that these factual films have been voyages of discovery both for himself and for his audience. "The wrecks are interesting in and of themselves—as objects, as pieces of engineering—but ultimately they're a doorway into another time. I think of the submersible, when we're doing this wreck diving, as a time machine.

Above all, Cameron is keen to celebrate the work of scientific pioneers. He is, after all, the son of an engineer. "I just want to be a cheerleader for legitimate scientific exploration. I think there's a necessity as a filmmaker to help get the message out, whether it's exploration, conservation, or respect for organisms and ecosystems.

"I'm driven by curiosity. I want to know how everything works, from the Big Bang onwards. There are still huge areas of curiosity to fulfill. When you've got a great story, whether it's a feature or a documentary, you've simply got to pursue it."

The latest fruit of his enthusiasm is *The Exodus Decoded*. Produced by Cameron, the program follows the presenter Simcha Jacobovici, who, after six years of archaeological research, has concluded that the Exodus described in the Bible actually happened hundreds of years earlier than previously believed. The tale of the Exodus lies at the core of Judaism, Christianity, and Islam. Cameron reckons it still strikes a chord. "Exodus is a story we all know. We were all raised with a biblical view of the world, which still has a resounding influence on Western culture.

"Simcha is brilliant at finding new evidence and making cognitive leaps that so-called experts aren't allowed to. Connecting the dots, seeing a pattern in disparate pieces of evidence and lateral thinking are all more the province of the filmmaker.

"Here, we've found evidence that may set the Exodus clock back two hundred years. We can shove this film in the experts' faces and start a dialogue. History is often told by the victors. It is edited by subsequent rulers, who chisel away at it to show themselves in a better light. History is a moving target, and we should not be afraid to be provocative about it.

"The challenge for documentary-makers is: how can we illuminate history and paint a clearer picture? Look at the *Titanic* site—steel can't lie. It is what it is. Regardless of what the newspapers said in 1912, the wreck is lying at the bottom of the ocean telling us its own story."

Having not directed a feature film for so long, does the filmmaker feel any added pressure? "No. There is always pressure to perform from one feature to the next. There are always high expectations.

"I remember going with a great sense of anticipation to each new Stanley Kubrick film and thinking, 'Can he pull it off and amaze me again?' And he always did. The lesson I learned from Kubrick was, 'Never do the same thing twice.' *Avatar* is not like anything else I've done—nor were *Titanic* or *Terminator* or *Aliens*.

"I always want to find something mentally engaging. I'll spend many months completing the special effects on *Avatar*, and it will not be released until the summer of 2009. It's quite a challenge—and for that reason, I embrace it."

James Cameron: A Life in Pictures

Francine Stock/2009

From an Alfred Dunhill BAFTA A Life in Pictures event, December 22, 2009. Transcript printed by permission of the British Academy of Film and Television Arts. Transcribed by Brent Dunham.

The *Titanic* may have floundered but James Cameron's film remains buoyant as the biggest box office success in history. Nothing this director does is modest in scale: he waited fifteen years for technology to catch up with his ideas to make *Avatar* in groundbreaking 3D. His previous, otherworldly films include *Aliens*, *The Abyss* and Arnold Schwarzenegger's trademark screen role, *The Terminator*. This is his life in pictures.

James Cameron: Thank you. Thank you for that.
Francine Stock: Let's start at the beginning: born 1954, Ontario, Canada—
JC: —I don't recall—

FS: —More or less. Not far from Niagara Falls.
JC: That's right, yeah. Actually, quite a bit north, it's probably closer to the Arctic Circle. We moved to Niagara Falls when I was I think two, two and a half. So my first memories are from there.

FS: So, the ultimate special effects right there on your doorstep.
JC: Absolutely. And I could hear the thunder of the falls just faintly muted at all times, twenty-four hours a day. So, the water on the brain thing has always sort of occurred to me as a result of that.

FS: And the water, obviously, is also going to recur during the evening here as well. So, if you were born in '54, it would have been the mid-sixties before you were aware of cinema. Is that right?

JC: I think when I was in the third grade or so, when I was seven-ish, I saw *Mysterious Island*, a Ray Harryhausen film, with fantastic creature effects in it. And really pretty mind-blowing stuff in its day and I recall that my response to that was to draw. Whenever I saw something that made a strong impression on me, I had to draw. But I wouldn't just draw the thing itself, I would start to embellish and create my own stories around it. There were these sort of trigger points: the Harryhausen films, and then that whole slew of sci-fi/B-movies that came. And then *2001* was a seminal moment in the late sixties, '68. It was not like anything I had seen before and that was the trigger point for me in wanting to emulate technique so I started making little models and lighting them in a contrast-y style against a black background, shooting them with my dad's Super 8 camera. And then a friend of mine had a camera that could do single frames so then we started doing animation. Then one thing led to another, I guess.

FS: Your father was a scientist, he was an engineer.
JC: Engineer.

FS: And you studied physics and English, I think, at college, although you had moved to California.
JC: Right physics first and then switched to English.

FS: Do you think you approach things in a scientific way?
JC: I'm pretty analytical. I was thinking about this the other day: I was sitting at a roundtable of directors and everybody said, "Yeah, you've got to go with your gut and you've got to have instinct. Your decisions should be instinctual." But I actually think that's a slight simplification of the directing process. I think it's a very analytical process, even on *Avatar*. I remember literally having a discussion with the editor saying, "Okay, look, in this battle sequence, every single time we've improved the battle, we've done it by putting like with like, putting the attack with the attack, the retreat with the retreat and grouping things that way." Well, that's a very analytical kind of approach and I realized that it's a balance between analysis and just pure, gut instinct.

FS: So you worked as Art Director for Roger Corman by 1980 on *Battle Beyond the Stars* so science fiction already right there from the beginning.
JC: This was right after *Star Wars*, and even before *The Empire Strikes Back*, and Roger was getting in there quickly, striking while the iron was hot.

And I got a job as a model builder, I was working in the model shop, and he came in and said, "Well, you haven't designed the main character's ship." And everybody stood there stunned and it sort of looked like it was going to be a quick bake-off to see who could come up with the design quickly enough. So everybody started drawing something and I figured, "It's a Roger Corman film, the main character's ship is a female personality, like HAL 9000 only sexy, right?" and I thought, "Okay, I'm going to draw a spaceship with tits." And that was my play and Roger came through the next day and he said, "What is this?" And I said, "It's a spaceship with tits, Roger." And he said, "You've got the job." That's how it worked.

FS: So, within just four years of that, you were actually directing your own big feature itself.
JC: Yeah, things happened fast

FS: *The Terminator*. Now is it true that you thought of the theme, or that the theme for *The Terminator* came to you in a dream?
JC: It wasn't so much of a theme as a seminal image. I was in Rome, I was broke, I had a high fever, and I was just having these weird dreams. I had this image of this kind of chrome skeleton, death image coming out of the fire, phoenix-like, and I just got up and sketched it. And around the nucleus of that, I started to create a story and sort of backfill: Okay, what is it? Where did it come from? Who is it after? And it all sort of fell into place fairly quickly.

FS: Well, we're going to see an example of it now and the moment is quite early on in the film, and it's a moment I'm sure you all remember it. It's when Sarah Connor is being pursued by this cyborg from the future, the Terminator, Schwarzenegger, and she hides in a nightclub. But, of course, he finds her pretty quickly but, luckily, somebody else is also looking out for her.
[Clip from *The Terminator*]
JC: So that's the governor of California shooting at the mother of my oldest daughter.

FS: Do you think science fiction should always have underlying ideas, you know really quite strong themes there, and, if so, beyond this idea of rage and getting the world to work your way, what is it in *The Terminator*?
JC: It's not really about machines from the future. It's sort of about our

relationship with technology. It's really kind of about our human potential for dehumanization. You see cops as examples. And the other idea is to not trust technology and to not trust the fabric of reality because by the second film, you've got this woman who's gone crazy, knowing that the world is a completely fragile place and it's all an illusion, it can all be torn away by this nuclear war. And I was sort of playing with that in the first film as well. There's this war, it hasn't happened yet, but if you know that, everything changes and all your priorities change. You know, ideas like that. And I think that comes from being a kid in the sixties. I remember the Cuban Missile Crisis clearly, having these fallout shelter houses, like that would do any good!

FS: So, the next place you go is into outer space with *Aliens*. Now, of course Ridley Scott had already done *Alien*, the first one, and set quite a strong pattern there, so how much of a challenge was it to follow on?
JC: It was kind of interesting because everyone was advising me not to do the film because Ridley Scott's a tough act to follow. And it just seemed like if there was anything good in the film that I made, it would be attributed back to the source material and anything bad would be attributed to me. And so it seemed like a "no-win" scenario. But I was such a geek-fan still, even at that point after having made *The Terminator* that I just wanted to make the movie. It seemed really cool. Sigourney seemed like she would make an amazing, evolved Ripley, because I took her forward with the post-traumatic stress syndrome after-effects of her first experience in the script that I wrote. And it just seemed like it was a really cool opportunity and I didn't want to pass it up.

FS: Do you feel that you took it in a different direction then? I mean, technically as well.
JC: Clearly, [*Alien*] was such an amazing film. I thought, "Alright, fine, what do I do? I do action. People know me from *The Terminator*, there's got to be a through-line from that." So I wanted to do some really kinetic scenes. And the second you put a kineticism into the backdrop of Ridley's design, now you've got a whole different film. It's going to be much more of a rollercoaster ride, much more of an action picture, less of a horror film.

FS: Well, let's see Sigourney Weaver in action here. And, as Ripley, she's returned to this planetoid, a particularly small planet, planetoid—
JC: LV-426.

FS: LV-426. Where the colony on LV-426 is mysteriously disappeared. And, of course, LV-426 is the place where the Nostromo crew saw the alien eggs. So, we know something's up. They find a child, who is a survivor of the colony but she's also having to deal and protect that child against an alien threat.
[Clip from *Alien*]

FS: To what extent with this film, and with the next film, *The Abyss*, did technical possibilities drive what you were trying to do?
JC: I was always trying to push. Look, I read avidly, I was a big fan of all the techniques of prosthetic and appliance make-up and visual effects, and if you could cheat them and use foreground miniatures and things like that, which we did on *Aliens*. I knew all the old cheats: the Shuftan shots, the glass paintings and all that. I used to love it when the effects department of a major studio was called the "trick department." You know? Because they were just tricks, tricks of the eye, they were *tromp l'oeil*, things like that. So, all the effects in *Aliens* are very crude by present standards, very simple and straightforward. Even the alien queen was just operated by people; it wasn't even hydraulic. There were off-camera puppeteers and there were two guys inside the body of the thing operating the arms and all that.

FS: But between *Aliens* and *The Abyss* you are starting to get that shift, aren't you? And computer generation is coming in, in a big way.
JC: We had all sorts of wild ideas: like projecting high-speed photography of water onto "claymation" and animating it frame by frame, all kinds of wacky stuff, and some of it probably would have worked just fine in the end. But it was proposed to me that we try it with computer-generated animation, and I knew nothing about that. So, I said, "Alright, show me a test. Show me something that looks even remotely like this." And two different companies, one was ILM with Dennis Muran and the other was Kleiser-Walczak, both produced a test and neither of them really looked that good. But one had the surface texture and the other one had the refraction and the movement and I thought, "If could put that with that, you could maybe do something really interesting." So, we kind of took this big leap of faith and went with the computer graphics. And I went with Dennis Muran at ILM and he and I became friends over the subsequent years and he worked on *Terminator 2*, of course, too, which is the natural through-line of that process.

FS: It is really interesting the way that computer generation evolves: so, it was water at that stage and then subsequently it was sand or fur or whatever. And you suddenly find a whole crop of films that come out at that time where everybody is saying that they can do this. But this, presumably, *The Abyss*, was really early on in this whole water thing.

JC: I can place it exactly. There was this film called *Young Sherlock Holmes* that had a CG character, the stained glass knight, but he was a hard surface model and he was just these floating panes of glass. But this was the first time that anybody had seen a soft surface model, and especially a human face that was animated, Mary Elizabeth [Mastrontonio]'s face went on the pseudopod, sticks out her tongue and it just sort of took it up to a higher level.

FS: We're just about to see that scene. But just to remind people, again for the setup for *The Abyss*: it's a nuclear sub that goes down in mysterious circumstances and then this crew are brought in to salvage the wreck. But there's great potential for tension within the crew. Let's see now this rare moment of harmony and a pseudopod.
[Clip from *The Abyss*]
JC: That stuff is so expensive, the CG. You can see it's all reaction shots, when the pseudopod comes into the room: one character reacts, then another, then another, then another... finally, we cut back to the thing. I think there's probably fourteen or fifteen shots in the whole sequence and they took nine months to do. And I think in the last two months of *Avatar*, in post-production on *Avatar* before final delivery, we had a thousand shots come in.

FS: So, obviously, *The Abyss* was a very demanding shoot. I mean you were shooting a little bit there in a not-yet commissioned nuclear facility.
JC: We were in what would have been the containment vessel of a nuclear reactor. It was a big tank and it held, I think, 7 million gallons.

FS: Also, [there were] discussions with the studio about the length of the film, I think. Does that always happen?
JC: Yeah, I always believe that to create fantasy with a sense of reality, you have to embellish it with a lot of detail. It's the small detail that makes it feel real to people.

FS: And so that whole idea of the three-hour film, which I understand you feel it needs the detail and the space, but do you know whether audiences like that?

JC: The only sort of reference point we had back in those days was *Dances with Wolves* which won Best Picture and it was three hours and ten minutes. But, historically, films that length just didn't work. And it wasn't until *Titanic* that we actually had a film that we believed worked at that length. Still, everybody was nervous about it, the exhibitors said it wouldn't work; we got a lot of pushback from the exhibition community. But we went with it anyway.

FS: And so *Titanic* begins, really, way back when you [were] diving, as you do, a lot. You go down to the wreck of the *Titanic* and shoot some documentary footage.

JC: Yeah, it really starts with me being a scuba diver and loving wreck diving and so on, exploring wrecks. And thinking, "What's the ultimate ship wreck? The *Titanic*." And the presentation I made to Fox was very simple: I walked in with Ken Marschall's beautiful book of paintings of the *Titanic*, whapped it open on Peter Chernin's coffee table in his office and this double-page painting of the ship sinking with all the lifeboats and the distress flares going off and I said, "Romeo and Juliet on the *Titanic*." That was it, seriously. Actually, it was my best pitch if you think about it. I'm usually pretty terrible at pitching. But my real goal was to actually go dive the shipwreck; making the movie was kind of secondary in my mind at that point. People make decisions for strange reasons. And my pitch on that had to be a little more detailed. I had written the script at that point and I said, "We've got to do this whole opening where they're exploring the *Titanic* and they find the diamond. So, we're going to have all these shots of the ship. Now, we can either do them with elaborate models and motion control shots and CG and all that which will cost X amount of money, or we can spend X plus 30 percent and actually go shoot it at the real wreck, and it will be a publicity coup and you can basically take it from the marketing budget." Which actually proved to be the case. I think the amount of free media that we got off of having actually dived to the wreck was pretty awesome and really helped the public awareness of the film right before the release.

FS: So with this tripartite thing, the historical detail, and, obviously, the spectacular effects and this very strong emotional story, did you approach *Titanic* in a different way?

JC: Well, I did a lot more research. I mean these other films [referring to clips shown earlier] were sort of fantasy/science fiction; I didn't need a lot of technical voracity or historical voracity to it. But with *Titanic*, I approached it very differently. I read everything I could read. I created an extremely detailed timeline of the ship's few days and a very detailed timeline of the last night of its life. And I worked within that to write the script and I got in some historical experts to sort of analyze what I had written and comment on it and I adjusted it. We wanted this to be a definitive visualization of this moment in history as if you had gone back in a time machine and shot it. But then, of course, overlaid and woven through that is this love story.

FS: The bit we're going to see now is actually Jack and Rose and it's early on when they don't really know each other, it's obviously Kate Winslet and Leonardo DiCaprio, and she is threatening to throw herself over the side of the boat because of this tremendous pressure from her family to go into a marriage she doesn't really want. And Jack extends a hand to help her.
[Clip from *Titanic*]

FS: I did read something once that you said that you felt *Titanic* had pushed the limit to how much time you can spend on character in mainstream filmmaking.
JC: I suppose what I was talking about is that it was a three-hour and fifteen-minute movie and by the time the credits are rolling on the majority of films, nothing pretty much has happened except he saves her here, they do a little spitting over the railing, he does a little drawing, you know? They fall in love, they run around the ship—it's really nothing but character and the development of a relationship for two hours. Then, a whole bunch of bad stuff happens. Which, structurally, is a very strange form, it's a very strange architecture for a movie but it worked because the only way all that disaster stuff later meant anything to you as an audience was because you cared about them. And I don't think the film could have sustained that if it wasn't—if you didn't know what was going to happen, if there wasn't in the back of your mind a sort of ticking clock and this sense of doom over the whole thing.

The innocence of that, the joyfulness of that, of their relationship, and just simply spending time on that wouldn't have worked.

FS: And, of course, as we know, it all worked out awfully well in the end.

So, at that point, that must have been when you came to consider the next thing somewhat inhibiting.

JC: What happened after *Titanic*, and bear in mind that I made the movie because I wanted to dive to the wreck. I basically got hooked on deep ocean exploration. And there was a thrill in that that was greater than the glitz of a red carpet, winning an Academy Award. I don't mean to diminish them; they're wonderful experiences but there was something very real and, yet, in a science fiction/fantasy kind of way, about exploring inner space and getting to actually do that. I always wanted to go to space. I couldn't do that. But I could go to the bottom of the ocean. So I wound up working with the Russian submersibles on six subsequent deep ocean expeditions over a five-year period, made four documentary films in that time. I always justified it to myself that I was perfecting the 3D technique to do a 3D movie in the future, and in fact that was true. We were doing that but also just having an amazing time. And raising a family, having children, I knew that the kind of commitment that I made to a movie didn't allow me to have any free time. I would just work seven days a week and it was completely consuming. I wasn't willing to do that either. So everything just kind of worked out the way it was meant to work out from my perspective. From the external view, it seems like I just sort of "went away" and then came back with *Avatar*.

FS: In fact, I think you had the idea for *Avatar* a long time back, didn't you?
JC: Yeah.

FS: The idea was the 3D one? Or the idea was the virtual reality?
JC: It was the virtual reality piece that wasn't there. The 3D we had worked out, even when we started *Avatar*. Back in '95, I wrote *Avatar* partially because it's something I had always wanted to do. It was a real dream project: the fantasy story taking place on another planet with all these cool creatures, it was going to be like the ultimate creature movie. You know? And just the design alone was what attracted me to the project. And then I shot *Titanic*, and after *Titanic*, my company, Digital Domain, was supposed to have all the answers for how to make this movie. I have given them two years after all and when I came back they still said, "You know, this isn't going to happen without a ridiculous amount of money and time." So, then, when it looked like the CG was beginning to mature enough that we could make *Avatar* if we were willing to push it a little bit to the next level, then we started the filming in '05. And we still

had two years of research and development to develop our performance capture pipeline up to our level, where we thought the characters would be fully believable.

FS: And this is where you used a head rig, basically, instead of using the little sensor things which people had used in performance capture.
JC: The mistake they had been making previously is that they put marker dots all over the body and they'd capture the body motion, but they'd use these little spherical markers, they'd glue them all over the actor's face. Well, you've got 200 some muscles in your body, half of them are in your face. So there's a whole order of magnitude, maybe two orders of magnitude more information, more data that is required about the face to actually make it real. And of course they weren't getting anything from the eyeballs themselves, the eye movement, because they weren't gluing markers on the people's eyes, at least not that I ever heard of. So, we decided to take a completely different approach, which was to create a head rig. The idea was that we would photograph the face in a close-up 100 percent of the time while the actor worked. But not just a close-up from a camera off somewhere, but locked to the head so it was essentially nulled out so that data could be put into the computer, and rates of change and edges, optical flow could be used to track all the features of the face as if they were markers. So, in essence, an infinite marker set.

FS: Well, we're going to see an example of it now. And I can't give all the context for *Avatar*, but essentially what we're going to see here is the avatar of the central character who is a Marine who would otherwise be in a wheelchair, but when he is on the planet, when he's on Pandora, he's this wonderful, ten-foot, lithe, bright blue creature. But he has to contend with various threats, which we're about to see.
[Clip from *Avatar*]

FS: So, Niagara Falls again there I see.
JC: Yeah, absolutely, there's got to be a waterfall. There are a lot of waterfalls on Pandora.

FS: I've got one final question for you, which is that, obviously, *Avatar* is a great showcase for all this groundbreaking new technology as you've done before. And we already know, although you may not say exactly what your next project is, but you're thinking ahead because that's how you work. What's the next big thing in cinema?

JC: I mean, for me, *Avatar* was such an experimental process. We made a lot mistakes, we went down some blind alleys and we meandered a bit and it took us a lot to work out exactly how to do everything. I think the next big challenge, honestly, is a process challenge for me. It's a challenge of being able to get the same end result as *Avatar* in less time, more efficiently, for less money.

FS: But the idea of "real" in cinema, as in—because Pandora is—

JC: It's meaningless now, the idea of what's real. I think the lines will just continue to blur between CG and photography until it becomes meaningless. Whether you capture something with a lens or you use imaginary photons in CG. The rules of lighting are the same: if you want sunlight, you create sunlight. You either do it with a Xenon light or 12k HMI or you do it with a sun source in global illumination in a CG scene file. It's the same thing; you have to imagine the sunlight. In neither case, usually, is it actually sunlight because all cinematography is a form of artifice anyway, masquerading as reality and the CG does the same thing. I just think it's going to become more seamless as we go along, and less relevant to dissect it or deconstruct it into what its component parts are.

FS: James Cameron, it's been a pleasure to talk about your life in pictures. Thank you very much indeed.

James Cameron

Tavis Smiley/2009

From *Tavis Smiley*, December 17, 2009. Transcript printed by permission of TS Media Inc.

Tavis Smiley: Pleased to welcome James Cameron to this program. The Oscar-winning filmmaker is one of the most successful directors, writers, and producers of our time, with seminal films like *Titanic*, *The Terminator*, and *Aliens*.

His latest is easily one of the most talked-about projects of the year, *Avatar*. The film opens in theaters around the country this weekend. As I mentioned at the top, it's up for four Golden Globe awards, including best director. Here now a sneak preview of *Avatar*.
[Clip of *Avatar*]

Tavis: I heard you whisper during the airing of that clip, "Interesting clip, good clip." Tell me why you said that.
James Cameron: I just—it was an interesting choice because it doesn't show the CG characters, it shows kind of the back story, with Stephen Lang, who plays the colonel, and it kind of sets up the world verbally, which is probably a good choice because he sort of lays it all out for you.

Tavis: So we're in now, so let's keep moving here. Since you are the director, this comes out of your mind, *Avatar* is?
Cameron: (Laughs) Well, the thing we're finding is that even when you've seen the film, people coming out say, "I don't know what I just saw." You have to go back.

Tavis: That's why I'm asking you. (Laughter)
Cameron: Well, it's a big action adventure movie that takes place on another planet but it's more than that, because it's also got a love story in

it and some kind of deeply felt kind of emotional moments in the film, and it's got a kind of environmental theme to it, I think, without being preachy, but I think something that people will be able to relate to these days with everything that's going on right now.

Tavis: When you have, James, all this bigness, all these special effects, some of us will get a chance in certain places around the country to see this in 3D. So when you have all this bigness going on, how do you keep the bigness from overshadowing the story?

Cameron: I think that's the biggest challenge of this type of film from a director's perspective, is to not get so absorbed in the nuts and bolts of the process that you don't pay attention to your actors. The funny thing that I've found with this performance capture stuff that we did on this film is that it actually sort of takes all that away, in a sense.

So it's just me and the actors, there's no lights, no cameras, no dollies, none of that stuff—none of the normal stuff on a film set that would distract me, keep me busy setting up the shot. I'm just working directly with the actor. So you're always dealing kind of with the heart of the movie every day. Then later, after we're done with the actors, then you work on all the visual effects and you fill in the scene around them.

Tavis: You're starting to answer a bit of what I wanted to ask a moment ago, which is you're not just known for being a good writer and a good producer and a good director, but you're an innovator. So for those who are going to go see this movie, in terms of innovation what is James Cameron giving us this time?

Cameron: I think there's two innovations in this film. One is the use of 3D just in general throughout the film and how it's used and the way it sort of draws you into the story. It's just a stylistic thing, really, without sort of poking you in the eye all the time and kind of reminding you, in the way that most 3D films do, that you're watching a 3D movie 100 percent of the time.

In fact, people have said they forget they're wearing the glasses. Part way in, a few minutes in they've almost forgotten it's in 3D although it's still working on your mind while you're watching it. The other really big innovation is the way we did the performance capture to drive these CG characters.

You didn't see it in that clip but we see these ten-foot-tall blue aliens called the Na'vi, and here you can see what we call Jake's avatar, which is the creature that he will project his mind into in order to go amongst the Na'vi and integrate with them. So they're done completely with CG, with computer-generated imagery.

Tavis: Tell me about the casting and how important—casting is important in every film; let me ask it a different way. In a film like this where so much of it is about, for lack of a better word, aliens and Na'vi and that kind of thing, tell me about the unique role that casting plays in a film like this versus *Titanic*.

Cameron: Yeah, well, look, I think casting is always super, super important to a film. Obviously it's important to a small film because that's all you see is the actors, but I think it's equally as important to a large film, and this particular film, because we're dealing with all these strange ideas, we're taking you into this exotic world, I felt that I needed somebody to play the main character, Jake, who's played by Sam Worthington, who was a very—just a grounded person, who is a very real person.

That's what Sam is. Sam was a bricklayer, comes from a blue-collar background, which is how he and I kind of related to each other, because I was a truck driver before I was a film director. He just feels like a real guy, and his approach to acting is to find authenticity in every moment, by whatever means necessary for him.

So putting him into this performance capture environment where there's not much there to work with, he found ways to make it real and I think that helps you on this voyage to this exotic world.

Tavis: Was it important for you, for the audience—is there any point beyond the fact that she's a great actress—for putting Sigourney Weaver in another sci-fi picture?

Cameron: Well, I actually think it produces an interesting irony, because, well, first of all, Sigourney and I have been friends since *Aliens* back in '86, and we were looking for some kind of project to work together on, and this turned out to be a really good one—a good role for her.

But there's an irony in the sense that in *Aliens* she was the human hero against the aliens, and in this film the humans are the invaders. They're invading the alien planet and the story is kind of told from the other side. So in a sense, she's one of the invaders, although she loves the Na'vi people, she loves the world of Pandora, and she means them only—means only to help them. But still, she's kind of on the wrong side, if you will, in this movie.

Tavis: You mentioned earlier a number of themes that run through the film. We'll talk about the environmental theme in just a second, because I assume that was deliberate, given that you were behind the project.

What also is fascinating for me about the project is to your earlier point here, in this *Avatar* film, the humans are invading. To my mind, at least, there's some interesting—I'm trying to find the right word here—some interesting commentary that you allow us, force us to wrestle with about who we are as humans, how we treat the planet, how we treat other beings.

Cameron: Our fellow humans.

Tavis: Exactly. Tell me more about that.

Cameron: Well, yeah, I think that was deliberate and it was one of the themes that I wanted to explore in this, and there are obviously references to Vietnam, there are references to Iraq, there are references to the American colonial period, and we've got a history—and not just America, obviously; we're talking about the French, the Spanish, the English, the Portuguese—of just kind of invading and taking what we need and forcing out and marginalizing indigenous cultures, and sometimes wiping them out completely, to the point that we don't have that many truly indigenous cultures left in this world. They're very, very tiny and there's a few in the Amazon, a few in Papua New Guinea.

Some of these languages are going extinct almost on a daily basis, some of these dialects. So we have a terrible history with this, and I sort of extrapolated even farther, to this idea of entitlement. We do the same thing with nature—we take what we need and we don't give back, and we've got to start giving back. We've got to start seriously and aggressively accepting our responsibility for stewardship of this planet.

Tavis: How do you give—my word, not yours—the proper treatment to the issues that you've just laid out now that we're all going to be forced to wrestle with when we see the film? As a filmmaker, I assume, at least, you want us to marinate on some of these things beyond the theater experience. How do you do that without being preachy?

Cameron: Yeah, it's a fine line. First of all you've got to put a whole bunch of spoonfuls of sugar in there to make it an adventure, make it visual, make it exciting. People are telling me coming out of the theater that they cried three times and they're having this big kind of emotional reaction, so that's part of it. The other thing is just don't make it preachy. Don't assume you have to give people information.

Assume that they've got the information already, and what we're going to give you is an emotional reaction to how we relate to nature and take you on a journey, not just a physical journey through the world but a kind of a mental journey, where you wind up looking at things from the side of the Na'vi, with their deep respect for nature, and then looking back at ourselves from that.

That's what science fiction does so well—it can hold up a mirror to all of us without pushing specific buttons of you're worse than—this guy's worse than this guy, you see what I mean? Science fiction doesn't really predict the future, that's not what it's there for. It's there to hold a mirror up to the present and look at the human condition, sometimes from the outside.

Tavis: You've been called crazy, I suspect, more times—(laughter) he's laughing already. I didn't mean that in a disrespectful way. I know you've been called crazy more times than you can count for the risk that you take.

Now, it seems to me that on demand, if you're going to be an innovator on demand, if you're going to be iconic on demand, you're putting yourself out there. I guess the question, though, is why—why take the risk to be innovative, to be iconic? People are going to talk about you and whether or not the gamble was worth it.

What I'm getting at is what is it about James Cameron that compels him to take that kind of risk?

Cameron: I think—look, I'm not a risk junkie, that sort of thing. I don't like jumping off buildings with a bungee cord tied to my feet.

Tavis: Although there was—let me cut in right quick—although there was a great quote I read, speaking of jumping. I don't want to forget this. You said that making this movie was like jumping off a cliff and knitting a parachute on your way down.

Cameron: Yeah, pretty much.

Tavis: I thought that was a great quote. (Laughs)

Cameron: Pretty much, and it looks like we made a good, soft landing, but there were a few times when it got away from us. But anyway, what I was going to say is that I'm not in it for the risk, but for me it's about curiosity. It's about wanting to see what happens. If we do this, if we build this thing what will happen? What can we create that people haven't seen before?

I think of the films that really got me excited when I was a kid, when

I was a teenager, they were images that I hadn't seen before and that I couldn't imagine for myself, and somebody had given me that moment of magical transport, whether it was a Ray Harryhausen film when I was really young, *2001: A Space Odyssey, Close Encounters, Star Wars*. These are big milestones for me—*Apocalypse Now*, just these kind of visions that I so enjoyed in a movie theater.

I thought, "Well, if you're going to do that sort of thing, you're going to be taking risks." And you have to be, almost by definition, as you were saying.

Tavis: Let me ask you to set your modesty aside for just a second. I hear the answer you're offering me now. Is it just about giving us, the viewer, the audience, a different, better experience, or does James Cameron process that this is part of the legacy, the film legacy that I'm going to leave is going to include exposing the audience to these kinds of things that they, had not seen prior to my being here.

Cameron: I think that's part of it. I think filmmakers generally like that sort of thing, if they can show you something you haven't seen before and you enjoy it. I've had good experiences with that. On *The Abyss* and on *Terminator II* we had some really groundbreaking tech that allowed us to do these liquid metal characters and so on, and I saw how fascinated audiences were with that.

So I thought, well, even just from a purely commercial business standpoint it's clear that people want to see something new, and you saw it again with *Jurassic Park*. I didn't make that film, but that shock of the new, that fascination.

So *Avatar* was a kind of an outgrowth of something that I started to do in the early nineties. I formed a company with Stan Winston, who was a good friend of mine and had designed the dinosaurs for *Jurassic Park* and designed *The Terminator* and the *Aliens* characters. We formed this company to take CG, the art of CG, to the next level, but we never really got to do the film that I wanted to do. After *Titanic*, I had written Governor already. It seemed like it still wasn't quite ready, the CG wasn't quite ready. So I waited a bit longer, started this film in 2005, when we thought we could sort of push it through the next barrier to get to this kind of photo-reality that we needed in these characters.

Tavis: How do you process at this point looking retrospectively at giving four years of your life—that's not including the writing of the script; as you said, you'd already written it. But four years actively of your life

bringing this thing to life; when you look back on that, you think what?
Cameron: I think it was worth it.

Tavis: You think it was worth it?
Cameron: Yeah. When I sit in a theater with an audience and see it, it's definitely worth it. The first two years was really spent on the design of the world and the design of all the creatures and the characters.

Tavis: Took God seven days; took you—six days—took you two years to design the world.
Cameron: Took me and two thousand other people. (Laughter)

Tavis: Two years to design the world, okay.
Cameron: Yeah. Well, we had a big team of artists, obviously, working on just the creatures, another team working on the plants and the Na'vi characters, like we're seeing Neytiri's character right now.

So I just surrounded myself with the most talented artists I could find, guys who I'd either worked with before or people that I had just respected for their work and wanted to work with for the first time. And then from that it goes to literally over a thousand CG artists who are now breathing life into this world and bringing it into focus.

Tavis: I think about all the issues that we were discussing a few minutes earlier in this conversation, James, from the environment to human rights and those kinds of things. I think of all those issues that you obviously care very much about, very deeply about, and I'm trying to juxtapose that with spending 500—all I can believe is the numbers that we're told, at least—but if this number is correct, $500 million to make this film. How do you respond to somebody who says that is an obscene amount of money, particularly juxtaposed against the issues that are so important? How do you justify $500 million for a film?
Cameron: Yeah, well, it wasn't that, that's not the right number. That number was arrived at even incorrectly in their own math by the—let's see, *New York Times*, I think, who added in all the marketing costs and all of the various promotions and sponsorships and all that stuff and got to this hugely inflated number.

But the point is that it is a big, expensive film, we know that. It's certainly in the top sort of five, if you will, and I would say the answer to that is every one of those dollars goes to a person, because it doesn't get fed into a computer and the computer makes the movie. It's humans, artists, working with computers that do all this work, and film crew, because we have live action shooting and so on, actors. People are making a living; a lot of people are making a living off this, so it's making jobs in a time of an economic downturn.

I don't feel bad about that at all. That's been the case on all my films. I get asked to make this type of film by the studios because they know they'll make money, it's good for business, it's good for commerce, and the thing is that right now, Hollywood is—its business is sort of retrenching to these big, milestone pictures because that's how the business is working.

Because television, cable, and so on has carved away a lot of the smaller stuff, and it's tougher now to get an independent film made.

Tavis: Just a few years ago it seemed that the studios were saying "We're not spending this kind of money on these big blockbusters anymore, we've got to get smaller budgets." That seemed to be the direction just a few years ago.

Cameron: Yeah, exactly, and then they found out that these are the kind of movies, as, by the way, the previous decade and the decade before that and the decade before that, these are the kind of movies that people want from Hollywood.

Tavis: You referenced earlier in this conversation that before you were a director you were a truck driver. That was a long time ago, given the films that you've been able to share with us. Take me back to those truck driver days, what that was like.

Cameron: Yeah, well, I was a truck driver, bus mechanic, I was a precision tool and die maker, I was a blue-collar guy and I was kind of happy, just driving a truck and living in a little house with a white picket fence with my first wife and life was good.

But in the meantime I was writing, drawing, painting, doing all this stuff—kind of the life of the mind, if you will. I never even really imagined I would be a filmmaker, even at that point. I was more of a film fan reacting to movies and creating my own stuff.

At a certain point the switch just got thrown and I just said, "You know what? I'm not going to do this anymore. I'm going to go try to be a filmmaker." And it seemed so improbable, but it happened.

Tavis: Tell me more about that turn, how you—pardon the pun—from being a truck driver to directing. (Laughter)

Cameron: Right, yeah, left turn signal goes on. (Laughter) Wait for opposing traffic.

Tavis: How'd that happen?
Cameron: Well, actually, a big catalyst for me was *Star Wars*, in two ways. One, when I saw the movie I realized that this was very much like imagery that I had been concocting in my own mind, and because the film was so successful I thought, "Well, if this is what a successful movie can be and that's the kind of stuff I'm imagining, I should be doing it."

The other thing is because *Star Wars* was successful it spawned a lot of knock-offs. A lot of people wanted to make science fiction films and so I wound up working for my first paying gig on a Roger Corman film, which was a knock off of *Star Wars*. A very cheap knock-off; it was like a $2 million film, but that was my first gig.

Tavis: You started reading sci-fi about eight years old, you got turned on?
Cameron: Yeah. I can't even remember when, it was pretty early.

Tavis: What was it, because everybody has their own things that we like and what turns us on and idiosyncrasies and all that. What was it about sci-fi that pulled you in as a kid?
Cameron: I just loved the fantasy, I love the characters, I like the idea of alien creatures, strange life forms. I like the idea of alien planets and the distant future and things like that. I had a very active visual imagination. So in those days we didn't have DVDs and video games and all that stuff, so you had to actually read something, conjure that image in your mind, and then my way of processing that was to then draw it.

What I read and imagined I would draw, and so I wound up with boxes and drawers full of all kinds of drawings of aliens and spaceships and all kinds of things.

So in a funny way I've been prepping for this movie since I was seven or eight years old, (laughter) in a very real way.

Tavis: You have been, as we know, writing, producing, directing—strange question here. I'm just trying to understand how your mind works and how your process works. Could you do the writing and the producing and not the directing on your projects these days, or do you have to direct because you have to shake this?
Cameron: Well, I've done both. I wrote *Strange Days* with Jay Cocks and

produced it for Kathryn Bigelow. I did the same thing on *Point Break*. I've written other things that haven't been produced but that were designed for other people to direct.

So yeah, I like to do that, but I don't have a voracious appetite for it. It's got to be a selected project. Kathryn and I worked together really well as a team back then, so I enjoyed that process.

Now I think from here on I'm going to focus pretty much just on directing my own stuff, just because frankly, I don't have a lot of time. I've made, what, six or seven films in twenty-five years and I don't know if I've got another twenty-five years. I might have fifteen years, something like that. So I've got to pick my projects carefully and stay focused.

Tavis: To your point now, because I'm always fascinated by how people make life choices, life decisions, tell me more about that last point. When you know that—I'm forty-five now, and unless I live to be ninety I got more days behind me than I got in front of me.
Cameron: That's right.

Tavis: I was just giving a speech about this. How, then, do you go about the process of making life choices when you got more in the rear-view mirror than you got in front of you?
Cameron: Yeah, right. Well, I just think you're careful. I think for me it's what's going to excite me, what's going to continue to excite me. I don't have some master plan. I don't even know what film I'm going to make next. It's just got to be something that excites me, that's something that I'm curious about, that I know I can learn from. That's critical for me. That's why I like doing these documentary films.

Well, here's an example of a life choice. When I finished *Titanic* I wound up doing six deep ocean expeditions and from that it yielded four documentary films over about a five-year period. My logic on that was I can't be running around in a zodiac boat in a twenty-foot sea when I'm eighty or seventy-five.

Tavis: Let's do this now.
Cameron: But I could still make a movie then. You see what I mean? So I thought all right, I'm going to go do this now, and then I'll come back to filmmaking later. Because I figured—a lot of people have thought, well, maybe I got scared of competing with myself or some kind of stage fright after *Titanic*, and that wasn't the case at all.

It was more like I had my FU money; I could do whatever I wanted at that point. (Laughter) I didn't think my directing career was going to go away just because I went off to do these other things, and it didn't. So I actually think that was a good call for me.

Tavis: I laughed when you said, "FU money." I think of Stephen Bochco, a former guest on this program, a great producer, as you know. Bochco once told me that, "Tavis, in this business, you either have to have FU money or an FU attitude." (Laughter)
Cameron: Or both.

Tavis: Or both. (Laughter) Ba-dum-bump, James Cameron. I don't know what the next—I had to clean that up because my mom is watching, and this is PBS, after all. I think you get the point.

I don't know, as he does not know, what his next film is; we know what the current one is, as if you don't know. *Avatar* is the one that's out now, directed by James Cameron. Good to have you on the program.
Cameron: Tavis, a real pleasure. Thanks.

Tavis: Glad to talk to you.

James Cameron Interview: *Avatar* Blu-ray; Also talks *Titanic 3D* and *Avatar 2*

Sara Wyland/2010

From Collider.com, March 24, 2010, http://collider.com/james-cameron-interview-avatar-blu-ray-also-talks-titanic-3d-and-avatar-2/20279/. Reprinted by permission of Collider.com.

According to director James Cameron, the groundbreaking sci-fi epic *Avatar* is not only the highest-grossing film of all time, but it is also the most pirated film of all time. However, that hasn't deterred its box office numbers and, if Blu-ray/DVD sales are any indication, it's not negatively impacting those numbers either.

In line with his strong environmental values, Cameron talked to press to promote the Blu-ray and DVD release scheduled for Earth Day (April 22) at a private estate in the hills of West Hollywood that makes use of solar paneling. During the interview, he was adamant that 16x9 is the best format for the film, previewed what fans can expect from the special edition, due out in November, explained why you won't see the Blu-ray in 3D for some time, and regarding *Avatar 2*, "the fastest we could imagine making another film is three to three and a half years, from the moment we start." He also said they're targeting a spring 2012 release for *Titanic 3D*.

It's a fantastic interview. Check out what he had to say after the jump:

Question: What makes Earth Day the right time to release this Blu-ray/DVD?
Cameron: What we've found is that so many people have responded, in different groups and causes, that are attempting to deal with environmental issues and issues of indigenous rights, and they come to us and really see *Avatar* as a focusing lens for all of these issues. The public has

really felt an emotional outpouring around these issues, so Earth Day is exactly the right time for us to premiere the discs. I just really want to express my gratitude to 20th Century Fox for throwing their weight behind these ideas.

I'm not trying to sell DVDs on the back of the hardship of the planet, as much as I'm hoping there will be a continued conversation around *Avatar* and around the needs and wishes that will elevate the consciousness and help us get the things done that need to be done. That's my new mission. I almost see it as an opportunity for *Avatar* to be helpful, as opposed to things helping *Avatar*. My wife said, "Honey, this is more than just an opportunity here. This is a duty and a responsibility." And, I actually see it that way now. I was always an environmental activist, but I've gone to a whole other level now, around the movie.

Q: How much of the April 22 release date for the Blu-ray/DVD has to do with the fact that *Avatar* is the most pirated film of all time?
Cameron: We're not even worried about piracy, at this point. I think people associate *Avatar* with a high-quality experience. Even while it was being wildly pirated, people were lining up and we were selling out in theaters. So, I think the wider public has made a decision that they want that premium experience. I see the same thing happening, in parallel, with the video release. Where normally Blu-ray pre-sales are at about the 15 percent level, we're already running 50 percent, so people are definitely excited about the Blu-ray release and pre-selecting for the most premium version in which they can see *Avatar* in a home environment. I see parallels between the two situations. How that translates to total sales, I can't say, at this point. We'll find out, in a month.

Q: What do you think the best format is to view this film in?
Cameron: The film was released in two formats. We released it in 16x9 and cinemascope aspect ratio. Obviously, the 35 mm prints were all in the scope ratio and with the IMAX stuff, we tried to take advantage of the height. The highest and best format for this movie is the 16x9, which plays beautifully. We finished the picture in 16x9 and then we vertically extracted the cinemascope when we were mastering the film for theatrical release.

In the theatrical release of the movie, it played in 3D in non-IMAX digital theaters in both formats. We did that by selecting whichever theater was going to look best in which format. But for the home, we wanted to go with the full picture. I really think it helps, with the sense of vertigo underneath the flying creatures, to have that little bit of extra frame down there, when they're looking down over cliffs. It enhances the sense of height.

Even though I love the cinemascope ratio compositionally, I actually found myself falling in love with the movie in 16x9, as we went along, and I prefer to watch it in that. Everyone thought the best viewing conditions for the movie were in 3D, but in 3D what we struggled with was the light levels. We struggled to get the light levels up, in the theaters. You get such a bright, crisp, dynamic picture on the DVD and Blu-ray. Something actually comes back to the viewing experience that you don't get in the theaters, with the colors and the strength of the contrast.

Q: The Blu-ray/DVD will only be in 16x9?
Cameron: Yeah. There will be no letterbox scope video.

Q: Will the 3D also be in 16x9 when it comes out?
Cameron: Absolutely, yeah.

Q: Why only include the film by itself on this edition?
Cameron: All these extraneous materials take down your bit rate. When you're a long picture like *Avatar* that barely fits on the disc, and you have to make room for a lot of other content, it starts to degrade the image quality. The quality, in terms of the resolution, has no noise and no grain. All of the visual elements of the picture are fantastic. Also, by the way, I have this unwritten deal with Fox that any time one of my movies makes more than a billion dollars, we leave all the crap trailers off of the Blu-ray and DVD, as a little service to the viewer. I can't stand watching them, any more than you can.

Q: Why won't we see the 3D Blu-ray right away?
Cameron: There just aren't that many players and screens yet. We have more of a long-term strategy, in that area. But I think it would be a shame to hold back the Blu-ray when people want it now, and I love it. I think it's a great format. I would recommend that, if people are thinking of buying a Blu-ray player around this time, make sure you get one that's 3D compatible because you're going to want it.

There's no significant cost difference to buy one that's 3D enabled, at least in some of the sets. The Panasonic set that uses the passive glasses, or Real D glasses essentially, has a little bit more of an up charge because of the cost of putting this polarizing film on the surface of the screen.

But, the other sets that use the active glasses have no significant additional cost in manufacturing because it's really just in the chip set that drives the image. I don't know exactly what all the price points are. I think most of them are up in the $1,500 to $2,500 range, just in size. If you're going to go 3D, go big. Get the biggest set you can, and then sit as close as you can stand. That's my advice. Get the coffee table out of the way and slide the couch over, right in front of the TV.

Q: What will be on the special edition Blu-Ray/DVD when it's released in November?
Cameron: It will have a lot of great features, making of stuff and behind the scenes stuff. You'll be able to do a branching experience where you can select if you want to watch the basic movie, if you want to watch the movie with six minutes of footage added back in, or if you want to watch an earlier cut of the film that has thirty or thirty-five minutes of additional footage. It will be an unrecognizable movie. You'll be going on a journey into a whole different version of *Avatar*. And some of the scenes won't be done because we won't have the budget to finish twenty or thirty minutes of CG stuff. We're taking the Greatest Hits six minutes and finishing that.

If you do that one experience, you'll watch a movie that's only about six minutes longer, but it's seamless. If you do the other experience, you're going to watch a movie that's much longer and has a lot of stuff in it that you won't recognize, some of which won't be finished. It will be a little bit more like some of the Disney stuff that they do where they leave pencil tests in for scenes that were never done. That's really more of a fan's exploration of what the movie might have been, or a lot of the ideas that fed into it.

You're also going to be able to look at a scene, and then look at the same scene with just the reference cameras of the capture. If it's a close-up in the final cut scene, it will be the close-up reference camera. If it's a wide shot, it will be the wide shot reference camera. We'll literally have a parallel cut, where you can watch it just in the reference cameras. The remarkable thing about that, and we've watched a few scenes that way, is it's the movie. It doesn't look like the movie, but the essence of it and the moment is exactly what you see in the final film. It's just people in black leotards. It's pretty wild. It's pretty amazing. The thing that I think is really cool is when you do it in a picture-in-picture, so you see the final image of Neytiri and you see what Zoe is doing, and it's identical. That's when you really get what the process is. You can talk about it for hours, or you can watch one scene in a picture-in-picture display and you'll get it.

Q: How is the experience of watching the movie different when you're sitting on your couch, as opposed to going to the theater?
Cameron: Go in the kitchen, make some popcorn, put your feet up and enjoy the movie. That's what the home viewing experience is all about. The richness, the vibrancy, and the dynamics of the movie are preserved in the home experience. People can't expect to have the same thing that you have on a fifty-foot screen, when you're watching a three-foot or four-foot screen. It's different. It just is.

Q: Do you think the story plays differently, when you see it in a more intimate setting?
Cameron: The story is the story. It still ends the same way. The bad guys die and the good guys win. It's just a different experience. It's immediate. You can put it in, any time you want. You can control your environment. You can pause it and go get a beer. It's a different experience. It's also the only way you're going to be able to watch it, when it's not in movie theaters anymore. When I'm cutting the movie, I'm working on a smaller screen that's about fifty inches. That's how I cut the film. That's how I lived with the film, for months at a time. So, I'm looking at the narrative and the storytelling.

The big screen experience is just a bonus for me, when I get to go, "Oh, this is cool. Wow, it's bigger." But, all of the creative aesthetic decisions are made on a smaller screen, anyway. Ninety-five percent of what I do as a director, in terms of supervising the design and the set construction, doing the photography, the lighting, working with the actors, all that stuff doesn't change. That isn't any different, no matter what screen it's shown on, down to some limit.

I don't feel that I'm making movies for iPhones. If someone wants to watch it on an iPhone, I'm not going to stop them, especially if they're paying for it, but I don't recommend it. I think it's dumb, when you have characters that are so small in the frame that they're not visible. I'm trying to make an epic. I'm not doing an episode of some talking heads, one-hour drama. To me, there's a limit that you wouldn't want to go below. I don't know. I've never watched *Avatar* on a laptop. I guess it probably works, but I don't recommend it. What I recommend is getting the coffee table out of the way and sticking your couch about four feet from your TV.

Q: You've made it clear that you're not a fan of the conversion from 2D to 3D. Can you explain why?
Cameron: Well, it's not a blanket statement. We're converting *Titanic*, but we're doing it right. What I'm not a fan of is a rushed or slap-dashed conversion that's not done right. And, I'm certainly not a fan of conversion when you could shoot the movie in 3D.

Q: Do you think more movies will be done through conversion for the cost savings, even if it's lesser quality?
Cameron: I don't know. How much quality do people want? The problem is that these decisions should be made by filmmakers. They shouldn't be made by studios. If it's up to studios, they're going to sacrifice quality for lower cost. Is that the right answer? Is that the principle on which movies are made by filmmakers? They don't get the cheapest lens. They don't get the cheapest camera. They get the one that does the job right and that satisfies their aesthetic requirements. If it was up to the studio, everything would be shot with a camcorder.

The decisions need to be made by filmmakers. Right now, they're being made by studios because all the filmmakers hung back and said, "Well, let's go see if Cameron hangs himself. Then we can forget about this 3D thing, and roll over and go back to sleep." That didn't happen, so now they've gotta go, "Oh fuck, maybe I have to think about doing a movie in 3D. It looks cool. It's a new art form. Let's go. Give us the money." That didn't happen, so now they're paying the price, which is the studio telling them to make their movies in 3D and they're caught with their pants down.

Q: What's it going to take for the power to return to the filmmakers?
Cameron: The filmmakers haven't done anything about it. They're not standing up. It's like, "Come on! Show some spine, guys." The studios have the power. They're going, "You're doing your movie in 3D. Guess what? You don't have a choice. You don't want to do it? That's fine. We'll get someone else." That's not how it was supposed to be. But, if the filmmakers take control of this thing, like they should, and like they control any other aesthetic aspect of their movie, then you'll have the quality and people will spend the money.

Q: If the technology had been there, would you have made *Titanic* in 3D, in the first place?
Cameron: Absolutely. Oh yeah, sure. That would have been awesome.

Q: Is the conversion of *Titanic* your next project?
Cameron: It's going to be done in parallel with whatever I'm doing next, over the next year. We're targeting for a spring 2012 release, which is the hundred year anniversary of the sailing of the *Titanic*. It's a nice marketing hook.

Q: Do you have another film you're looking to do next?
Cameron: There are plenty. I've got a number of projects. I just have to decide which one I want to do.

Q: Do you want some breathing room before a sequel happens?
Cameron: I think the breathing room is a given. The fastest we could imagine making another film is three to three and a half years, from the moment we start, and we're not planning on starting tomorrow. It's not about me needing breathing room. It's that these films take time. There's going to be a natural breathing room. People will have forgotten about *Avatar*, by the time we get a sequel done, and then they'll go, "Oh, *Avatar*. Yeah, that would be cool." It's not like *Iron Man 2*, coming out the year after *Iron Man 1*. It ain't going to work that way.

James Cameron Interview! Talks *Avatar* Re-release, Sequels, 3D Conversions, and Working with Del Toro

Jim Dorey/2010

From *MarketSaw* (blog), August 7, 2010, http://marketsaw.blogspot.com/2010/08/exclusive-james-cameron-interview-talks.html. Printed by permission of Jim Dorey. Transcribed by Brent Dunham.

Jim Dorey: Today I have with me mega-director James Cameron, whose highest-grossing movie of all time, *Avatar*, is being re-released on August 27 with an additional eight minutes of highly anticipated footage for us. Welcome, Jim.
James Cameron: Hey, thanks for having me on.

JD: You bet.
JC: I guess it's inevitable that I talk to you.

JD: Yeah, yeah. A lot has happened since the last time we spoke.
JC: The failing advocacy of the 3D medium.

JD: You got it right. Well, we're all excited with the re-release but I do have some 3D housekeeping questions I'd like to start off with.
JC: Okay.

JD: I know that you said that producing engagements will be few and far between for you, but we've heard that you may be producing [Guillermo] Del Toro's *At the Mountains of Madness* in 3D. Is there any truth to that rumor? Can you shed any light?

JC: It's absolutely true. Yeah, Guillermo and I are doing this. It came up pretty quickly, just two or three weeks ago. And he had come back from *[The] Hobbit* and we were talking about stuff he might be wanting to do. Usually when we get to that phase, either when I'm thinking of what I'm going to do or when he's thinking about what he's going to do, and this is a twenty-year friendship, you start reading each other's scripts. We were talking about one thing and I said, "Hey, what about *At the Mountains of Madness*? Are you still doing that?" And I wasn't even angling to produce it; I just wanted to sort of know where his head was and what he was doing. And he said, "Oh, I want to make that film so much! That's my passion film!" And I said, "Well, why don't we make it?" And that conversation led to, "Okay, here's a concrete plan, let's do it. Let's go talk to Universal." So we went over there, we pitched it with me producing on a fast track and so hopefully we'll be going second quarter next year.

JD: That's absolutely amazing.
JC: And in 3D.

JD: Yeah, and in 3D. So, obviously, you'll be native 3D.
JC: Oh, absolutely. I'm not into conversions. I mean I'm into conversions for classics but unless you have a time machine [they] can't be in 3D otherwise. Like *Star Wars*, *Indiana Jones*, and all that stuff. I don't know what the plans are for those but those are films that should be done.

JD: Sure.
JC: And we're doing *Titanic* for a 2012 release.

JD: Yeah. So will the Fusion cameras be used on Del Toro's [film]?
JC: Sure, absolutely. We're constantly improving those so we'll probably have a new generation of that camera by the time he starts.

JD: Excellent, excellent. So you've seen what we've all seen with regards to *Clash of the Titans* and *The Last Airbender* and now audiences are reacting. They weren't the best 3D conversions, really.
JC: Yeah, there's no way you can convert a movie in seven weeks, it's ridiculous. You know, *Titanic* is going to take us eight or nine months, maybe a year. You can't rush it and you certainly can't rush it if people don't know what they're doing. And, I think, unfortunately, *Clash of the Titans* showed a fundamental lack of knowledge of stereo space in addition to the shoddy work that comes from rushing. And, by the way, I

didn't want to hate the movie and I didn't hate the movie, I just hated the conversion of the movie. I'd be happy to watch the movie in 2D; I actually liked the film from a directorial standpoint and Sam [Worthington]'s work and so. I just think you can't charge a premium ticket price, a two or three dollar up charge, when you're delivering a crap experience.

JD: Basically, I knew you were going to say that but I had to ask. Do you think Hollywood has learned its lesson?
JC: Well, you know, *Clash of the Titans* made a lot of money, so what's the lesson to be learned? I think we're going to have to see a consistent pattern of the audience realizing that they're getting hoodwinked. And then, hopefully, Hollywood will learn its lesson. I think there's enough discussion out there at workshops and symposia and all these other various get-togethers where people chatter on endlessly that Hollywood is getting the sense that they better step up with quality if they're going to charge extra for a special experience. So, hopefully, this will all be just a bad dream.

JD: Yeah, it's been remarkable how [the audience] has become more and more educated about what the 2D and 3D process is and that time is a huge factor. So, obviously the impact on the conversion on *Titanic* won't be all that much because I think that will probably be part of the marketing; perhaps some of the messaging that you'll be putting out is that "We're taking our time. It's a masterpiece and we're putting together a life's work here."
JC: Yeah, we're going to use the better techniques for mapping the geometry and rotomating the geometry so that we've got moving forms to map onto. You can't just cut out edges; you're going to get flat people moving. And I'll use all my knowledge of stereoscopic photography to put things on the right depth planes. I think that's where a lot of this stuff goes off the tracks. We did tests for *Titanic* where we had seven different vendors do the same shots for conversion. I don't think anyone else has done that. And we got seven different answers as to where they thought things were, spatially. You know, some of them were not bad guesses and some of them were ridiculous. So, the problem is when you put a human in the loop, and it's entirely subjective, and they're just sort of sitting there guessing where things are based on perspective and other clues in the image, they're not going to do very well. As opposed to, I was there, I know where everybody stood, I know how big the set was, I know how far away things were, and I've got a pretty good sense of where

things should be. Plus I've got a trained eye for analyzing stereo space and so do the other members of my team so I think we're going to do a pretty good job on it. But if you don't step up with all of that, with the money, with the resources, with the time, you're going to get garbage.

But I think this whole conversion argument, honestly, is going to go away. And here's why: a couple things, one, you've got 3D TV sets coming from all the major consumer electronics companies, right? So now the TV sets are here before there's content for it so how's the broadcasting community responding? All the cable networks and satellite DirecTV and ESPN and everybody are all announcing 3D channels, right? So now you're going to have sports and stuff pouring in to these sets over the next year or so and it's all live production. So how are we going to handle this content gap? Well, we're going to make a whole boatload of cameras, right? So now you're going to have hundreds, if not thousands, of cameras out there, hundreds of productions, many, many operators, many trucks, lots of live feeds. And when that's the case, there's going to be a lot of fits and starts in that, there's going to be a lot of mistakes made, but cut to two years from now when there's thousands of people shooting 3D live, how can a producer turn around to a studio and say, "I can't shoot 3D. It's too difficult, there are too many problems, it costs too much, it adds six months to post-production." You can't say any of that stuff, that's all garbage. How can you say it when there's people right down the street doing it right now with the same cameras? You can't. So it's going to go away; the whole argument for conversion will go away. And all the arguments against conversion that have been cropping up over the last month that are becoming apparent to everyone are going to even strengthen. I think at that point, you know, conversion is not going to be considered a particularly viable alternative for high-end 3D. You know, people may look back through their catalogs and say, "You know, I'd like to take—" this is an example, this is not something that's really happening, "—but let's take the entire four or five seasons of *Battlestar Gallactica* and turn them into 3D and reissue it as a 3D DVD." Well, hell, I'd buy that! If you can figure out how to do it cost effectively. So, I think people will look at those things down the line, and certainly they should be looking at certain types of titles—*ET*, *Jaws*—let's see those in 3D, that would be great but you've got to do them right. The filmmakers should be involved. I've said this to Steven [Spielberg], "Make sure that you supervise this stuff and then it can be great."

JD: Definitely. The director's input has got to be there. Just going forward, you mentioned a while back going under Pandora's oceans for *Avatar 2*—

JC: Before you go down that path, one other thing about what's happening right now in 3D, and think about what this is: you've got a pulse of 3D stuff coming into the marketplace that was very successful between *Avatar*, *Alice in Wonderland*, and *How to Train Your Dragon*, right?

JD: You bet.

JC: And you've got the Hollywood community reacting to that but they weren't able to react in the short run, like, "Let's make movies natively in 3D" because that puts you on a one-year to eighteen-month horizon before they're going to make any money. They want to make the money now. So they're looking at what they've got. "What do we have? What's coming out this summer? What's coming out in three months? Let's turn that into 3D." But that's a knee-jerk decision based on a specific moment in history, it's not necessarily a pattern for what will happen on an ongoing basis. So, yeah, hopefully they've learned their lesson and hopefully they'll start making movies from scratch in 3D. And we see a lot more of that happening right now. In fact, over at the shop in Burbank, we can barely keep a camera in the place. We're going to build fifty new ones but we can't keep them in there. I went through there the other day and there were only two rigs in the whole shop when there are normally like forty sitting in there and they're all out on movies and sporting events.

JD: Yeah, I was just talking to Vince Pace just a while back and he was in Australia and he was flying over to London and the man's up to his neck. It's amazing.

JC: Well, I saw him a few days ago and he looked like he hadn't slept in a week. And two years ago, we were having to lay everybody off and we were down to like three people because nothing was happening. Now you've got the opposite problem, which is a good problem to have. Okay, so you were going to ask me something about the sequel.

JD: Yeah, just jumping to *Avatar 2*, do you have any overarching themes yet? I know Sam [Worthington] was mentioning that you haven't really started writing yet, that you have ideas but you haven't started putting pen to paper.

JC: Yeah, sure. I have an overall narrative arch for *[Avatar]* 2 and 3. And there's some modifications to that based on my experiences in the last few months from having gone down to the Amazon and hung out with these various indigenous groups who are actually living this type of story for real and that's influencing a little bit, having talked to their indigenous leaders. But it's not changing the overall pattern. I haven't got the script done yet, that's going to be a ways out; right now I'm focusing on the novel and that's going to take me the next couple months. The novel corresponds to the first film.

JD: A lot of people have been asking about that novel, wanting to get some information.
JC: Yes, it's happening. I'm not sure exactly when it's going to come out, maybe before the end of the year but probably the first quarter [of next year].

JD: *Avatar 2*, any Pandora aliens other than humans?
JC: Oh yeah, there's going to be a whole bunch of cool new stuff and I'm not talking about it at all. [Laughs] It's going to be just like the first movie. We didn't let anything out.

JD: So, the re-release of *Avatar* includes eight extra minutes—
JC: It's actually nine.

JD: Oh, it's nine?
JC: Yeah, I added some.

JD: Awesome, that's good to hear.
JC: I added some since that press release. Yeah, it's all CG, none of it is boring shots of people sitting around an office at the base, drinking coffee. It's all out in the rain forest, some of it is at night. There's a big hunt sequence that's got a lot of flying, a lot of Banshee stuff, riding Direhorses, very high-energy, high-impact action. There's a very powerful emotional scene toward the end that's been added back. It's got the best CG in the film in terms of facial performance. There's some stuff where the Na'vi sort of counterattack after the bulldozers destroy the willow glade. That's a night attack scene which has been put back in. And then the aftermath of that, how the humans react to that, it's got steps leading to the war. There's some stuff with Grace and the school in the jungle. There's another creature called the Stingbat that is brought back in. There's a Sturmbeest, which is the animal they hunt; we see hundreds of those. Sturmbeests are really cool animals and I really missed them when

we took them out of the film. There's some little bits that have been put back into the end battle, including the Quaritch fight with the AMP suit and some stuff in the actual battle itself.

JD: So there's more [Stephan] Lang scenes?
JC: Pardon me?

JD: More Lang scenes, Quaritch?
JC: There's little bits here and there, little action beats, and there's a little bit added to the love scene in the willow glade at night and there's some other night stuff with Flying Fanlizards, it's really just kind of beautiful and magical. It's all top-quality stuff; it's all on par with the best of the rest of the film. We had plenty of stuff to choose from. I said, "If we go back, let's put back the best of the best." Because I didn't want to completely off-balance the movie with changes of pace and stuff, making it suddenly twenty or thirty minutes longer. It still wants to be for a general audience and some people may have never seen the film, or certainly not seen it in a movie theatre so I didn't want to change the experience too much. We knew that we weren't getting any criticism of the film's length in its original release version, we weren't putting people to sleep. So I figured I was safe adding back six or seven percent beyond the original running time, which is where we're at right now. It's sort of a sweetener or a turbo charger, if you will. I don't think it fundamentally changes the movie. And why would we want to?

JD: Exactly. Is this re-release—
JC: I got to wrap it up. I'm getting the hook.

JD: Okay, I just wanted to ask you about the 3D Blu-ray—
JC: Well, there's no announcement yet. We're not making an announcement now about the 3D Blu-ray because it's a ways out. We're waiting to get a bigger base of people with screens and players. It's a bit of a "chicken and the egg" problem but we want *Avatar* to be a good seller when it comes out in 3D. And, by the way, I've seen the 3D master run on high-quality sets, both the Panasonic and the Samsung sets, and it looks amazing, it looks really spectacular. Of course, I told them I want one delivered immediately [laughs], which I believe is being set up fairly soon.

JD: Well, I can't wait to see the new footage and watch *Avatar* edge closer and closer to that $3 billion mark. Thank you, Jim Cameron.

JC: I don't know about that. You know, people have said, "Oh, you're just a bunch of money grubbers trying to squeeze the last drop of blood out of the turnip." I don't think so. It's really about giving the people what they want. People have said they want more Pandora, we've got it, and we kind of got edged out of the 3D market prematurely because there weren't enough screens to accommodate *Avatar* plus *Alice [in Wonderland]* plus *How to Train Your Dragon*. So, why not give people that opportunity to see it one last time on the big screen in 3D? I think it's going to be really cool.

JD: Thank you very much and thanks FOX for the time. I appreciate it.
JC: Sure, thanks, Jim.

Index

Alba, Jessica, 141–42
Alice in Wonderland, 211, 214
Alien, 14, 16, 20, 22, 159, 181
Alien 3, 167
Alves, Joe, 87
Apocalypse Now, 194
Apollo 13, 82, 135
Arnold, Tom, 69–70
Asimov, Isaac, 101, 118
Assonitis, Ovidio G., 59, 122
At the Mountains of Madness, 208

Ballard, Robert, 155–56
Batman, 34
Battlestar Gallactica (TV), 210
Beauty and the Beast (TV), 51
Ben-Hur, 104
Bennett, Peter, 94
Beringer, Tom, 51
Bewitched (TV), 88
Biehn, Michael, 8, 16, 26–27, 32, 39, 61, 66
Bigelow, Kathryn, 34, 72–73, 88, 102, 162, 198
Blade Runner, 14, 22
Bogart, Humphrey, 59
Bogdanovich, Peter, 18
Bonnie and Clyde, 116
Borders, Gloria, 103
Bradbury, Ray, 101
Brainstorm, 72

Brynner, Yul, 11
Buff, Conrad, 162

Cameron, James: on *The Abyss*'s ending/ Special Edition, 27–28, 36–37, 88–92; on the audience, 4–5, 11, 26; on breaking into the film industry, 6, 9, 45–47, 85–86, 97, 117, 119, 122–23, 129–30, 147, 163; on budget, 19, 104–5, 195–96; on casting, 7, 12, 60–61, 98–99, 141, 148, 191; on collaboration, 6, 31–32, 73, 102, 121, 123, 145, 162, 195; on directing, 151; on diving, 30, 33, 45, 96–97, 136–37, 169; on documentaries, 169–70; on "the drowning rat," 24–25, 37–38, 94–95; on the environment, xiv, 171, 192, 200–201; on film vs. digital, 164–65; on filmmaking strategies/problem solving, 9–10, 28, 29, 46, 79–81, 153–54, 182, 187; on his childhood, 44–45, 110–13; on his crew, 57, 65; on his goals as filmmaker, 4, 16–17, 21, 24, 34, 107, 118, 127–29; on his influences, 3, 14, 17, 32, 59, 100–101, 111, 116–19, 165–66, 170, 179, 193–94, 197; on his parents, 17, 58, 110, 117–18, 179; on his relationships, 18, 31, 63, 70; on his work ethic, 33, 123–26,

130–31; on human behavior, xiii, 4, 39–40, 52–53, 72; on marketing, 25, 91–92; on meeting people's expectations, 24–26, 144; on music, 167–68; on the origins of *The Terminator*, 3, 10–11, 47–49, 60, 180; on the press, 27–28, 83, 104; on producing, 161–62, 197–98; on production design, 22, 33, 82, 119; on school, 18, 45–46, 85, 111–12; on science fiction, 72–74, 144, 193; on space exploration, 133–38; on special effects, 5–6, 31–33, 82, 102–3, 126, 157–58, 175, 183, 188; on technology, 75, 99–100, 108–9, 128, 149; on television, 139–43; on theme, 14, 23, 39–40, 55–56, 72, 95, 99, 163, 180–81, 192; on 3D, 190, 201–2, 205, 207–14; on violence in the movies, 7, 13, 16, 164; on wanting to be a storyteller/filmmaker, 8–9, 114–16; on working for Roger Corman/New World Pictures, 6, 9, 18, 47, 59, 86–88, 119–21, 147, 179; on working with actors, 20–21, 27–28, 30, 32, 96, 141–42, 145, 190; on working with Hollywood studios, 7, 10, 38, 57, 60–62, 91, 103–4; on writing, 5, 14, 47, 50–53, 56, 100, 102

Works: *The Abyss*, 23–28, 29–34, 36–39, 44, 64–66, 79, 88–96, 101, 106–8, 127, 144–45, 150, 166, 182–83, 194; *Aliens*, 7, 14, 15–18, 19–22, 25–26, 31–32, 36, 39, 50–51, 63, 89–90, 106–7, 144, 149, 155, 159, 166–68, 177, 181–82, 191, 194; *Aliens of the Deep*, 156; *Avatar*, 157–58, 174–75, 177, 179, 183, 186–88, 189–99, 200–206, 207–14; *Avatar* sequels (planned), 200, 211–12; *Battle Angel Alita* (planned), 161, 172; *Battle beyond the Stars*, 6, 9, 47, 86, 179–80; *Dark Angel*, 134, 139–43, 152, 162; *Escape from New York*, 6, 9, 47, 87; *The Exodus Decoded*, 174–77; *Expedition: Bismarck*, 151, 154, 166; *Galaxy of Terror*, 6, 9, 47, 87; *Ghosts of the Abyss*, 147–68, 170, 175; *Last Mysteries of the Titanic*, 169–73, 175; *Piranha Part Two: The Spawning*, xii, 3, 13, 35–36, 47, 122–23; *Point Break*, 34, 88, 198; *Rambo: First Blood Part II*, 7, 14; *Solaris*, 144–46, 162, 164; *Strange Days*, 71–76, 102, 145, 197; *The Terminator*, 3–7, 8–14, 15–16, 31–32, 36, 39, 47–49, 52, 60, 87, 97, 99, 122–23, 127, 145, 148–49, 159, 177, 180; *Terminator 2: Judgment Day*, 35–40, 41–49, 50–56, 89, 98–99, 103, 105, 107–8, 150, 163–64, 182, 194; *Titanic*, 77–109, 110–32, 142, 145, 149–51, 157, 166–68, 177, 184–86, 194, 198, 205–6, 208–9; *True Lies*, 57–70, 98, 108, 155; *Xenogenesis*, 9, 46, 86, 106, 161

Cameron, Mike, 63, 66, 80, 149–50
Card, Orson Scott, 100–101
Carpenter, John, 87
Carpenter, Russell, 162
Carrere, Tia, 69
Catch-22, 116
Charlie's Angels, 167
Chernin, Peter, 184
Clark, Arthur C., 101, 111
Clash of the Titans, 208–9
Cleopatra, 104
Clooney, George, 145, 164

Close Encounters of the Third Kind, 63, 90, 194
Cobb, Ron, 22
Colossus: The Forbin Project, 99
Commando, 52
Conan the Barbarian (fiction), 101
Conan the Barbarian (film), 98
Contact, 144
Coppola, Francis Ford, 18
Corman, Roger, 6, 8, 9, 16, 47, 86–88, 119–20, 147, 179–80, 197
Costner, Kevin, 105
Cousteau, Jacques, 170
Cox, Jay, 102, 197
Curtis, Jamie Lee, 68–69

Daly, John, 60, 99, 123
Dances with Wolves, 91, 184
Dante, Joe, 9, 13
Darth Vader, 12
Das Boot, 10, 32
Davison, Jon, 9
Day After, The, 14
de Bont, Jan, 103–4
De Niro, Robert, 32
Dead Zone, The, 5
Del Toro, Guillermo, 208
Diller, Barry, 91
Dilley, Les, 31
Dirty Harry, 11, 13
Doctor Zhivago, 83
Doors, The, 102
Driver, The, 14
Dune, 15

Easy Rider, 116, 119
El Cid, 104
Ellison, Harlan, 62, 111
Empire Strikes Back, The, 106, 179
E.T.: The Extra-Terrestrial, 142, 250

Felachek, Frank, 93–94
Fern Gully, 101
Fincher, David, 167
Finnell, Mike, 9
Forrest Gump, 107
Furlong, Edward, 39

Giddings, Al, 79
Giler, David, 14
Godfather, The, 116
Godzilla, 103–4
Goldin, Dan, 137–38
Gone with the Wind, 83
Graduate, The, 116

Hamilton, Linda, 8, 14, 36, 39, 60, 180
Harold and the Purple Crayon (book), 124
Harris, Ed, 27, 29–30, 32, 95, 107
Harryhausen, Ray, 179, 194
Henriksen, Lance, 59–60, 62–63, 98
Hill, Debra, 87
Hill, Walter, 14
Hobbit, The, 208
Horner, James, 168
How I Made a Hundred Films in Hollywood and Never Lost a Dime (book), 147
How to Train Your Dragon, 211, 214
Howard, Robert, 98, 101
Hurd, Gale Ann, 6–7, 10, 16–18, 31, 63–64
Huston, John, 150

Indiana Jones (films), 208
Interview with the Vampire, 82
Invasion of the Body Snatchers, 51
Iron Man, 206
Iron Man 2, 206

Jackson, Peter, 175
Jacobovici, Simcha, 176
Jaffe, Steve, 102

Jaws, 87, 250
Jimenez, Neil, 56
Johnny Utah (Point Break), 34, 88
Jurassic Park, 150, 194

Karate Kid, The, 15
Kassar, Mario, 67, 104
Kennedy, John F., 134
Kubrick, Stanley, 17, 44, 116, 177
Kylstra, Johannes, 92–95

Lamont, Peter, 22
Landau, Jon, 68
Landis, John, 13
Lang, Stephen, 189, 213
Ligado, Rob, 82
Lord of the Rings, The (fiction), 101
Lord of the Rings, The: The Two Towers, 158
Lovecraft, H. P., 101
Lucas, George, 4, 49, 74–75, 117, 119

Madigan, Amy, 30
Making of 2001, The (book), 115
Marschall, Ken, 184
Marsh, Ed, 65
Mastrantonio, Mary Elizabeth, 26, 65, 183
McCarthy, Kevin, 51
McDowell, Andie, 106
McNeely, Joel, 168
Mead, Syd, 22
Medavoy, Mike, 60
Miller, Valerie Rae, 141
Muren, Dennis, 182
Mysterious Island, 179

New World Pictures, 9, 18, 47
Newton, Sir Isaac, 85
Nicholson, Jack, 18
Nietzsche, Friedrich, 92

Night to Remember, A, 83
Niven, Larry, 111

O'Bannon, Dan, 20
Octopussy, 22
Out of Sight, 145
Outland, 14

Pace, Vince, 211
Paxton, Bill, 63, 155, 157
Perfect Storm, The, 145
Platoon, 51
Predator, 52
Prochnow, Jürgen, 12

Raimi, Sam, 146
Regan, Ronald, 16
Reiner, Rob, 164
Reinert, Al, 134
Right Stuff, The, 9, 33
River's Edge, 56
Road Warrior, The, 14, 88
Romero, George, 36
Rydstrom, Gary, 103

Saldana, Zoe, 203
Savage, Doc, 161
Sayles, John, 18
Schwarzenegger, Arnold, 7, 8, 11–12, 38–39, 49, 52, 60–61, 67–70, 98–99, 104–5, 148–49, 180
Scorsese, Martin, 18, 32, 119
Scott, Ridley, 20, 159
Screenplay (book), 45
Sememeyevich, Anatoly, 79
Shakespeare, William, 144
Silent Man, The, 18
Simpson, O. J., 98
Soderbergh, Steven, 145–46, 162, 164–65
Solaris (original), 164

Spartacus, 104
Spiderman, 146
Spielberg, Steven, 74-75, 87, 90, 175, 250
Stallone, Sylvester, 14
Stand By Me, 164
Star Wars, 21, 49, 59, 85-86, 101, 116-17, 144, 179, 194, 197, 208
Stone, Oliver, 51
Sturgeon, Theodore, 101

Tarkovsky, Andrei, 144
Terminator 3: Rise of the Machines, 148-49
Thomas, Jim, 52
Thomas, John, 52
Three Kings, 145
Titanica, 79, 158
2001: A Space Odyssey, 17, 44, 58, 115-16, 133, 179, 194
2010: The Year We Make Contact, 15

van Vogt, A. E., 101, 111
Vanja, Andy, 104

Waterworld, 105
Weatherly, Michael, 141-42
Weaver, Sigourney, 17, 20-21, 39, 106-7, 191
Westworld, 11
Winston, Stan, 194
Wizard of Oz, The, 101
Wood, Beatrice, 130
Woodstock, 116
Worthington, Sam, 191, 209

Young Sherlock Holmes, 33, 183

Zemeckis, Robert, 107

www.ingramcontent.com/pod-product-compliance
Lightning Source LLC
Chambersburg PA
CBHW021838220426
43663CB00005B/296